MEMOIRS OF A RUGBY-PLAYING MAN

Also by Jay Atkinson

NONFICTION

*Ice Time: A Tale of Fathers, Sons,
and Hometown Heroes*

*Legends of Winter Hill: Cops, Con Men,
and Joe McCain, the Last Real Detective*

*Paradise Road: Jack Kerouac's Lost Highway and
My Search for America*

FICTION

Tauvernier Street

City in Amber

Caveman Politics

MEMOIRS OF A RUGBY-PLAYING MAN

Guts, Glory, and Blood in the
World's Greatest Game

JAY ATKINSON

THOMAS DUNNE BOOKS

ST. MARTIN'S PRESS ☙ NEW YORK

The names and identifying characteristics of some persons described in this book have been changed.

THOMAS DUNNE BOOKS.
An imprint of St. Martin's Press.

MEMOIRS OF A RUGBY-PLAYING MAN. Copyright © 2012 by Jay Atkinson. All rights reserved. Printed in the United States of America. For information, address St. Martin's Press, 175 Fifth Avenue, New York, N.Y. 10010.

www.thomasdunnebooks.com
www.stmartins.com

ISBN 978-0-312-54769-1

First Edition: April 2012

10 9 8 7 6 5 4 3 2 1

For my nephew Matt Berry,
North Shore Rugby Football Club

*As I remember and write, I grin, but not unkindly,
at my distant and callow self and the absurdities
which constitute his chronicle.*

Siegfried Sassoon,
Memoirs of a Fox-Hunting Man

MEMOIRS OF A RUGBY-PLAYING MAN

Introduction

"First Blood"

How dull it is pause, to make an end
To rust unburnished, not to shine in use
—Alfred, Lord Tennyson,
Ulysses, 1840

Thinking about it now is like watching a jumpy old newsreel, an event that occurred eighty or ninety years ago, not just thirty-five. Like so many other North American sportsmen, the first rugby match I ever saw became the first one I played in. It was April 1977, a chilly Saturday in Wolfville, Nova Scotia, on a lush green field encircled by pine trees. I was assigned to the right wing for a match between my school, Acadia University, and the men's club from Stellarton, Nova Scotia, an old mining town populated by some very hard fellows.

A couple of guys on the rugby team asked me to play; I went to a few practices on a muddy field behind Crowell Tower, acquiring a rudimentary grasp of the rules and strategy while "getting a run in with the lads," if nothing else. Since I was a philosophy major, on that particular morning I broke off studying Thomas Hobbes (who wrote that life was "nasty, brutish, and short"), threw my soccer boots and mouthpiece into a kit bag, crossed over Highland Avenue and walked along Main Street to the park. Setting out that morning I thought I was in for a vigorous workout that might fill the hours before dinner, followed by a rack of beers at the local tavern and a few laughs. As I passed along the row of downtown shops I had no idea that I was entering a new life: that I was about to embark on a sporting odyssey passion that would dominate my time and energy for the next three decades, and beyond.

For me, rugby would become like a good marriage, and this was my wedding day: an initial burst of euphoria that included a distinct sense of tradition and ceremony, followed by a kind of sporting honeymoon, filled with early successes and achievement. Then came the inevitable ups and downs, the good days and bad ones, and, while grinding it out over the long haul, a mounting succession of painful insights, injuries and failures. But, somehow, there was always the will to pick up and keep going—the feeling that it was all worth it. *For richer or poorer; in sickness and in health.* For years, I soldiered on, still playing long after I'd given up the sports of my youth; through ignominious defeats, both private and collective, and more numerous than I care to remember; if only to participate in a handful of brilliant victories, some of them fleeting moments of personal vindication in what appeared to be meaningless games, and a few, rare occasions in championship matches when the referee whistled full time and I ran wildly over the grass, leaping and tumbling on the ground in huge pileups with my teammates, my blood brothers. But all that was still far ahead of me.

Down at the field on that cold gray Nova Scotia morning, I skinned off my sweats, pulled on a team jersey, and laced up my boots, shivering in a pair of white canvas shorts and high blue socks. Jogging onto the pitch, I stole a glance at the coal miners from Stellarton in their black shorts, black socks, and dark blue and black striped jerseys. We were a bunch of college kids, lean and fit and cocky, but they were *men:* broad chested and stubby legged in the forwards, with close-cropped hair and tree trunks for necks and grotesquely truncated ears. Out in the backs, where I'd be making my debut, they were tall and rangy, with longer hair and missing teeth; passing the ball to one another and running up and down at incredible pace, they spoke in low, confidential tones, laughing as they warmed up.

I kept telling myself that I'd been in tight spots before, as I ran around the pitch with our scrumhalf, Rob Murray. Rob was himself from Stellarton and had arranged the match; he was fast, daring, skillful and tough, our best player, and the main reason why I was on that field in an Acadia jersey, watching his kinsmen pass by in a tight, fearsome bunch. An easygoing and charming fellow, I had seen Rob Murray around campus and he'd encouraged me to come out for rugby. At scrumhalf, Murray was supposed to deliver the ball to the backs from out of the scrum, running with it or kicking it downfield when necessary, while on defense harassing the other team's forwards and scrumhalf like a rabid terrier. Rob was the first of the "rugby types" I was to meet over my years playing the game: self-deprecating, wry tempered, affable, and on familiar terms with a barstool, but hard as penny nails on the rugby field, and loyal to a fault.

Most everything I had tried in college came easily to hand, but I understood that rugby was going to be different somehow. Thin lines of sweat ran down my back despite the chill and, though I was ill at ease, it gave me some comfort to be kicking the fat, oval ball to Rob Murray while catching his towering spirals in return. He could take on any man in the park—singly, or in twos and threes.

I'd played hockey against some pretty rugged kids back in Massachusetts, and here at school I was on the varsity wrestling and soccer teams, exposed to superior competition in practice every day. Still, my first thought was that the stakes were higher on the rugby pitch. I had the sense this was going to be more than just a game—it was a *contest*. To buck up, to gird myself for what was coming, I had to reach beyond my recent sporting experience to draw on my heritage.

I have a distinctly Anglo-Saxon name and my ancestors, on both sides of the family, came over from England and Ireland and Wales by ship in the early part of the twentieth century. On my paternal grandmother's side, I had a great-uncle Jack, who, like his sister Dorothy several years before him, left his untidy little village in northern England and came to America looking for a fresh start. John L. Maynard, or Jack as he was called, from being the most all-round workingman in the county, was a robust, dark-haired, smooth-featured, prizefighting sort of fellow, who lived mainly by his wits, which he exercised across a long and diverse career— seafaring man, steam- and pipe fitter, carpenter, plumber—pretty much anything that required the sweat of his brow. Handy with his fists and a favorite among the ladies, Uncle Jack was a handsome rake with a solid frame; someone I'd seen only a few times when I was a boy, the family apparition, dropping in with his sea bag and ribald stories, then disappearing just as quickly. With a wink and a crooked smile, off he'd go, whistling an old sea chantey. My dad, himself just shy of six feet and over two hundred and fifty pounds, used to say that Uncle Jack was "tough as whale shit, and twice as stinkin'."

So Uncle Jack was foremost in my mind, as the referee inspected our boots and whistled Rob Murray and the Stellarton captain to midfield to go over the rules. When the other team ran back onto the pitch, I slipped in my mouthpiece, made the sign of the cross, and squared up to the opposition, herded together a scant fifteen yards away. Rugby, I already knew, demanded physical courage and, by all accounts, Jack Maynard had that in spades. I bent over to pull up my socks, swung my arms back and forth loosening my shoulders, and then straightened up, punching at the air. Biting on my mouthpiece, with a feeling of dread rising in my chest that I would become intimate with over the next many years, I realized that I was motivated by fear: a fear of failure, of not wanting to embarrass myself or my teammates or my school. I was determined to handle the situations—the moments—that were presented to me. And as the kickoff rose into the heavy, gray sky, I had the faintest inkling that something auspicious was under way.

During the Stellarton match, I only touched the ball twice. The first time, I dashed along the sideline with it until I was pushed out of bounds. Then, late in the second half, with the score tied 6–6, Rob Murray gave me a signal and, in a move we had practiced, took the ball from our mauling forwards and threw a long, American football–style pass across the field. Running into the gap, I caught it like a flying brick against my shoulder and sprinted downfield into open territory. Just as Stellarton's last defender tackled me, I spun the ball back inside to the onrushing Murray, who had nothing but empty space to the goal line. But the referee blew his whistle, awarding the ball to Stellarton and saying I had illegally passed it forward. Standing on the wing in the blue and white striped jersey with the Acadia crest on it, I waited confidently for the ball to come my way again.

It never did, but that didn't matter. I was hooked.

The legendary origins of rugby can be traced back to 1830s England. In the midst of a football match at the Rugby School in Warwickshire, a disgruntled lad named William Webb Ellis reportedly picked up the ball and began running with it, dodging his angry schoolmates. Gradually a set of rules was encoded and the sport became known as Rugby football and spread throughout Great Britain. After an extended period of trial and error, rugby matches eventually became divided into two forty-minute halves with a short water break in between; each side, or team, is made up of eight forwards and seven backs, with limited substitution and a compulsion to move the ball forward by running or kicking only. Points are scored by touching the ball down in the end goal, known as a try, which is worth five points, and by drop- or place-kicking the ball between the goal posts, worth three. Full-on brawls are a bit less frequent than they were in the early days, and onlookers are discouraged from joining in the occasional donnybrook that occurs when tempers run high. Then again, to play rugby often requires that a player get pissed off fairly often.

In the decades after William Webb Ellis's epiphany, the game flourished nearly worldwide as British soldiers and sailors carried it to the limits of the Empire. (In this country, it evolved into American football, or gridiron as the British call it, and a try became known as a touchdown.) One element of rugby has never changed: as soon as you tuck the ball under your arm and set off running, the other team becomes incensed and tries to knock "your fuckin' 'ead off."

In the Anvil Tavern after my first game I approached the referee, who was drinking beer and laughing with some of the players, and told him that I had not thrown the ball forward—it was a lateral. "That's all right, son," he said, in a soft brogue. "A sideways pass isn't legal, either. It's got to travel backward."

In the old Irishman's simple explanation I learned that things happened fast on the rugby field, but with consequences. All around us in the tavern, there was a din of boisterous talk and deep, heartfelt laughter. As the beer flowed toward evening, and the referee in his stocking feet raised his voice in song with players from both teams, I could see that rugby was a game rich in history and chivalric tradition. It was a blood fraternity, and starting that day I was a member.

Atkinson lore has it that I ended up at Acadia University in Nova Scotia because our family doctor, a bow tie–wearing gentleman named George Dawson, who lived around the corner from us, had graduated from there in the 1930s. Apparently, when I was brought into his office as a newborn, Dr. Dawson said, "This kid is going to Acadia," which my dad never forgot. I was the first Atkinson to attend college, not only in my immediate family but also in previous generations. My grandmother Dorothy Maynard had immigrated to Methuen, Massachusetts, from England in 1922. A few years later, she married my grandfather Wray, who made pork pies in his cellar and sold them from a horse-drawn wagon. During the Great Depression, Wray and his brother Harvey pooled their resources to open a full-service bakery and liquor store on Broadway in Methuen. As a boy, my father toiled long hours in the bakery, raised and slaughtered pigs, and then enlisted in the army straight from high school. Later Dad sold insurance for John Hancock, going door to door in the 1950s and early 1960s, until signing on with a small local company as a broker. The history of the family, like that of many immigrants, was therefore of steadily increasing comfort. The rest of the Atkinsons had scrapped and hustled and sacrificed, and I was the one reaping the benefits.

My father and mother, Jim and Lois, were happy to pay for my education—one that they never had the money or leisure time to pursue for themselves. They expected that I would study hard and after a few years of preparation, enter some honorable profession. Engaging in sports, as far as my parents were concerned, was some vague aspect of the college experience that would perhaps make me more well rounded. So they had no objection when, in addition to the rigor of my studies, I dedicated myself to various athletic pursuits; in fact, my father enjoyed bragging about my humble exploits during Rotary Club meetings. For my part, I had always loved gymnasiums and ice rinks and playing fields, and the occasional black eye served to distinguish me from the other philosophy majors. But

I was attracted to rugby most of all because playing the game required fierce commitment, skill and discipline: the perfect little "grubber" kick, feathered into an open space on the field. The occasional punch in the face, given or received. The postgame drink-ups and sing-alongs. Rugby gave me a sense of authenticity; there was something hard-nosed and vigorous about it that heightened my sense of who I was and where I had come from. And I soon learned that running full tilt into the opposition was an existential moment that could not be faked.

Our rugby coach at Acadia was a pasty-faced old English gent in a tweed overcoat and soft hat. He was a tall man with big hands and feet and huge red ears, who stood mostly silent during the rainy practices I attended, occasionally shouting out garbled and incoherent phrases as encouragement. He nipped at a flask throughout our sessions, and gave apparently wise counsel to those players experienced and bold enough to approach him. I recall one enterprising fellow standing beneath the coach's umbrella, nodding and listening intently, happy to be out of the cold Nova Scotia rain.

Running around the field making little pop kicks and then gathering the ball in my outthrust arms, I felt like one of those barnstorming athletes who lived on porridge and stout, a slippery ace with a jutting chin and razor-sharp cleats. My grandparents had come to North America from the land of clammy weather and strong backs, and when I ran onto a rugby pitch for the first time I had a strange sense of déjà vu—it was like a homecoming. Rugby was classic and elegant, sport in its pared down essentials, fifteen kindred souls with no equipment except a mouthpiece and no substitutions except for injuries.

Over the past three and a half decades, I've played in close to six hundred rugby games—at least forty-five thousand minutes of competition, including various league championships, tournaments, and all-star matches. I've circled the globe, toting my rugby kit to England, Scotland, Wales, Ireland, Northern Ireland, Australia, Fiji, Chile, Argentina, Mexico, and Canada. That's more than six hundred hours when I was, at various times, exhausted, exhilarated, intimidated, vengeful, and often enough, triumphant. Each appearance on the rugby pitch was a test of nerve, where just showing up earned me a passing grade. I began playing rugby long before the Internet and cell phones and the whole notion of continuous partial attention that prevents us from living in the moment; there is no such thing on the rugby pitch. Add up my time there and it amounts to an entire month, night and day, where I was supercharged with purpose, completely and irrevocably alive, and never for a moment bored or listless. A lot of people can't say that.

I've played for the Acadia University Rugby Football Club; Mile High RFC of Denver, Colorado; the University of Florida RFC, where I attended graduate school; Burlington Centaurs RFC of Ontario, Canada, who invited me on my first international tour, to England and Wales; and the fabled Boston Rugby Club, which was established in 1960. For the past twenty-eight years, my home club has been Amoskeag RFC of Manchester, New Hampshire; and over the past fourteen years, I've also been playing for the Vandals RFC, an invitational side based in Los Angeles and made up of players from across the country and around the world. There have been occasions when I've wanted to quit and long stretches where my rugby was dispirited and lackluster. But the sport has steered me through some rough times: childhood friendships that dissolved, thwarted ambitions in love and work, and the deaths of friends and family. Nor do I think about my gray hair or minimized cash flow when I'm in a scrum; everything happens so fast, there's no time to feel sorry for yourself. Playing rugby means participating in an accelerated, extrasensory form of life, where every action you perform is filled with meaning, every blade of grass individuated and portentous, and things off the field—social problems, career and business worries, even thoughts of mortality—disappear like smoke.

Years of high-pitched competition have, of course, led to a few injuries: torn cartilage in my knee, broken cheekbone and eye socket from a blindside punch, a detached retina, cracked ribs, compressed disks in my neck, a ruptured hamstring, root canals in all my front teeth (one of which has been replaced altogether) from blows to the head, torn ligaments in both ankles, and dozens of stitches, bruises and blisters. I'm determined to wear out all my stock parts and to that end, have had right knee surgery, left ankle reconstruction, and two operations on my left eye. Many times I've been laid up in bed or in the hospital, punchy with morphine, cataloguing my accumu-lated woes and swearing off rugby forever. But I've always come back. Once, when I was a mere kid of thirty-three, my mother was quite ill and we were all sitting around the house on a Sunday. My right eye was blown up and purple; I was walking with considerable difficulty, and for the first and only time my mother told me that I should con-sider giving up rugby. I was getting killed every week, and I certainly wasn't getting any younger. Why do that to myself?

I remember that moment quite clearly. I was lying on the floor, watching a football game on television with a pillow beneath my sore shoulder and an ice pack on my bothersome left hamstring. Struggling to sit up, I told my mother about playing rugby in Chep-stow, Wales, and listening to the choir after the game in my club tie and blazer, clutching a pint of ale under the dusty portraits of for-mer internationals and their old championship teams. The voices of the Welsh rugby players so sweet and clear it was like angels were singing under the eaves. Leaning up from the floor the words just tumbled out, all the things about rugby I had never articulated to anyone but felt in my heart. Drinking kava in the Fiji Islands, some-one was playing calypso guitar and I was the only white person in the village, but completely at home among so many rugby players. Hurtling in a darkened cab through the streets of Belfast during the Troubles, on my way to play behind the fortified walls of the North of Ireland Rugby and Cricket Club. And how satisfying it was to sit with my longtime Amoskeag teammate, Greg "Duke" Cronin, after our games and go over every play, every moment, dissecting them one by one, very lovingly and with great attention to detail. The re-telling allows us to believe it, since the games whirl by so fast they are hard to hold on to.

"To us, it's poetry," I said.

My mother was dying then, I knew, in the last stages of emphy-sema. She wiped her eyes and looked steadily at me, the tube from her oxygen machine looped over her ears. "You shouldn't quit any-thing that makes you so happy," she said.

"Happy" is a relative term. Rugby practices have always been little pockets of socializing and tribal networking interspersed with lung-searing pain and the foreboding of full contact without adrenaline.

After one training session when I was pushing forty, I was driving the coach home and he stated an opinion that stayed in my mind for a long time afterward. Rugby players who are twenty or twenty-one years old are best suited for the game, not just for physical reasons but because "they're full of piss and muscle and their lives are uncomplicated in a way that a thirty-two or thirty-five year old's isn't," he said. "They live for rugby at twenty-one."

It occurred to me that certainly I was living for rugby at age twenty, and more than three decades later, I'm still fixated on the sport—as a *player*, not a coach or administrator. The rugby life at age forty came with far greater mental, emotional, physical, and financial strain than it did when I was just starting out. Now, at age fifty-two, after having ankle reconstruction surgery and facing an entire year of recovery, I'm wondering if I'll ever be able to play again, to go once more around the paddock with my old teammates. My rugby pal Chris Pierce has said that if I have the stomach for it, he'll set up a rehab program that'll put me back on the rugby field. It sounds crazy, I know. But once the matches begin, particularly if I take a hard shot early and the adrenaline makes me fearless, I can still play like a kid.

Back in 1984, in my first A-side game for the Boston Rugby Club, we played against Philadelphia-Whitemarsh and in the pack with me was the legendary Chris Vale, a tall, lanky forward with a shaggy mane of gray hair who had once played for the vaunted Eagles, the U.S. national team. Late in the second half with the score tied, Vale picked up a loose ball and drove into three members of the opposition, got stopped five yards short of the goal line, and dished the ball to me. Everything froze and the sound disappeared from the field as the pass came from Vale's hands. I could read "Mitre" on the side panel, caught the ball, was in the air for an eternity and landed hard in the end goal without feeling any shock. I leaped up and threw the ball away and had to keep telling myself *You just scored*, like I used to in hockey and soccer games, turning upfield already disbelieving the sheer joy of it.

Afterward in the Hammond Lounge near Cleveland Circle, pressing in among all the sheet rockers and laborers watching football on TV, I was headed for the men's room when Vale grabbed me by the arm. Then in his late thirties, Chris Vale was known as the gray-haired messiah of rugby, absolutely fanatical about the sport and imbued with its mystique. He braced me around the shoulder, summoned the barman, and bought me a glass of beer as several other young players looked on with admiration and awe. "Son, you did a yeoman's work out there today," said the aging star, a compliment I'll never forget.

People say that money is ultimately without value, because you can't take it with you. It's also true that you can't take peak experiences with you, either, but that misses the point of having them in the first place. My life as an itinerant athlete and writer who has amassed no fortune, purchased no real estate, and contributed little to the civic good has been viewed by some as a tragedy of lost potential. But few wage slaves have ever whooped with their all-star teammates after a last second victory over the Quebec provincial team, or scored a try in the Mexico City stadium where U.S. Olympic long jumper Bob Beamon set a world record. Once I entered a pub in Dublin accompanied by a pretty blue-eyed Clondalkin girl and the doorman tipped his hat and said, "That's the Rose of Tralee you've got there, lad." The next day we won our match, and as I jogged past the grandstand little kids stuck out scraps of paper, clamoring for my autograph.

At the start of World War II, my grandmother's kid brother Jack, tired of going to bed hungry, ran away from home and enlisted in the Royal Navy. Leaving port for the first time many of his young shipmates were terrified, crying in their bunks, but for sixteen-year-old Jack Maynard it meant great bowls of milk in the galley and a new pair of shoes. Over the next two decades, Uncle Jack served intermittently in the British and Canadian navies, and was torpedoed and relegated to the lifeboats in each of two wars. Nearly forty years after Jack Maynard first shipped out, denting a wooden floor with my cleats in that Nova Scotia bar, I was mixing it up with a rough bunch of lads, something I now had in common with my tough old great-uncle from Yorkshire County.

Reparations

There are the things we do for love, and the things we do for rugby, which are pretty much the same, at least in my case. Over the past few months, my fifty-two-year-old left leg has been x-rayed and examined more than a Saudi Arabian's carry-on bag at Logan Airport. Finally, in March, I go in for surgery to repair some of the damage that rugby, soccer, wrestling, ice hockey, hiking, and trail running have done to my left foot and ankle over the years. Arriving early at Cambridge Hospital, I find a quiet, sunny corner and spend forty-five minutes visualizing the successful completion of the operation and doing some deep breathing exercises. Soon I'm dressed in a gown and rolling on a gurney along an interminable hallway, watched over by an operating room nurse.

"How do you feel?" she asks, before they begin the IV.

"Relaxed and confident," I say.

Just then the surgeon, Dr. Jay Phillips, appears in his light blue scrubs. "Feeling good?" I ask. "Everything all right at home?" The affable Dr. Phillips, a tall, dark-haired fellow who treats me like his cousin, pokes me in the arm and laughs. "See you later," he says, going off to talk with his associate, Dr. Marcoux, who will assist.

I'm one of the less than 5 percent of patients who opt to remain conscious for this particular surgery. Inside the large, brightly lit operating room, the anesthesiologist gives me a spinal and begins the sedation. He says it'll be like a glass of wine, but in less than a minute it feels like I've been hit with the entire vineyard. There's a screen across my waist, a yard of dark blue fabric that prevents me from seeing what Dr. Phillips and his colleagues are doing. But at one point early on, they hoist my foot off the table. I can't feel a thing; it's like being presented with a mannequin's leg.

The operation begins at noon. To keep my mind occupied, I interview the anesthesiologist at some length. He's Chinese, early middle age, thin and bespectacled, in pale blue surgical garb. His wife is a doctor, too, practicing in New York. They have one child, a daughter, et cetera. The sedation seems to grow stronger as my questions become more personal. I glance up at the clock and realize I've been lying completely still for two and a half hours.

I put on some headphones and begin listening to Bob Dylan and Tom Waits. At intervals I can hear the saw whirring as they cut through the calcaneus bone in my foot; it smells like something's burning. Then I lose consciousness, descending into a strengthless black void that must be like an atheist's death.

I wake up at 5:30 P.M. in recovery. The resident or someone there says that I've vomited, but I don't recall that. (Under x-ray, the five titanium screws in my foot look like a bunch of hardware dropped into a bony pot of dough at Home Depot.) They move me to the surgical recovery ward on the sixth floor and start me on a morphine drip. This drug really messes with what the charge nurse calls my "sleep architecture." The hours pass by on the wall clock: 10 P.M., midnight, 1 A.M., 3 A.M., 5 A.M., gray runny streaks of dawn, and finally I'm exhausted and garbling my speech, watching one staff member after another pass through the room while I doze and wake and gape at them in my morphine reveries and then fall into semiconsciousness again.

Following this, I have a string of waking hallucinations that make morphine the drug of choice among rugby's surgical veterans. In the most compelling of these, I check into a large hotel with Vandals RFC captain Frank Baker, where we meet up with my old rugby pal and roommate Surfer John Hearin and teammate Billy Bishop and throw our bags into the room and head out to make further travel arrangements; we're flying out west to play rugby in a tournament somewhere.

The hotel lobby is connected to an airport, where we run into Stormin' Norman Litwack, my old Acadia pal Drew Cooper, Super Dave Laflamme, Dan "Original Sully" Sullivan, Duke Cronin, and a bunch of other forwards. Everyone is trying to book flights but there's terrible weather, and one by one the gates are shutting down. We're sitting in a bar on the concourse when our tighthead prop, Butch McCarthy, who hates to fly, walks up smoking the stub of a cigar. Butchie tells us to finish our drinks because he found an airline that's still flying.

Baker and I are the last ones out of the bar and ahead of us, the other Vandals are passing beneath a sign that reads JUNK-O JUNKETS.

I ask Baker where we're going and he says that we're taking a flight on a wild charter that specializes in drunken college kids heading for spring break. What kind of pilots do they have? I want to know.

They don't have pilots, says Baker. Somebody just flies it.

In the hallucination, I just shrug and follow Baker onto the plane. That's rugby for you: Choose your sides, believe in your teammates, and say fuck it. I'm laughing with Baker when I wake up.

A few weeks after my ankle surgery, they sawed off the first of two hard casts; my left foot was bruised and flabby, crisscrossed with nasty scars from the three incisions Dr. Phillips had made. "That looks awful," I said.

"But it's going to work great," said Dr. Phillips. "You're a 'max' kind of guy, so we gave you a 'max' repair."

Phillips noted that he "was the only guy in this town" who would've gone so far in performing multiple repairs: the triple fusion in the mid-foot; the cutting of the calcaneus bone and repositioning of the heel with titanium screws; and the ligament repair, made with a natural material called Pegasus, which comes from a horse's pericardium. A typical surgeon would've just performed an ankle fusion and let it go at that, said Phillips. "But like I was saying, you're a 'max' kind of guy," he said, in case I hadn't been listening.

After eight weeks in a cast, and three weeks in the boot—a black, buckled, medieval-looking contrivance that rose to my knee—I stood in front of Chris Pierce, a first-rate physical therapist and present-day captain of my old rugby club, Amoskeag RFC. Grinning like a maniac, Piercey summoned my left foot, bruised and trembling, onto the carpeted floor of his clinic in Windham, New Hampshire.

"You don't need this anymore," Piercey said, tossing aside my crutch.

Crew-cutted, bespectacled Chris Pierce is a well-hewn sculpture of a guy, a positive thinker of the old school; he can get his patients to walk through walls for him. But my left leg from the lower quadriceps to the floor was as straight and thin as a rake handle; what appeared to be a dead crow was tied to the end of it.

"I don't know, Piercey," I said. "It feels pretty shaky."

Under Piercey's knowing eye, I had just completed two weeks of gradual weight-bearing exercise. Trying to actually walk on the thing is the inevitable "last step."

"Go for it," Piercey said.

With a profound ache in my mid-foot, and what was left of my calf muscle shaking like a pudding ("*Did you ever catch them rustlers?*" "*What rustlers?*" "*The ones that stole your calf*"), I made it unassisted across the room, heel to toe, my Achilles tendon stretched to the breaking point. It was like watching a fifty-two-year old toddler going from the couch to the ottoman.

"Way to go, speedy," said Chris.

After ten minutes of walking, sidestepping, and toe raises, I finished for the day. Sweating in rivulets, I looked down at my foot and ankle, which was reduced to a swollen purple mass of fused bones. "Fuckin' A, Piercey," I said, dropping into a chair. "I can't imagine ever running on this foot, let alone playing rugby."

My ankle was stiff and creaky, like that of an old woman who has fossilized at the bingo table. But my calf horrified me the most: it looked like a narrow bag of petroleum jelly. How was I ever going to play rugby on *that*? After all, I hadn't been able to run a step in almost two years. The possibility of a last rugby hurrah seemed remote.

While I was down on the floor laboring over ankle rotations, I was visited by an image of playing rugby: the easy movement and change of direction, the well-thrown lineout ball, and perfectly executed scrum. There on the rug in Chris Pierce's clinic I felt a surge of the pure joy I felt playing alongside Frank Baker and Solly and Spencer Cackett; the total acceptance I always took for granted when I was on the field with the Vandals. Nobody ever says a word about it, but you can sense the respect for your skills and what little piece of competence you bring to the game and the approbation you feel in doing it.

Grunting and sweating over such a basic movement, my fantasy was suddenly eclipsed by a wave of doom—the fear that my ankle was never going to improve enough to walk normally. At that moment, rugby seemed like a distant aspect of my past. But I called over to Piercey through gritted teeth, and said, "I wanna make the next Vandals trip."

Chris regarded me for a moment, his hands on his hips. "I can do that," he said.

At the true beginning of my rugby adventures, during graduate school at the University of Florida, my life was certainly uncomplicated and I was full of the piss and vinegar that would later be at a premium. I sort of drifted into Gainesville on a whim—a lucky accident, as it turned out. But I ended up playing more than fifty matches in the Gators' white jersey with orange and blue hoops, drinking up an ocean of beer in the process and chasing coeds with the zeal of a young Sinatra. My time there became the extended foreground of a long career, the place where I gained my footing as a writer and learned the game that would take me around the world. It was the most fun a guy ever had.

After my ankle surgery, it appeared that the fun was over. So perhaps F. Scott Fitzgerald was correct when he wrote that there are no second acts in American life; but the old Princeton man never said anything about an encore. Because, in the end, rugby has actually demanded very little of me, and given back so much. I've played the sport on five continents, and enjoyed the friendship of people from all walks of life—the sort of friends that a man is lucky to have, and will cherish until the grave. This book is a testimony to those friendships, and to rugby football, the greatest sport on God's green earth.

Chapter 1

The Vandals

A few months before Dr. Phillips screwed my ankle back together, I was at the Mardi Gras tournament in Louisiana playing for the Vandals. Fifteen minutes into our first match, the sky was low and dark as we spread across our goal line, waiting for their forwards to attack. The referee marked the spot and they ran a fake to the right, freezing the stiffest part of our defense, the heavyweights. Then their biggest player—roughly half my age and twice my size—charged straight at me as the scrumhalf flipped him the ball.

At 52, most guys are watching their kids play high school sports or riding in carts across the local golf course. But as the young behemoth tucked the ball under his arm and hurtled forward, I bit down on my mouthpiece and lowered my center of gravity and scrambled toward him. I didn't have any real thoughts, just an instinct to step into the gap. In rugby, you lace 'em up and take your chances. . . .

Five miles east of downtown Baton Rouge, Louisiana, Independence Park is a vast, flatiron complex of athletic fields and jogging paths, with five rugby fields lined and laid out beside the main parking lot. That weekend, I was competing in the annual Mardi Gras Rugby

Festival as part of the Vandals RFC, a team assembled by my old friend Frank Baker, an Associated Press editor in Los Angeles. Shortly before our first game, Baker announced the starting team and after pulling on the red and black Vandals jersey, I swigged from a gallon of water and set off at a jog, past the concession stands and the medical tent and a portable stereo playing zydeco music. In the stench from the local oil refineries, I ran along with the pancakes from breakfast leaping around in my stomach, trying to steady my heart rate and take the edge off the jitters.

If all sports are really about war, then rugby is an eighteenth-century epic of bayonet charges and hand-to-hand fighting. On an expanded football field without any yard lines, the teams line up facing each other like infantrymen wearing cleated boots. And every few minutes the combatants must steel themselves for a fresh assault into the teeth of the enemy. Faintheartedness is easy to spot: the player who shirks contact is hooted from the sidelines and often injured. I've been playing rugby since Gerald Ford was president and these days I'm the oldest guy on the Vandals roster, an invitational side made up of players from all over, many of whom are in their twenties and early thirties. Current Vandals hail from Ireland, Australia, Kenya, New Zealand, Uruguay, Cuba, Rhode Island, Colorado, Louisiana, Tennessee, Florida, Massachusetts, and the District of Columbia. It's a pretty good club, one of the best I've ever played for.

I hear the voices on occasion, saying that I'm too old and too slow, my best rugby long gone. Certainly I have the responsibility of a career, a sixteen-year-old son who needs and deserves my attention, and a body that's intact but constantly on the verge of major breakdowns: ankles, knees, neck, hamstrings, upper back, and the rest. But rugby gives me something that I can't get anywhere else: the feeling that, while I'm out there, I'm living the truth. Sure, it's a young man's game, but that's no reason to surrender something you love. What compels my passion for rugby at this age is the dividend from grit: the months of training exchanged for one or two golden moments of performance.

After jogging half a mile, I stopped among some trees and pissed on a holly bush, coming out to a baseball diamond to stretch in the dust near home plate. Away in the distance I could see the rugby fields grouped together and the other Vandals moving back and forth in a red-shirted mass. Seven of this year's nineteen Vandals come from my home club, Amoskeag RFC of Manchester, New Hampshire. Then there's thirty-one-year-old Tom "Reggae" Rege, who was born in Kenya, and Lyle Jones, thirty-three, from Renova, Mississippi. My old college roommate Surfer John Hearin from Cocoa Beach, Florida, and Super Dave Laflamme of Rhode Island, and Spencer Cackett, a commercial deep-sea diver from Australia. Tennessean Daniel Carter, who talks about as fast as a possum does arithmetic, enjoys regaling us with stories about his hometown. "In 'Sweet Lips' you order food and they bring you gravy—whether you want it or not," says Carter, who owns a coon-hunting mule named Festus.

But the undisputed chieftain of the Vandals is forty-two-year-old Frank Baker, the son of a newsman who's originally from Upstate New York. With his mobile features and white-blond hair, Baker looks like a younger and more rugged version of the actor Ed Begley, Jr., and was once a four-letter man for the Voorheesville High Blackbirds. A couple of times a year, he invites his favorite ruggers to join him under the banner of the Vandals, and players converge from various points to witness Baker's monumental place kicks and offbeat sense of humor.

Baker invented the Vandals back in 1995, when he was playing for Amoskeag, by combining our sturdy pack of forwards with Providence RFC's shifty backline, which produced a tournament victory in Portland, Maine. (I didn't play in that first game, but I've played for the Vandals on just about every trip since.) The idea caught on and soon, excellent rugby players with exceptional social skills—funny, charismatic guys that Baker had encountered over the years—were clamoring for a Vandals' invitation. As he roamed the country in various assignments for the Associated Press, he added ruggers from the Deep South, Washington, D.C., and California and Colorado to the mix. It was a perfect rugby storm for me: high-level tournament competition two or three times a year, with representative level players who didn't take themselves too seriously and loved to have a good time. I'd tried Old Boys rugby with various over-thirty-five and over-forty teams and it wasn't for me. Fat guys huffing and puffing around the field, sloppy play, and bad jokes; nothing like the kinetic, forward-driven rugby I'd always thrived on. And just when you caught on to the joke and relaxed, some 230-pound moron would knock you senseless. Fuck that.

Even in a public place, a rugby team is a closed society, talking in a kind of shorthand that outsiders are never privy to. On this particular trip, several of the Vandals visited Bourbon Street in New Orleans and as we proceeded among the masked revelers and funky, pie-eyed tourists, Baker jerked his hand upward, pointing to a middle-aged woman on a balcony overhead. She had a cup of beer in her hand and a pair of red plastic horns attached to her head.

"A housewife from Ohio is, in fact, the devil," said Baker.

"Get behind me, Mrs. Satan," I said, as we went past.

Minutes before the opening kickoff, I joined the other Vandals beneath the goalposts with a sense of mortal dread running through my veins. There's a fair chance you'll get hurt or maimed in a rugby game, and a remote possibility you'll be killed. Over my career, I've known three very athletic guys who ended up in wheelchairs and before every game I kneel down, make the sign of the cross and whisper, "Dear Lord, please keep me, my teammates and our opponents free from injury and help me play to the best of my ability, as a glory to God. Amen."

Being in a scrum, especially right up front—at hooker, where I play—is particularly dangerous. The two packs line up a yard apart, a total of eight men on each side intricately bound together with three men forming the front row, the hooker in the middle. When the referee shouts, "Ready. *En-gage!*" and sixteen guys collide with the thump of bone on bone, there is absolutely no way to remain half interested in what's happening. As soon as the scrumhalf puts the ball into the tunnel between the two sets of forwards, it's my job to hook the ball back with my foot, at the right speed and in the right part of the tunnel, so our scrumhalf can get it out to the backs. Once the two packs come together at that velocity and with that much force, the joy of risk crowds out the dread.

The two props—the Argentines call them *pilars*—are expected to protect the hooker no matter what. That weekend in Louisiana, I was playing between two longtime teammates from New Hampshire. Butch McCarthy, six foot one, 285 pounds, is a former Plymouth State College Academic All-American in football who lives by the credo: *high intensity, short duration*. Like-sized Fred Roedel played football and rugby at Norwich University and has the on-field temperament of an enraged moose. I'm five foot nine, 165 pounds and for the past twenty-three years, I've trusted life and limb to Freddie and Butch. In the scrums, we hang on and squeeze until our fingernails bleed.

Our first match was against a team of buzz-cutted navy flyers from Pensacola, Florida, who won their preliminary game by a score of 67–0. They kicked off and Bill Bishop caught the ball and the onrushing Pensacola boys hit the breakdown and we all went down in a heap. In rugby, the area surrounding you is exaggeratedly clear, absent of sound and slow moving like syrup. Outside that circle everything whips past at incredible speeds. The game moves with the quickness of thought, the ball spun from player to player, suddenly appearing in your hands. Decisions are made on the crest of an instant—run with it, pass it, take a tackle or go to the ground—and mistakes bring that blurry violence right to you.

The first few scrums of the Pensacola games were tight and breathless; all I can really think about is doing my job, executing the skills I've acquired over the years in precise little steps. I'm not a star, and never have been; I know what I'm supposed to do and do it without any fanfare. In the rest of life, my role is a little uncertain, but here, in the midst of what looks like utter chaos, I know exactly what's expected of me. I know who I am.

Against the navy boys I did what I needed to in the scrums, the lineouts and the loose play, waiting for the younger guys to tire, for the game to come back to me. But when we committed a penalty about eight meters from our goal line, we were forced to retreat and they played the ball off the ground from the referee's mark and charged at our line. Our defense was stretched thin and they handed the ball to a young, sturdy-looking prop who took it on the dead run and came straight at me. In a nanosecond I stepped forward, dropped my shoulder and tried to get underneath his chest. But he was running low and the broad blade of his shoulder struck the top of my head, glanced off, and crashed into my left side, throwing an electric charge from my jawbone down the length of my spine.

The sky turned black, and I went ass over teakettle and landed on my head in the end goal. Somewhere in the blur of our collision, the Pensacola man flicked the ball to a teammate and it was that fellow who scored in the corner. Butch McCarthy came over and yanked me to my feet. "Physics," he said.

My neck felt like it had been cranked downward a few notches, and my shoulder was killing me. Since the early 2000s, I've barnstormed with the Vandals twice a year and spent the rest of the time getting fit. I train pretty hard six days a week, limit myself to a couple of beers, and go for regular medical checkups. With all those hours in the gym, the last thing I wanted to do was take myself out of the game.

A few minutes later, I got whacked in the head with somebody's boot when I was rucking the ball from a pileup. Sinking to one knee, I asked the referee for a minute of injury time. Fred Roedel came over and put his hand on my back and asked if I was all right. We stood up and I walked in a little circle, jangling my neck loose. Then I stepped through the knot of players and slung my arms over my props' shoulders, preparing for the next scrum. My heart was hammering and my breath came shallow and fast. I leaned hard against Butch's hip, the two packs slammed together jarring my vision, and the ball came skittering into the tunnel. I struck with my right foot, heeling it toward the back of our scrum. We drove over the ball, securing it, and Fred said, "Good job."

Although we trailed by only three points with a few minutes to play, we ended up losing to the navy boys 34–23 and got bumped into the consolation bracket. In the next game, we defeated a team from Oklahoma City 37–0 but I further telescoped my neck in a mismanaged scrum and had to come out. After the match, I limped over to the medical tent and asked one of the physical therapists to examine my injuries. I felt a pinching sensation behind my left ear and the trapezius on that side was tense and weak. The therapist probed around with her fingers and discovered two knots of muscle behind my shoulder blade.

"Take some aspirin and ice it," she said.

We were scheduled to play Lafayette in the third-place match the next day. "Can I play tomorrow?" I asked.

The therapist shrugged. "I don't know."

That night, it was time for kangaroo court, an ongoing stream of banter, where your rugby pals zero in on your weaknesses for the entertainment of the assembled. One man was accused of laundering and ironing his jersey between matches. Another was mocked for being thrown out of the game just minutes into his Vandals debut. In rugby, no one is innocent. As Judge Baker worked his way through a crowded docket, I nursed a can of beer and worried about my neck.

After the court session, most of the Vandals ambled down to the casino, which was a big riverboat tied up near the hotel. At my age, important matches don't come around very often and I wanted to play in the consolation final. So I went back to my room and watched an old Steve McQueen movie with an ice pack on my neck, praying for a fast recovery.

Early the next morning, we gathered in the lobby for the drive out to the fields. When we heard gospel music coming from a conference room, fellow Catholic Tom Turner and I walked down to investigate. A short, powerful-looking man from the Christian Interfaith Ministry greeted us at the door, shook our hands and welcomed us inside. A drum kit stood at one end of the narrow hall, flanked by an electric organ and three female singers in their Sunday best. Facing the musicians were several rows of chairs but none of the tiny congregation was seated: white-gloved ladies were swaying back and forth with their arms raised and a man who looked seven feet tall was clapping his hands like thunder.

They were singing the Lord's Prayer and the organist punctuated the final bars of the hymn with cries of "Thank you, Lord!" while the congregation shook their hands at the ceiling. It occurred to me that I'd traveled to many exotic places and experienced many incredible things because of rugby. And as the hotel conference room erupted in "Amen!" and the vocalists held the last, trembling note, I said my own little hosanna to the fellowship and mutual esteem that are the hallmarks of our sport.

Out at the pitch, I felt pretty good after stretching out and receiving deep pressure massage at the medical tent and informed Baker that I was able to play. We went down into the shade at the north end of the park and ran some ball drills and practiced a few lineouts. Then the referee came over and inspected our boots and gave us a few perfunctory instructions. "Two minutes," he said.

Baker drew us into a circle. "The Vandals have never entered a tournament without winning a piece of hardware," he said. "Let's get that plate."

The referee blew his whistle and we ran onto the field and lined up to take the kickoff from the Lafayette Rhineaux. Even after giving up a fluke try in the opening minute, we knew we were going to win. "Steady, boys," said Damian MaGuire, our hard-charging Australian center. "Hit it up in there."

For several minutes, everything we did turned to gold: swift, beautiful scrums, clean pickups and hard running into the gaps. I sprinted from one joyous breakdown to the next, digging the ball out like a fox terrier, and in the continuous, switchback manner of good rugby, twenty-six-year-old Marc Murray from Amoskeag scored three tries in succession. Walking back to midfield, gnarly-eared John Solomon from Washington, D.C., slung his arm around my neck and Bill Bishop came alongside and grinned like a matinee idol.

"That's the stuff," Billy said.

On that chilly afternoon in Louisiana, we defeated the Rhineaux 48–14. At the final whistle, the Vandals all crowded around and mussed each other's hair and spat on the bayou mud we'd been wallowing in. Then we gathered round, making a bouquet of our fists and gave three cheers for Lafayette and three for the referee, and I felt young and strong. I felt alive. Past the age of fifty, I was grateful for every second on the field, and for every moment I spend on this earth.

Not long after that trip, Surfer John and I played for the Vandals again in the Fort Lauderdale Ruggerfest, with several of our old buddies from U of Florida watching from the sidelines. They were hooting at first, making fun of my gray hair and pretty much ridiculing everything I did. But we played a solid match against a bunch of young studs from the metro New York select side, losing by a converted try. Afterward our former teammates greeted us with some cold beers.

"You're still playing real rugby out there," one of them said.

Not long after that, I injured my left foot in a mountain climbing accident, suffered through the ankle surgery, and then an eye operation for a "cataract by trauma," which was caused by a vicious sucker punch in a rugby game nine years ago. Now, facing all that physical therapy and with my sporting future in doubt, I can't help thinking about how much I love rugby, and how it all got started.

Chapter 2

We Are the Boys from Old Florida

In my mind's eye, I can see myself clearly, as though I am walking along a few feet to one side and in possession of my former self at the same time. It's early September 1980 and there I am, in aviator sunglasses, tan corduroy shorts, wrinkled oxford shirt, and toting a backpack as I veer off the broiling sidewalk on SW Thirteenth Street in Gainesville, Florida, and pass beneath the ancient trees shading Norman Hall, angling toward the browned over athletic field where the University of Florida Rugby Football Club is practicing. My heart rate is ascending and the first thin stream of adrenaline is loose in my bloodstream.

It's Tuesday evening, near the end of my first week in graduate school, and after seeing a flyer on a telephone pole, I'm eager to meet someone from rugby and get a toehold on the club. Jostling around in my bag are a few notebooks and pencils, my old soccer cleats and a pair of canvas shorts, my Peabody Nautilus T-shirt, and a form-fitted mouthpiece. I'm ready to step in and play, if asked.

A grassy embankment borders the north end of the rugby pitch, a million insects massing around the bank of klieg lights. Before descending to hunt for the coach, I pause at the crest with my Chuck Roast bag over one shoulder, scanning the lines of motley clad players running up and down. Nearby, two groups of forwards practice scrummaging directly on the berm, using the gentle incline to provide extra resistance.

Just as the heavier, more skillful A-side pack shoves their opposition up the embankment with a combination of prowess and grit, the eight-man pops his head out from between the second rows, looks over at me and grins.

"Hey, pardner," he says. "Wanna play some rugby?"

I can't help smiling back. "Right on," I tell him.

The eight-man is bound in at the rear of the pack, the main conduit to the scrumhalf, and usually a pretty big guy who runs the ball and tackles like a madman. After the initial shove, he detached himself from the rest of the pack and ambled over to introduce himself and shake my hand. Upright, Dave Farwick was a tall, broad-shouldered, well-built fellow, with a thick neck and an athlete's easy gait. We talked for less than a minute, though it was as if we'd known each other for years. Soon I was dropping trou as coeds streamed past on the sidewalk, hopping on one foot as I tugged on my cleats, in a great hurry to meet the coach, Jon van Blokland, who Farwick had pointed out.

I'd been in Gainesville since the end of August. After graduating from Acadia, I'd spent the next year fumbling around in Denver, most of that spent gazing out a classroom window at the nearby Rockies, wondering what the hell I was doing in law school. Other than being anointed the best street hockey player at the downtown YMCA (until a guy from Michigan showed up), the highlight of my stint in Colorado was playing wing and inside center for the Mile High Rugby Football Club. They practiced in a manicured park not far from the University of Denver Law School and one of my classmates, a guy named Colin Campbell (a former rower from Princeton, and half brother to Brad Dourif, the actor who played Billy Bibbit in *One Flew Over the Cuckoo's Nest*, among other memorable roles), and I escaped from the tedium of our studies as often as possible to get a run in with Mile High RFC.

Mile High played an early season match in Evergreen, Colorado, hometown to President Reagan's would-be assassin, John Hinckley, Jr. The town and the rugby pitch, as I recall, were located on a lovely plateau in the foothills of the Rocky Mountains, and that morning both teams were employed in shoveling off a thin blanket of fresh snow to reveal the touchlines and markings so our game could be played. It was memorable for a couple of reasons. In the first half, our bandy-legged scrumhalf, Jerry van Valkenburg, picked up a ball from a ruck and took it alone to the weak side of the field, where only a single defender blocked his path to the try zone.

Van Valkenburg was several years older than Colin and me, a lawyer by trade, and a voluble, opinionated fellow originally from back east, New York, I think, which made him a natural antagonist to someone from the Boston area. Van wasn't very big or fast, but he had quick feet, an agile mind, and the kind of moxie that suits the man playing that position, which is somewhat akin to the quarterback in football, except that the scrumhalf, like everyone else, never leaves the field to talk to the coach and look at Polaroids of what just happened.

As Van raced at the husky young player waiting in the gap, he suddenly put on the brakes, skidding to a stop like a roadrunner in a cartoon. Halting a yard or two from the Evergreen defender, Van pointed at the sky above the kid's head and cried, "Look!" The dumbfounded wing followed Van's arm with his gaze, up toward the armada of clouds floating past, whereupon our cagey scrumhalf tucked the ball under his arms and dashed forty yards for the go-ahead try, laughing as he went.

We won the match and afterward convened at an old saloon on the town's rustic main street. Drinking at the bar, I realized that I wanted to play rugby with characters like Van Valkenburg for as long as I possibly could, and damn the rest. So right after Christmas, I quit law school and holed up at a friend's place in Boulder, writing a short story that I would use for applying to master's programs in creative writing. The story was based on an epic fistfight I'd engaged in while at Acadia, with a knuckle dragger named Lloyd who hailed from Cape Breton. It's a rough part of Nova Scotia and he had at least twenty pounds on me, but with my pals Drew Cooper and Ronnie Martin and Jeff the Ghetto looking on, eventually I wore Lloyd out, bringing him to the ground with a double-leg takedown, tying up his arms and knocking him senseless with four or five noggin-denting head butts. (I was bleeding from several cuts on my face and Coop thought it would be a great idea, at 2 A.M., to bring me over to the dorm room of Marjorie MacDonald, a gorgeous varsity swimmer from Newfoundland, so she and her roommate could help me clean up. I was head over heels for Marj and did not object, but what strikes me now is that Coop had a steady girlfriend, Sheila, who he's been married to now for more than twenty years. Like a good rugby buddy, he was always looking out for me.) On the strength of this submission, the University of Florida accepted me to their master's program.

Arriving in Gainesville with only a couple hundred bucks in my pocket and, due to my late application, no promise of a teaching job to help pay the bills, my initial outlook was pretty grim. I rented a room in a seedy boardinghouse off NW Thirteenth Street, with a rusted iron bedstead, no television or stereo, and an obese, nosy, lecherous old landlady, Mrs. P, who had a habit of knocking on my door after midnight to inquire whether I had any tea bags. Tea bags, my ass.

Dave Farwick was the second friendly face I encountered on that red-letter day. The University of Florida is spread over two thousand acres, and without even a bicycle transportation, I'd set out on foot to locate my classroom buildings, the bookstore and the gymnasium. Showing up unannounced in the English department, I wandered among the maze of tiny offices searching for the graduate student adviser. Jack Perlette was from the northeast, a wiry, bespectacled former hockey player who took pity on me, and my rapidly diminishing stake. He called a friend at the English Language Institute, which happened to be located in Norman Hall, arranging for me to interview for one of their positions teaching English to foreign students. It was a stroke of good fortune, and my trip to Norman Hall and its adjoining rugby field took on a dual purpose.

I was able to join in for the final thirty minutes of practice, long enough to get sweaty before my night class and to catch a wild elbow to the face from somebody. When Coach Van Blokland keened on his whistle to mark the end of the session, I hurried out of my cleats, pausing to tell Farwick, who was the first-side captain, that

I'd be back on Thursday. I had no idea at the time that I'd just been introduced to four or five guys who would play major roles in the ongoing dramedy of my life—over the next two and a half years in Gainesville, and continuing to the present day—or that two or three more would appear within a few months. I was too busy hustling across the darkening campus to my fiction writing class, which my printout informed me was being taught by some guy named Harry Crews.

Chapter 3

In Praise of First Things

A wide boulevard lined with enormous palm trees and the occasional live oak formed the quickest route to my classroom from Norman Field. The campus was deserted at that hour, as the 7 P.M. classes had just begun; the large, porticoed stone buildings along either side were illuminated here and there by spotlights or otherwise wreathed in the early darkness, and the scent of flowering plants wafted on the close, humid air. Most of these streets, which were patrolled amiably by the campus police, were limited beyond a certain point to foot traffic and I hurried down the center of the roadway, in my curious ensemble of rugby shorts and socks, a pinstriped oxford shirt, and running shoes. My cleats and a notebook and pencils leaped around in my backpack as I jogged toward the GPA classroom building, a nasty mouse forming under my right eye where I'd been struck with an elbow; my heart booming, a doubled-branched river of endorphins and adrenaline pouring into my chest from the brief rugby practice, and the notion that I was late for my first-ever graduate writing class.

I bounded up six flights to the third floor of the new-looking classroom building, the sound of my footsteps ringing on the metal treads. Emerging at the end of a long hallway, I overtook a large, jut-jawed fellow in a battered golf shirt and cheap dungarees limping past the departmental office, which had closed up for the night. The fluorescent lighting threw a sickly cast over the man's face: his gray-black hair, cut short and badly, was plastered down on his Cro-Magnon forehead. His hooded blue eyes were set deep inside his skull, above prominent cheekbones, a nose that had been broken a few times, and a thin, cruel mouth. By the looks of it, the university recruited its janitorial staff at moldy old boxing gyms and soup kitchens. The man paid me no mind, stumping along the corridor with his head angled down at the floor.

"Hey, chief," I said. "You know where fiction writing is?"

With a baleful glare, my latest acquaintance directed me into a nearby seminar room with the flicker of his hand and a bestial grunt. Inside the small, well-lit chamber were a dozen or so fresh-faced young grad students, and a couple of middle-aged guys that must have been taking the class for enrichment or something. The fellow with the limp came around to the head of the table and made a profane remark to a thin, wiry guy in his thirties, who just laughed and shook his head. Apparently the fellow I had mistaken for a custodian was the professor, which wasn't the last mistake I would make that night.

A prodigious talent with a short-fused temper and a fuck-you attitude, Harry Crews is the author of more than twenty-five books, including *The Gypsy's Curse, A Feast of Snakes, Car, A Childhood: The Biography of a Place, The Knockout Artist* and *Body*. Born in hardscrabble Bacon County, Georgia, in 1935, Crews first came to the University of Florida in in the late 1950s, after a hitch in the Marine Corps. With the assistance of his mentor, the writer and teacher Andrew Lytle, a hard-drinking Southern gentleman in his own right, Crews began to develop his unique literary voice, which is articulate, gritty, and raw, like a pissed-off Shakespearean rustic with a dagger sunk into his breast, keening his death song center stage.

Over the past fifty years, Crews has written and optioned Hollywood screenplays (though none has been produced, thus far); appeared in a riveting cameo in Sean Penn's directorial debut, *The Indian Runner*; contributed dozens of articles to major magazines like *Esquire* and *Playboy*; written a stage play titled *Blood Issue*; and participated in tumultuous friendships with the likes of Penn, his former wife, Madonna, the musician Levon Helm, and actors Charles Bronson, Ed Harris, and Harry Dean Stanton, as well as dozens of his former students. At the time that I met him, Harry had published ten novels in ten years, and he hadn't done it quietly or humbly, awakening a rabid lust for schadenfreude among many of his academic colleagues, most of whom Crews had no affinity for. Harry Crews is not for everybody—now that he's retired and ailing, he's practically been erased from the University of Florida English department's history, like one of those Russian bureaucrats who suddenly goes missing from archival photographs of the Politburo. Despite his enduring unpopularity among some of his under-published peers, a significant number of writers owe their careers to Harry, myself included. For it is as teacher and mentor to three generations of aspiring writers that Crews has truly distinguished himself—a distinction that has been often overlooked in the forging of the Crews legend.

Of course, I didn't know any of this back then. I had arrived in Gainesville because it was the only creative writing program that would have me; I literally had no place else to go. So when the gruff, squinty-eyed Crews plunked himself down at the conference table in the writing room and outlined his teaching method in that thick Georgia drawl, I couldn't translate his soliloquy fast enough to write much of it down. Rubbing the tattoo of a hinge on his elbow joint, Crews asked us if there were any questions, while wearing an expression on his weather-beaten face that said he didn't wish to entertain any.

You could tell right away that Harry Crews was not all sun-warmed raspberries and puppy dogs, but I'm nothing if not stubborn, raising my hand to say, "Excuse me, Professor, but I couldn't understand what you said because of your accent. Could you repeat it, please?"

At the end of my comment an undercurrent of tension electrified the room. A female student emitted a tiny gasp, and several people shifted in their chairs. For a long while, Crews just stared at me, his face a blank mask. "I don't much like your accent, either," he said, in a low, menacing voice. "We can go outside and settle it, if you want."

Around the table there was more shuffling of feet and examining of cuticles. This was the damndest graduate school I had ever heard of, where the professors and students were expected to adjourn into industrially lit hallways to fight like dogs. I noticed that an old gent with a gray crew cut, Western boots, and a pearl-button shirt had also narrowed his gaze on me. He turned out to be a retired physician who had been trying for years to complete a western novel filled with gunfights and brawling cowboys. It seemed he had a scientific interest in the path of bullets fired into the human body at close range and other violent esoterica, which was not matched by his narrative gifts. He was watching both of us closely, his chin lifted toward me in professional surmise.

Harry Crews was a big man, half a head taller and at least fifty pounds heavier than me. The whitened scars gathered over the ridge of his brow indicated that he'd been in his share of fights, and I speculated briefly on how many of those had started in class. But I've been known to get my Irish up on occasion, and was high on the naturally occurring chemicals racing through my bloodstream from rugby practice.

"Fuck it," I said, rising from my chair. "Let's go."

At the far end of the table, the small, wiry guy who Harry had spoken to earlier started in his chair, uttering a tiny sound. Annoyed, Harry cut his gaze over that way, and asked, "Why, what do you think of his fucking accent, Costello?"

His name was Mike Costello, a decorated combat veteran and a favorite of Crews's who had spent most of 1968 in Vietnam with the 199th Light Infantry Brigade. In platoon operations, his unit was transported by helicopter into the boonies, where they would remain for days, walking, camping, and looking for trouble.

Costello looked over with a sad little smile, and said, "Jay's accent is memorable, Harry. Just like yours."

Harry continued to glare at me for another moment. "All right," he said. "Fuck it." We both sat back down. There was more uneasy silence, and then Crews asked if anyone had a story to read. Nobody spoke up, and finally I raised my hand and Crews waved in my direction, saying "Go 'head."

It was the only story I'd written to that point: "The Fight." It was pretty awful, but it contained men, darkness, fear, rage, joy and blood, all of which were presented in a cinematic way. As I read the six or seven pages, Crews listened with his eyes closed and a smile playing over his lips. When I was through, he extended his hand across the table and I shook it.

"Harry Crews," he said, in that gravelly, inimitable voice. (He always pronounced his name as *Harr-a Crooze*.) "We're gonna get along just fine, son."

My first encounter with Crews dramatized an essential component in the mentor-student relationship—that the teacher must challenge the apprentice and the apprentice must rise to that challenge. Beyond this fact, Harry is one of those rare individuals who embody the rugby personality without ever having played the game, a rare trait in my experience, as the varying combination of grit, aggression, physical courage, loyalty, chivalry, insouciance and comic self-awareness typically develops from time spent between the lines. You can often tell a rugby player by the way he walks: one hip thrust forward as he ambles along, grinning at what the world presents to him.

But learning to write is also a contact sport, certainly not an occupation for the weak willed, or anyone who is easily discouraged or offended. Harry called it "a nasty, bloody business," yet thanks to my innate competitiveness and blue-collar background, I kept returning to his office over the next two and a half years, where he would hand back my failed stories without a mark on them and then proceed to discuss the scenes, characters and dialogue contained therein with a depth of understanding and subtlety that a more selfish person would've saved for his own work. Harry would shove the pages across the desk at me, and then prescribe *The Heart Is a Lonely Hunter* or *The End of the Affair* or *Wise Blood* for what ailed my writing. I'd take my medicine without protest or apology. And then he'd dispense the only useful advice that a writing teacher can give: Go fix your ass to the seat of the chair.

I studied with Harry Crews for six consecutive semesters when he was known to take a drink, and once said to me, "I've had off days. Hell, I've had off *weeks*." But Crews with a terrific vodka hangover remains the most definitive, charismatic authority on writing and literature I've ever known. All his classes were filled to overflowing, as the student ghetto rang out with news of this guy who dressed like a hobo and lectured like a king. From the very start, I ran to Harry's classes, scrambled for a place up front and hung on every word like it was Holy Writ. When I tell my own students that I used to follow Harry outside, jotting down everything he said, and then hurried to an actual bricks-and-mortar library to check out the books he mentioned, they stare at me like I was Saroyan's haberdasher, or played football with Hemingway.

In Harry's mind, what we were doing on the third floor of the GPA building was no different than joinery or glassblowing, and if an apprentice was blessed with a smattering of natural talent and some luck, and then pressed onward in the face of all obstacles, he or she might rise to the position of journeyman. I would walk home after class, thinking about that fact.

It could get lonely at night those first two or three weeks, with Mrs. P. rumbling around in the hallway and local teenagers hotrodding past on NW Thirteenth Street. I didn't have any money to go out, and though there were thirty thousand students at the university, I only knew one so far: Dave Farwick. But I had the definite sense that I was in the right place at the right time, for my writing and my rugby, and that before long there would be men, darkness, fear, rage, joy, blood and girls, lots of girls—all of it presented in a cinematic way.

Chapter 4

The Girls in Their Dolfin Shorts

After four years of those Canadian girls, the swimmers especially, bundled up in their Hudson Bay sweaters and peacoats, mufflers wound four or five times around their necks, and their lithe torsos and fine long legs hidden beneath bulky turtlenecks and woolen trousers; and then the prim Denver secretaries in flat shoes and ski vests, hoisting their cowhide messenger bags as they paraded along Colfax Avenue, I was not at all prepared for what occurred at the University of Florida on a gorgeous September afternoon when classes let out. At ten minutes to the hour, chatty torrents of half-naked female flesh came pouring from the vaulted doorways of every building on campus—an event that appeared to be staged for my benefit the first time I witnessed it. As the bell tolled from the zenith of Century Tower, thousands of girls came rushing out in a graceful troupe, brunettes and redheads for sure, but mostly blondes, blondes in every shade of wheat, amber, and gold, in their hiked up, diaphanous shorts, a veritable army of honey-dripping marauders: the slim brown shoulders and slender arms, their nails painted fire-engine red, legs firm and tanned and lovely. With skin-tight FLORIDA tank tops riding up to expose an inch or two of midriff, gold bracelets jangling, their faces unlined and unworried and marked only by a touch of mascara and lip gloss, all of them speaking to one another in a low sibilant buzz of indistinguishable meaning but, paired with their light floral scent, this hourly promenade of coeds was one of God's little miracles, assuring the regional propagation of the species to a mathematical degree of certainty that would have impressed the guys in the statistics department.

The best place to witness this hourly migration was from a bench on the campus's great central park, the Plaza of the Americas. The rugby players called it the Plaza of the Dirtbags, since during classroom hours various corners of this greensward were occupied by Hare Krishnas kitted up in their orange bedsheets, dispensing free ladlefuls of vegetarian succotash along with their harebrained cosmology; soapbox proselytizers railing against Ronald Reagan and his ranch hands—foreign trade, the current economic meltdown, industrial pollution, and what-have-you (One afternoon while I was sitting on the plaza with a handful of rugby players, one of these habitual protesters, a short, pudgy, bespectacled fellow, came bustling along with an armful of pamphlets and a bullhorn. Somebody asked him what the burning issue was on that particular day, and he said, "Unsecured federal bonds" out of the side of his mouth without even slowing down.); and homeless young troubadours playing their guitars and bongos, or else bench-pressing rusted sets of weights they carried in each day from who knows where, shirtless and tanned so dark they looked like muscle-bound Al Jolsons in blackface, and smelled like livestock. There was also a handsome young guy in a customized wheelchair; a mysterious, charismatic fellow named Seamus, who usually sat in the shade reading a book, attended to by a shifting retinue of helpmates. We often wondered what his story was.

In those first weeks, I was so preoccupied by this horde of tender young things I just sat down, either on a bench or a stone wall or beneath a tree, knocked off my pins by this cavalcade of cheesecake, letting it rush by on all sides until it abated, at a few minutes past the hour. Talk about your embarrassment of riches. I felt like a fisherman so awed by a running school of blues he forgets to throw his line out. Most of these coeds were undergrads from Miami and Fort Lauderdale and Tampa-St. Pete, sorority girls and ex-cheerleaders and those that played a mean game of tennis at Daddy's club; not that they were too good for me, exactly, but we had very little in common for the most part, and I was three or four years older than the majority of them, which seems like no big deal now, though for some reason it did back then.

Moreover, what few women I had encountered in the graduate school were plain, eyeglass-wearing types, a Bible thumper, a couple of married broads, and a nutty, barefoot girl who cornered me at a reception for new master's candidates, going on for twenty minutes about minimalism, post-modernism, and sexual repression in Virginia Woolf. Two of these gatherings in the first week, and it was plain that I really didn't fit in there.

Having secured a teaching gig, I spent a good portion of each evening in my room on the third floor of Mrs. P's rickety old boarding-house, seated at a tiny desk working on a new story that I imagined would impress the editors at the *New Yorker* or some other prestigious magazine, leaving me on the same familiar terms with Harry Crews as Mike Costello and old Doc Shoot-'em-up.

The story was called "Gainesville Blues," and gazing down at the trash-strewn alley, crisscrossing telephone wires, and the auto parts stores and taco stands that formed my vista in that quarter of the city, I had no trouble drawing on a reservoir of colorful local experiences in fashioning my tale, along with a dash of self-pity. Like any good apprentice, I tried to utilize the materials at hand and, feeling like a character straight out of the 1930s, a figure conjured up by Ring Lardner, Jr., or S. J. Perelman, I filled up the pages in a blue, stiff-backed University of Florida notebook with my own misadventures and those of the folks I met on the plaza.

That first semester I was teaching two courses of rudimentary English, which lowered my tuition, paid the bills, and left me with about two hundred bucks a month in spending money. I attended the required literature classes during the day, Harry's fiction seminar on Tuesday nights, and kept busy playing soccer for the English Language Institute team (it was loaded with flashy Brazilian and Venezuelan players from my classes, who were eager to share the ball with their maestro), while also attending rugby practice on Tuesdays and Thursdays over at Norman Field.

The University of Florida Rugby Football Club was a bit of a misnomer in those days, as the team included several local players who
no longer attended the school, if they ever had. Though the vast
majority of the fifty or so athletes out to those early training sessions were matriculating at UF and our coach, Dr. P. Jon van Blokland, a charismatic, fortysomething Englishman, was a professor
of agricultural economics, a handful of older players formed the
backbone of the first side and controlled the selections. Since I was
busy with varsity sports at Acadia, and had played only one fall
season in Denver, my rugby education was accelerated in Gainesville because the fine weather allowed us to play straight through
from September to May, essentially doubling the number of matches
played by northern clubs. Also, since college sides were fairly scarce
in Florida at that time (UF, Florida State, U of Central Florida, and U
of Miami), we competed in the men's division against hardened
club teams in Jacksonville, Winter Park, Orlando, Boca Raton, Fort
Lauderdale, and elsewhere. It was a tough schedule.

UF fielded two sides, and with many more than the thirty players
required for that practicing over those first few weeks, it was incumbent upon new arrivals to somehow make an impression on the
coach, and the first-side veterans. Van Blokland worked us like rented
mules in that early September heat, a series of wind sprints, ball-
handling drills, calisthenics and ruthless shuttle runs, all the while
keeping up his cheerful repartee: "Go on, then. One more time up
and down the park. That's right, Martin. You've got no bloody business being tired. You're a bloody West African, aren't you? Okay, all
right, we're set now. Would you prefer the hand, the whistle, or the
'whee' to start you off?"

The first half-dozen training sessions the field was crowded with
freshmen and sophomores in cutoff football pants and old mesh
jerseys, former high school studs just a little too undersized, or a
step too slow, for NCAA Division I football, but impressive nevertheless. Also running around Norman Field were prissy frat boys in
their mail-order rugby boots and starched white shorts; a handful
of muscle-head types who walked off in the middle of all that running and never came back; and another intriguing little group, a
freewheeling bunch of rookies who joined up the same week I did,

four or five easygoing dudes who arrived on motorcycles and mountain bikes and skateboards and, while the other players were looking all serious and pissed off, warmed up by throwing a Frisbee
around barefoot and doing backflips, or walking on their hands in
the middle of the field.

These guys weren't very big, my size mostly, five nine, five ten,
170 to 185 pounds, shaggy-haired, unkempt, smelling of pot every
day, but agile, boisterous, outgoing and friendly, in old short-sleeved
rugby jerseys from other cities, other countries even, teams and
clubs I'd never heard of, La Plata Juniors and Bermuda Schoolboys
and West Point and Rossall College. Compared to what I'd seen thus
far in my brief career, and most definitely in contradistinction to the
dour, bearded older guys on the club, these whiz kids were a different type, some kind of rugby player X, and definitely entertaining to
watch. They were the new blood, and I wanted to be part of that.

One way to get noticed was to stand out during the live, fifteen-
on-fifteen scrimmages that Van Blokland officiated on Thursday
evenings, pitting the A-side returnees against a shifting cast of second team players. Since our opening league game was still a couple
of weeks away, these mini test matches were a welcome break from
the tedium of ball drills and sprints. I've always been a fitness
hound, and though taken aback by central Florida's heat and humidity, was coming off four years of strenuous workouts at Acadia,
where in October and November I was required to attend four-hour
workouts every day: soccer practice from 4 to 6 P.M. in the raw, chilly,
Nova Scotia weather, a brutal wind coming off the Bay of Fundy, and
then wrestling practice from 6 to 8 P.M. in the airless and overheated
cracker box of the War Memorial Gymnasium.

In the four-corners drill at Norman Field, with van Blokland at
midfield blowing on his whistle, I'd be sure to stay with the first
group, running from push-ups in the try zone a hundred yards to the
other end of the park for squat thrusts, across the twenty-five-meter
width in a diminishing cluster of players to the crunches and sit-ups,
and back down the long one-hundred-yard touchline for jumping
jacks; around and around until a couple of guys started puking and
Van Blokland decided we'd had enough. I was pretty fit and could
handle the ball all right so Farwick and second-row forward Cary

Vick and a center named J.T., who consulted on selections, installed me at inside center on the second side.

Going live against the A-side was serious business. My opposite number was Jim Thul, who was known by his initials, J.T. There was no mistaking him on the rugby field: his blue and white practice jersey, his dark socks pulled up high, his stiff-footed gait, and above all, his half-insolent air proclaimed who he was. A stocky, bearded man, Thul had played lightweight football at Penn State in the mid-seventies, and resembled a Civil War general with his bushy whiskers, stubby lower teeth and obdurate manner. J.T. was the exact opposite of his new, barefoot, Frisbee-throwing teammates, and though he and I were both from the Northeast—Thul had grown up in New Jersey—we took an almost instant disliking to one another.

J.T. played club scrimmages like he was trying out for the national team: no joking around, half-speed run-throughs, or brother-in-law tackling. He also had the advantage of being surrounded by the club's best players, and a knowledge of what they were likely to do in any given situation—both conditions that are integral to success in rugby, the ultimate team sport. On my side of the ball, several rookies were making their debut, which was a disadvantage. In particular, the B-side fly half, playing next to me and charged with distributing the ball to the backs or kicking it, couldn't get out of his own way, or anyone else's. He was just awful: dropping good passes from our scrumhalf, running into his own forwards by mistake and kicking the ball directly to J.T. and the redheaded Danny Marvel on the other side, who counterattacked it straight down our throats.

During a brief pause in the scrimmage, while fresh players were being rotated in, I called over to one of our flankers, a tanned, fit, athletic-looking kid with blond hair who had already made a few good tackles and generally finished ahead of everyone in the conditioning drills.

"Hey, surfer, can you play fly half?" I asked, out of earshot of the guy currently occupying the position.

"Yeah, sure."

"Good, 'cause this dude is killin' us."

The kid I was talking to looked like somebody right out of a 1960s surfing movie: blue eyes, sun-bleached hair worn over his collar, with a square jaw, high cheekbones and shiny white teeth. He didn't say much in those first few weeks, at least not to me (we were both following that time-honored athletic tradition of keeping your mouth shut on a new team and letting the quality of your play do the talking), but he was easygoing and friendly and had that sporting jack-of-all-trades look and attitude that I took pride in myself. So when I suggested the change in fly halves, he just ambled over in the midst of the general rotation and put himself there.

The surfer was capable of getting the ball out quickly and cleanly, seldom kicked it and wasn't afraid to run into the first tackler just as he off-loaded the ball to me, which created a little space to run. We made a couple of nice breaks and gang-tackled J.T. once or twice, with help from the other flanker, a lanky, ginger-haired newcomer who had grown up playing rugby in Bermuda. When the scrimmage ended and Van Blokland was lining us up for wind sprints, the surfer dude walked past me and we shook hands.

The B-side scrumhalf was a veteran second-teamer in his mid-thirties named Staley. Often missing from practice because of work, he was a quiet, loosely built, average-sized man, with a smattering of gray at the temples and a pencil mustache. He played rugby in tennis shorts, which was odd, and in addition to being the oldest guy on the team, he had the further distinction of owning a local bar. Friday Night Live was a couple of blocks north of Mrs. P's boardinghouse on NW Thirteenth Street, a small, rectangular, windowless joint sided in dark wood with a slanted parking lot that could accommodate maybe a dozen cars. After practice on Thursday night, Staley would put on a keg for the rugby guys and we'd load up on one-dollar drafts before heading out to more populous nightspots.

The interior of Friday Night Live was dank, unadorned and dim, smelling of stale beer and old cigarette smoke while lacking any furniture other than the tall wooden bar across from the only door. Several pillars obstructed your view from here to there, and a small parquet dance floor was dimpled and dented and scuffed with a thousand black heel marks. It was a punk rock bar, just as that short-lived musical phenomenon was fading from view. The house band was The Irritations, a mangy little trio with a short, vascular,

slightly hunchbacked front man who screamed out the lyrics to ditties like "Blitzkrieg Bop" and "Turning Japanese," leaping around
the makeshift stage like a spastic chimpanzee. Slam dancing was in
vogue then, often incited by The Irritations lead singer, who was
quick to jump into the mayhem, while the few skinny, black-clad,
Mohawk-wearing punks that made up the bar's regular clientele
usually regretted the moment when the rugby players joined in.
One of the first rugby guys I met was a polyester-clad, jug-eared
forward from Okeechobee by the name of Keith Platt, who we nicknamed "the Epitome" since Coach Van Blokland had remarked in
practice that Platt, a nasty fellow on the pitch (though quite pleasant
off it), was "the epitome of American violence" and would rather
knock someone on his ass, twice, than score a try.

By ten o'clock on my first night at the bar I was pretty lit, and
along with Keith Platt, the guy from Bermuda, and a couple of determined locals, was taking speedy room-length sprints onto the dance
floor, smashing into whatever obstacle presented itself: punks, pillars,
members of the band and guys on the rugby team. Staley was watching from the end of the bar, smoking a cigarette with his foot up on
a case of empties, while The Irritations put out a racket that sounded
like a cross between the bombing of Dresden and a sawmill.

I don't remember exactly what happened after that. I was tucking
my right shoulder and charging into people, an activity that seemed
to be encouraged at Friday Night Live, and next thing I knew, I was
off my feet, rolling on the floor and trading punches with somebody. Staley had a bouncer working on Thursday, Friday, and Saturday nights, a nonmatriculating lunk head in a tight T-shirt and crew
cut, with a safety pin through his cheek and one razor-serrated
eyebrow. There was no tribal connection between these knuckle
draggers and the rugby club, and when he reached down to yank
me upright I thought it would be a great idea to throw a punch at
him—a sober, well-built, humorless misanthrope who had been
pitching out unruly drunks every weekend for a couple of years. So
I was soon disavowed of this notion, and got my ass kicked.

I am not a tough guy, by any definition. For most of my childhood
and early adolescence I was a dreamy, undersize kid whose idea of
a good time was attending a matinee performance of *Mary Poppins*

at the Palace Theater in Lawrence, Massachusetts. However, the kids in my neighborhood loved sports and so did I. Every day after school we played football or baseball in the street; and on odd-shaped parcels of land and in driveways, we entertained ourselves for hours with homemade contests like "running bases" and "outs" (where you threw a rubberized baseball against a set of cement stairs, and if your opponent caught it in the air or on a clean bounce, that was an out), or the self-explanatory "kill the man with the ball." I found that I didn't mind getting knocked down all that much, and enjoyed trying to tackle older, bigger kids.

But these kids were my buddies, for the most part. When we ventured out of our little enclave down to Howard Park, I was often terrorized by a local bully who liked to sneak up on me and hold my head underwater in the playground's concrete pool. (I honestly thought that I was going to die in that warm dirty water, someday.) In the winter, I wouldn't go down that way much, but the summers were horrible: it was the only place to cool off, and I lived in mortal fear of this kid. Let's call him Shabboud, a chunky, black-haired and beetle-browed evildoer who was probably getting the shit beat out of him on the second floor of the tenement where he lived and was looking for someone to take it out on. I was a logical target, I suppose, a couple of years younger and ten or fifteen pounds lighter, with no older brothers to defend me, or teach me how to fight.

Round about fourth grade, when the threat from Shabboud had dissipated for some reason, I began to figure out that you just had to be *willing* to fight, and most kids would leave you alone. One of the toughest kids in my grammar school, Dave Pandelena, was spoiling for a fight at recess one day and the other kids were shying away, even a few sixth graders I knew from the John Street bus. The Ashford School in those days was divided into two groups—the "hoods," in their pegged jeans, black engineer boots, T-shirts and slicked back hair, and the "collegiates," essentially proto-preppies, who favored short-sleeved madras shirts, penny loafers, and wide-wale corduroys or khakis. Pandelena was most definitely a hood, big and rangy for his age—he was probably thirteen in the fifth grade—with a brother, Mike, who was even bigger and had a five o'clock shadow by lunchtime.

I surprised everyone, including myself, by saying that I would fight him. Even Pandelena tried to talk me out of it: what a mismatch. But the object of my affection, Betty Jean Coco, was over by the hopscotch courts in her white stockings and navy-blue sailor dress, intent on the proceedings. Everyone had heard me say it. I shook my head grimly: *Let's do this thing.*

Pandelena gave me a quick and thorough beating. But he helped me off the ground and if we weren't altogether friends after that (I was somewhere in the vicinity of the collegiates), he never bothered me again. In fact, I didn't get in another scrap for two years, when we moved across town and I had to fight the toughest kid in the Searles School, on the very first day of sixth grade, which again proved to be strategic, though it cost me a pinstriped, double-breasted suit jacket.

All of this history telescopes down to the parquet floor of the sole remaining punk bar in Gainesville, Florida, where a huge welt is forming on my cheek and blood is seeping from a cut beneath my eye. Being a 165-pound wiseass has always been a dangerous occupation. But my two most recent bouts had been successful: I pretty much KO'd the bigger, heavier Lloyd from Cape Breton in front of Seminary House at Acadia, and in my final match as a 142-pound wrestler for the Axemen, had pinned a stout-looking middleweight from the University of Newfoundland (in the first round of a match I was not expected to win) at the Maritime Collegiate Championships in Halifax, Nova Scotia. And those points were the difference in earning Acadia the team championship.

What I had failed to remember when I'd thrown a telegraphed haymaker at the punk rock bouncer was that, overall, in street fights, playground brawls, hockey donnybrooks and varsity wrestling matches, my career record was something like 18–33. Not exactly championship caliber, and I was reminded of that ignominious fact when Staley and the bouncer got me under the arms, rushed me through the heavy wooden door and deposited me on the scarred and broken pavement in front of the bar. There I stayed for what seemed like a considerable length of time, ruminating on my social debut with the rugby club, my dwindling finances and a buxom girl named Darlyne who I'd worked with at the Jewish Community Center day camp the previous summer.

Half a minute later the door to Friday Night Live opened and I heard footfalls on the pavement. I looked up with my good eye: it was the surfer dude from rugby practice.

He regarded me for a moment and said, "That was probably ill advised," as he helped me to my feet.

We stood gazing at the stars over NW Thirteenth Street as I rubbed my sore jaw. Beyond the shadows of the parking lot, the strip of fast-food joints and convenience stores was bathed in the ethereal glow of neon light.

"Feel like a burger or something?" Surfer asked. "I'm hungry."

I spit out a gob of blood, mumbling about being low on cash.

"I got you covered," he said, and we set off for the bright lights of Thirteenth Street.

Chapter 5

The Last Free Saturday

After Surfer treated us to a midnight snack at Whataburger, we wandered toward the sound of rock music emanating from somewhere in the vicinity of Mrs. P's boardinghouse. It turned out to be a rambling wreck of a place, an old dingy Federal-style building marked by indecipherable Greek letters. Most of the fraternities were located on campus, a row of immaculately maintained antebellum mansions on a curved, sloping lane, separated from one another by beautiful emerald lawns and an occasional gigantic palm tree or live oak. Situated on a nondescript street a couple of blocks north of the university, Sigma Nu was a dumpy two-story house with crooked shutters and hundreds of empty beer cans lining the front walk. Inside, a couple dozen scruffy guys milled about talking to four or five girls, and Surfer and I helped ourselves to the keg, loaded the turntable with Springsteen records and picked up the conversation we'd started in the parking lot of Friday Night Live.

My new buddy's name was John Marshall Hearin, and he'd enrolled at UF after getting tossed out of West Point halfway through his junior year. He hailed from Daytona Beach, where he had grown up in a trailer park with his mother and sister, playing baseball and soccer at DeLand High while hitting the waves every chance he got.

At UF, he was majoring in aerospace engineering and planned on becoming an astronaut, just like the clean-cut former military pilots he'd occasionally run into near Cape Canaveral when he was scouting the surf. Getting pitched out of the United States Military Academy would deprive him of the free training as a jet pilot that would've been part of his minimum eight-year military commitment. But Surfer John Hearin was nothing if not enterprising, and had traveled to Gainesville to work on plan B.

The critical event at West Point had occurred in the summer before his junior year, when he'd just graduated from helicopter school at Fort Rucker in Alabama, and was heading off the base to celebrate with two classmates who'd also just earned their wings. One of the other cadets had a bag of pot and the MPs found it during a routine search at a checkpoint and they were all instantly, irrevocably in the shit. You were expected to drink up a river of booze in the service of the United States government, but Uncle Sam was not then, and probably never will be, down with the ganja.

Although Surfer was considered a model cadet before the pot bust, he had a bull's-eye on his tunic when he returned to West Point. Over that fall, he was written up for a torrent of minor offenses, ultimately leading to expulsion when he was spotted in the crowd at the Army-Navy football game. He was supposed to be working off demerits by "walking the area," marching solo with his rifle on the parade ground, and a classmate reported him to a superior. His stint in the army finished, he'd worked as a lifeguard all spring and summer, grown his hair long, and turned up for rugby at UF after playing the sport during his two and a half years at the Point.

Surfer was in the frat house kitchen talking to a coed in a pink miniskirt, and I was sitting in a moth-eaten chair in the deserted living room, my old, battered Houston Astros cap pulled low over my eyes, nursing a beer and grooving along to "Darkness on the Edge of Town." As might be imagined, I was more than a little surprised when a girl sat on the arm of the chair and yanked up the brim of my cap.

"Hi. What are *you* doing here? Oh, that's a nice black eye. You should get that looked at."

The voice close at my right ear came from an attractive, fit-looking girl with ringlets of blond hair strung with beads on one side of her smooth, pretty, well-tanned face. She had large, expressive brown eyes above a pert nose and full lips, and she laughed merrily at my initial remark—"I'm a fuckin' hobo. Leave me alone."—cuffing me on the shoulder like we'd been pals since kindergarten. Karen Koffler wore a pair of light green Dolfin shorts over a one-piece flesh-toned bathing suit, and when we both stood up to shake hands, she was as tall as I was, with the wide shoulders, narrow hips and lovely firm legs of a competitive swimmer.

Koffler, as I immediately began to call her, was from West Islip, New York, out on Long Island, an eighteen-year-old freshman water polo player who planned on becoming a physician. She was confident, friendly and well built, with strings of beads around her neck that accentuated her wide, full, upright breasts and an array of gold and silver and figured turquoise bracelets that jangled when she touched my arm or brushed away her hair. She smelled like the beach: of salt and sand, coastal breezes, suntan lotion and crushed oyster shells. We talked for over an hour, about our families, our childhoods, future plans, secret dreams and whether there was a heaven and what you would have to do to get there.

Koffler said she knew there was someone from up north in the house when the music changed abruptly to Springsteen, and that she figured out who it was by using the scientific method: eliminating each of the fraternity brothers she'd met her first week on campus, cross-referencing them against the other undergraduate men in their khakis and Top-Siders, finally developing her hypothesis based on the hard data provided by my facial abrasions, baseball cap and Peabody Nautilus T-shirt.

"Didn't your mother teach you not to talk to strangers?" I asked.

Koffler laughed. "There was just something different about you," she said. "You didn't exactly fit in."

Koffler was one of those people, like me, who is fascinated by the teeming minutiae of life, by new acquaintances, by spur of the moment adventures, and the absurdity of gender roles (aggressive = men; women = passive); rightful ascendancy expectations (a four-bedroom colonial on a leafy cul-de-sac as a hedge against anxiety, ennui and death); and social norming (the beautiful daughter of a blue-chip

Manhattan tax attorney should not, by any reasonable standard, be wearing a bathing suit after midnight in the ruined living room of Sigma Nu talking to the likes of me). On the whole, I found her to be intensely curious, forthright, intuitive and devoid of pretense: like a rugby player, only with nice tits.

During that magical hour, the frat boys and their girlfriends and hangers-on seemed to morph into statues and recede into the far corners of the room. All the sound dimmed out except for our conversation; I could barely hear Bruce rasping out the lyrics to "4th of July, Asbury Park," though the stereo was going full blast. I didn't know it back then, but in the space of a single evening I'd made two of the best friends a man was ever likely to meet.

Around 2 A.M. Koffler and I went onto the porch of Sigma Nu and stood for a moment examining the stars ranged above the city. We hugged at the top of the stairs, promising to stay in touch. "Bye-ee," Koffler said.

"See you in the funny papers," I said.

Surfer had long since disappeared, presumably with the girl from the kitchen. None of us had a telephone number to give out (this was a time, regrettably lost forever, before the onset of cell phones, online dating services, reality television and AIDS), though I knew I'd be running into Surfer at rugby practice the following Tuesday. When Koffler darted back to give me a peck on the cheek and then disappeared into the gloom, it occurred to me for the first time that there was nearly thirty thousand students at UF and our academic paths brought us nowhere near each other.

I trudged home beneath the mossy oak trees. There was no rugby game that weekend—the last free Saturday I'd have for quite a while—and I was flat broke. I had one class the next day, and that evening I was back at the little desk by the window, scribbling at "Gainesville Blues" and gazing out the window.

My neighbor across the hall at the boardinghouse was a good ol' boy from Tavares, Florida, named Scott Duncan. A loose-built, rosy-cheeked twenty-three-year-old architecture student who stood six feet five inches tall, Duncan smoked menthol cigarettes, listened incessantly to Molly Hatchet and Lynyrd Skynyrd at full volume and tugged an orange and blue Gators ball cap over his mass of curly hair the minute his feet hit the floor each morning. He had a steady girl back home, Miss Nancy, who he visited every other weekend in his big boat of a Dodge, and later that fall, when I was alone on Thanksgiving, he took me along to the family dinner and his mother's homemade corn bread stuffing.

Just two nights after the debacle at Staley's bar, I was working at my desk when Scott rapped on the door. Dave Mason's "Look at You Look at Me" was coming from this little eight-track player I had lugged down to Florida, and after Scott had filled the doorway for a couple of minutes, puffing on a Newport, he said, "I can't stand listenin' to this Yankee music. Let's go somewhere."

My room was roughly the size of a jail cell, about fourteen by eight, and on soft, fragrant nights like that one, I couldn't wait to get out of there. When I took my jacket down from a peg on the wall and looked up, Scott slapped me on the side of the head. "I'm fixin' to teach you about real music, boy. Southern rock."

After class one night Harry Crews had given me his address, inviting me to drop by anytime while hinting he'd look more kindly on an impromptu visit if I brought along a couple quarts of beer. Harry was pretty well known on campus and Scott was eager to meet him. We thundered down the back stairs to his car and were soon driving along West University Avenue, squinting at the house numbers in the dimness.

We stopped in front of a little square-framed clapboard house where Harry, after being thrown out by his bodybuilder girlfriend, Maggie, had a few weeks earlier taken up residence in a furnished room. It was on the second floor, considerably larger than the ones that Scott and I inhabited at Mrs. P's, with two broad-paned windows on each of the exterior walls, a full bath, double bed and a long, heavy wooden table that supported Harry's old manual typewriter and a stationery box half filled with manuscript pages from the new book he was working on. The room was otherwise undecorated, and smelled of sour laundry and roach spray. Empty quarts of Miller High Life lined the windowsills and rolled around on the floor as Scott and I entered the room, each of us carrying a bag with two icy, sweating quarts of Miller in it, as requested.

The three of us exchanged greetings and handshakes, and after giving one of the quarts over to our host, Scott and I took up positions on either side of the unmade bed, with Harry occupying the only chair in the room. He was dressed in a pair of flared Sears Roebuck jeans, cheap boat shoes and a baggy golf shirt with a little penguin embroidered on it, his hair mashed flat from lying down and his eyes red-rimmed and weary. He'd been reading *Hamlet* from a large folio of Shakespeare's plays and after we'd begun drinking the cold, sweet beer, Harry took up the leather-bound volume and read one of Horatio's speeches from near the end of the play.

Harry had an excellent reading voice; he often held the class spellbound with his dramatic renditions of Flannery O'Connor and Carson McCullers, and to hear him read aloud from a story being workshopped, which didn't occur very often, was like a young playwright having his lines run by a Tony-winning actor.

When Harry finished the speech, he put the volume on the table, and then patted it with his hand. "He sure was an indecisive sumbitch, but once he got moving, ol' Hamlet put some of those fuckers *down*."

The beer disappearing as quickly as our enthusiasm arose for a more crowded, convivial location, Harry suggested one of his favorite watering holes, Lillian's Music Store, just a few blocks away. Getting to our feet was the only requirement for departure; Harry didn't even lock his door.

Scott drove us there in the midst of a light drizzle. Situated on a cobblestone square in Gainesville's old downtown, Lillian's is a spacious, well-lit public house on the ground floor of a historic brick building. Large plate-glass windows etched with Victorian designs framed the entrance; inside, an ornate wooden bar ran the length of the right-hand wall, and a dozen or more tea tables draped in linen were arranged in rows over the main floor. Several parties occupied these tables and a boisterous din arose from there, and from the swells in twos and threes standing at the bar. Harry was on familiar terms with several pretty young waitresses and both of the bartenders, who greeted him with profane jocularity and poured his first vodka tonic without being asked.

Soon we were seated at a table in the center of the room, and after the beers and vodka were delivered, Harry began to hold forth on a variety of topics. Carrying twenty or thirty extra pounds, Harry used to enjoy telling smaller guys like me and Mike Costello, "You're lean, but you're *light*," giving you a hard shove while enunciating that "T" at the end with the elocution of a British schoolmaster. He would also challenge you, after a couple of drinks, to feats of strength: arm wrestling matches, and what he called knuckle wrestling, where the seated contestants would reach across the table and take hold of one another using only the middle finger of the right hand, and after a prearranged signal begin twisting or rotating their closed fists in a clockwise direction, until one or the other was forced into submission.

Lillian's is a classy, big money place, certainly the swankest joint in Gainesville that Scott or I had visited thus far, and hijinks like we were engaged in drew a fair amount of attention. At first Harry defeated both of us right-handed (Scott beat him lefty), but after he'd had another vodka, I put him down arm wrestling, and then twisted his middle finger so much beyond six o'clock that he fell out of his chair onto the floor when he capitulated. My victory did not go unnoticed.

Though Harry was a regular at Lillian's and threw his money around pretty good, duking the bouncer and hostess, this latest spectacle was enough to get us ejected. A steady rain was falling in the street, and as Scott headed for the door, I pulled Harry up from the carpet, slung his left arm across my shoulder, and cinching my right hand around his waist, helped him outside. It was like balancing a side of beef on a roller skate. Harry was practically deadweight, and as we lurched onto the sidewalk, Scott was torn for a moment between helping me keep Harry upright and going for his car, which was parked up the block.

The square was deserted but for a rusted pickup idling at the curb in front of the bar. While Scott, Harry and I stood in tableau against the falling rain, a young man in a lacquered straw cowboy hat leaned out of the driver's side window of the truck and sneered at us.

"Harry Crews is nothin' but a lousy drunk," he said. "Big shot writer! You're a fuckin' loser and a bum."

I tipped Harry onto his own feet and walked over to the truck. "What's your fucking problem, buddy?" I asked. "Harry has done more in his life than you'll ever do."

Behind me, Harry crashed to the pavement and rolled off the curbstone into the gutter, where the slough of rainwater drenched his pants and the back of his shirt. After emitting a pathetic groan, he lay there motionless, watching the proceedings with his uppermost eye.

The redneck in the cowboy hat was in his early thirties, with a long, bony face, short hair and a prominent Adam's apple that bobbed up and down as he continued his apoplectic denunciation of my mentor. In the front seat beside him, a mousy blonde in a jean jacket fussed at his elbow, telling him to just forget it and drive away.

"Yeah, why don't you just fuck off?" I said.

But when I got within arm's length of the truck, the driver reached into the shadows and took up a heavy-looking pistol, extending it through the open window. It was a silver-plated .38, the barrel of which reached almost to the bridge of my nose.

"Why don't *you* fuck off?" the guy said. "Fuckin' Yankee."

In the reflected light from the bar, I could see partway down the barrel of the gun. An enormous sense of calm overtook me, shoulders square to the window of the truck like the man inside was about to do something as harmless as taking my picture. There was no fear, as I've been lucky that way most times in my life when I should have been afraid. Nor was there a diorama of significant past occurrences rotating across my field of vision. I was possessed, most of all, by a strong sensation of curiosity over what was going to happen next.

The girl was screaming and tearing at the man's shirt, begging him to drive away, though all that seemed to be happening at a distance. An inner clock ticked off the final seconds of my life, as if a championship game was about to end, a portentous thing decided. It was a trivial thing to die for, I knew, but plenty of people have been killed for less.

Just then Scott sidled up to the truck, a yard or two off to my left. In a quiet but firm voice, he said, "You don't really want to shoot anybody, man. If you pull that trigger, your life is just as over as his."

Between her sobs, the girl pleaded with the cowboy to listen. He seemed to waver for an instant, the gun barrel trembling along with his hand. Then he retracted his arm, placing the gun somewhere beside him in the dark. "All right, Charlotte," he said.

The threat suddenly removed, my inner peace was supplanted by a mounting rage fueled with buckets of adrenaline. I reached across the cowboy's torso, my fingers closing on what felt like the pistol. I pulled my arm back and threw what I had in my hand onto the sidewalk behind me. But it was just the empty holster. *Oh-oh.*

This bold action incited the redneck to probe around in the darkness for his gun, but Charlotte caught it up before he could find it, pulling open the glove box at the same instant and locking the .38 inside. "Let's just go," she said.

"I ain't leavin' without that holster," said the cowboy, opening his door.

Under the streetlight he was six feet tall, pigeon-chested and clad in dusty jeans, boots and a T-shirt, his arms knotty with muscle and badly sunburned. The brim of his straw hat was tipped well over his eyes, leaving them in shadow, and when he came forward, I moved along with him, as though I intended to assist with his errand.

At the appropriate moment I bent down, reaching the tooled leather holster before he did, and grasping it in my fist I sprang up, using my legs to generate some momentum, and threw a long, looping uppercut that caught him on the point of his jaw. Somebody puts a gun to your head, and suddenly he's unarmed, well, you try to get at least one good shot in. "Fuck you," I said.

The redneck staggered back, surprised. Miraculously, the cowboy hat remained on his head. Executing a little two-step to keep his feet, he ran over to get his .38 but Charlotte refused to unlock the glove compartment. Scott continued to speak a placating version of redneck to him, and reluctantly the guy climbed into the truck, put it in gear and rumbled away.

Scott and I retrieved Harry from the gutter, where he was now thoroughly soaked from the runoff, his teeth chattering. With the storm drains rising in a chorus beneath the roadway, we loaded Harry into the backseat, and Scott drove back to his place. Harry got out under his own power, staggered into the house without uttering a word, and Scott threw the Dodge into gear and raced off with the stereo blaring.

We were babbling at each other like two idiots, trying to make sense of what had just occurred, with Scott puffing away at a Newport, stubbing it out and lighting another. When I began fishing in the backseat for what remained of the six-pack we'd started the evening with, he took a hard left onto SW Thirteenth Street, thrusting me against the passenger-side door, nearly throwing it open; then a quick right onto the darkened, dripping campus, where we barreled along an interior road at close to fifty miles an hour.

"Harry *fucking* Crews," said Scott, letting out a rebel yell. He snapped open a can of beer. "That's one ol' boy who really knows how to party."

Blue lights revolved behind us, and there was the quick sharp roar of a siren. Scott pulled over beside the School of Management, and two campus police officers walked up on us.

"What the heck are you guys doing?" one of them asked. His partner informed us that, even if this particular roadway was open to vehicular traffic, which it surely was not, the speed limit on campus was eight miles per hour. We'd been clocked at fifty-six.

Scott and I each had an open container of beer in our hands. It was one of those occasions where your only hope was the truth, and after a quick glance at me, Scott told the two cops what had happened outside Lillian's.

There was a short silence, where one of the cops looked at the other and shrugged, and then asked where we lived. Scott gave him the address of Mrs. P's boardinghouse, which was less than two blocks away, and the cop said, "Turn around, go on home, and stay there."

"Yes, sir," said Scott, easing into gear. "Y'all have a good night."

As we swung around, illuminating the crabbed underside of a palm tree, it occurred to me that graduate school was already paying off. Half of what I needed to know was in the library, and the other half was on the rugby field and in the street. Beyond that, I'd begun to understand that there were people you could love, people you could trust and a very small percentage that fit into both categories.

Chapter 6

The Friday Afternoon Drinking Club

My greatest contribution to the legacy of Florida rugby and to the hospitable climate of the Sunshine State in general, was in establishing a local chapter of the Friday Afternoon Drinking Club, the vaunted FADC, a singularly convivial social organization founded by a group of vagabonds and visionaries in Wolfville, Nova Scotia, in the year of Our Lord, 1975. I'd been invited to attend a few of their meetings during the spring of my senior year at Acadia, where the group's elders would often regale me with the history of the club, and as I began to make fast friends with a particular segment of the rugby team at UF, it was only fitting and altogether natural that we would open up a southern front, where I'd be charged with passing on a sense of the FADC's venerable tradition.

As far as anyone can tell, the first meeting of the FADC was held at Coolen's Trailer Park on Gaspereau ridge overlooking Acadia's campus, some time in late November after the football season had ended. The original attendees were a handful of Axemen football players, several of whom also played rugby, including my close friends Bill "Dag" Fullerton, who grew up in Halifax, Nova Scotia, and whose two front teeth are edged in gold; Quincy, Massachusetts, native John "Pinky" Stevens, a fellow Boston-area guy; my wrestling teammate Terry Tapak, a woolly-headed 240-pound mammoth with a friendly, laid-back manner; and the legendary Ralph Stea (pronounced *Stay*), a lanky, loose-limbed and nimble wide receiver for the Axemen who also played several years of representative rugby at center and fullback. I knew of Ralph Stea more than I knew the man himself; when Dag Fullerton asked you for a bottle of beer, and you tossed it across the room to him, he'd catch it with soft hands and quote Ralph, using a trio of sayings common to gentlemen requesting the ball from a teammate on the rugby field: "With you. [catch] Well threw. Thank you." Of course, I shared the general history of the FADC with the Florida enrollees as they joined up, but I also made sure these new conscripts were well versed in the bona fides of Ralph Stea, since his legacy is as important to the FADC as Benjamin Franklin's was to the equally mysterious Free and Accepted Masons.

FADC began operating just as I arrived in Wolfville, and when it was in its formative stages I hadn't yet made the acquaintance of Dag, Pinky, Drew Cooper and the other stalwarts, since I was busy cutting weight to wrestle at 142 pounds, and attending two daily practices while keeping up my studies in philosophy, art history and literature. But I hadn't been on campus very long when I first heard Ralph Stea's name mentioned. He was a kind of friendly ghost by the late seventies, a free spirit who seemed to disappear when football was over and then rematerialize at training camp the following August. In point of fact, however, Stea was a fixture on the Eastern Canada college football and rugby scene for more than a decade, and by the time I showed up at Acadia he was best known for a caper he had engineered playing football at Mount Allison University, located one hundred miles away in Sackville, New Brunswick.

That year, the Mounties ended yet another disappointing football campaign with a season-ending game at home. They were on the wrong end of a lopsided score but had the ball near midfield in the closing minutes. Playing split end, Stea, who was one of the few bright spots on the Mount A team and would soon transfer to Acadia, knew that he could beat the opposing defensive back on a post pattern and, in the huddle, convinced his quarterback to forgo the play the coach had sent in and throw the ball deep instead.

Ralph sprinted along the home sideline, threw a little head fake about fifteen yards downfield and then shifted into a whole other gear. His QB lofted a pass over the middle of the field and Stea, outrunning all the defenders, veered left, caught the ball in midstride and flew into the end zone without being touched. And he kept on running, between the goalposts, over the cinder track, through the open gates at that end of the stadium and onto Sackville's main street.

The home crowd's ragged cheering turned into laughter. But what made Ralph Stea run? Just before the previous set of downs, Stea had gone over to an injured teammate on the sideline in his street clothes and asked for five bucks, which he shoved down his pants. Gambling on a breakaway touchdown and a clear path out of the stadium, Ralph sprinted toward the liquor store a half block away, in helmet, cleats and all, the pigskin still tucked under his arm, and asked the stunned counterman for a five-dollar bottle of wine. A minute later, he reentered the stadium with the wine held aloft like the Olympic torch, as he took a victory lap and the crazed mob of Mount A fans screamed its approval.

Memorable events during that initial season of the FADC included an acid-fueled night culminating in a frantic search across campus for Terry Tapak's golden retriever, a bitch in heat; the template for a new game called Wineby, which consisted of two teams of fifteen players facing each other on a rugby field, whereupon each team would guzzle a gallon of cheap red wine in as few players as possible, recapping the empty bottle and tossing it along the line rugby-style, until the wing at the end ran it to the opposing try line and deposited it there—first team to go through fifteen gallons wins, with limited substitution (I actually attended the first Wineby match as an innocent bystander, a spectacle worthy of the fall of Rome); as well as the collaborative writing of a short play presented at Acadia's spring variety show titled *Why Can't We Be Friends?*

After the first year, most FADC meetings were held at the so-called Yellow House, located at 53 Highland Avenue in Wolfville.

The Yellow House was known for its funky smell, bowling alley-shaped living room, legless parlor furniture, and at least one kitchen wall stacked floor to ceiling with empty beer cases. I remember one occasion in the spring of '79 sitting on the curiously stunted furniture and drinking Alexander Keith's India Pale Ale with Dag, Pinky, Dan-o McNally and Scooter Riddell, an easygoing outside linebacker from Ontario who would later act in beer commercials, no doubt using the Stanislavski method to tap into his FADC experiences. Cable television in those days consisted of two channels from northern Maine and at three o'clock on a Friday afternoon, we were stuck with a syndicated religious program out of the Deep South, hosted by a bombastic nut job of an evangelist named Ernest Angley.

Angley claimed to be able to cure people of diseases over the airwaves, exhorting viewers to "put your hands on the [TV] set" when he was fixin' to start the healin'. Scooter was pretty hung over that day, trying a little hair of the dog as a remedy, and when Angley urged him to come forward, Scooter placed his oversize mitts on either side of the rabbit ears.

"Alcohol demons: come out!" bellowed Angley, reaching toward one of the in-studio cameras.

Nothing happened. Scooter shuffled back to his legless easy chair, retrieved his beer and pointed at the television. "That guy isn't cool," he said.

The first Gainesville chapter meeting of the FADC occurred in the driveway of a run-down bungalow on the edge of the student ghetto. By late fall, I was tired of the ass pinching Mrs. P, and Scott Duncan and I violated our leases at the boardinghouse by moving two blocks over to a cockroach-infested place I dubbed the Mansion, which rented for $350 a month. Scott only stuck around for one beer that afternoon since he was going home to visit Miss Nancy, so there were just three attendees at that inaugural meeting, all of them rugby players: myself, Surfer and an eighteen-year-old flanker named Conrad Merry.

While Surfer, industrious as usual, fiddled around with a tiny, three-legged charcoal grill he'd found in the weeds behind the Mansion, Conrad sat in the dust of our elongated front yard, barechested and smoking a cigarette. He was one of the Frisbee and hacky sack–playing newcomers, a collection of avant-garde ruggers who just sort of found each other and then adopted me and Surfer: Dave Civil, who had played for Bermuda's under-nineteen national rugby team and whose father was a U.S. Navy pilot; a tightly muscled little guy from Pompano Beach named Steve Smith, who had the quick, light patter of a street hustler and an overactive libido, even for a twenty-year-old rugby player; Greg Taylor, a former high school wrestling star from Maryland; and Carlos Ballbe, a shifty fly half from La Plata, Argentina, who talked like an erudite Speedy Gonzales, and whose brother, Gaston, a sometimes wing, was nicknamed "Get Stoned" by the other players. Carlos only weighed 135 pounds but I'd seen him bench-press 235, an amazing feat of strength for a skinny guy with long arms. He had started playing rugby at age nine, in La Plata, just outside of Buenos Aires. The youth rugby fields were in the *bosque,* or forest park. When you joined the team, Carlos said, you were stripped naked and baptized in the "Mississippi River," which happened to be a creek used for discharging waste from a nearby zoo.

Conrad had walked over from his dorm in nothing but a pair of dingy white rugby shorts, a small gold stud in his left ear and a rawhide cord around his neck hung with a metal washer. He had the aura of a Cockney orphan, a white kid whose family owned a large cocoa estate in Trinidad and who'd also lived in Venezuela, but who'd been packed off to an English boarding school with his older brother Frank at a tender age. Sitting in the dirt with his mop of curly brown hair and British accent, Conrad looked like a demented fifth Beatle.

He was tanned to a cinnamon hue, with a spare upper torso and the thick, sturdy legs of a habitual footballer, his feet blackened and tough from going around without shoes. While Surfer loaded the tiny grill with briquettes we'd pinched from an absentee neighbor, soaked this pyramid in lighter fluid well beyond the recommended amount and then tossed in a match that plumed upward with a theatrical whoosh when it reached the coals ("*Fire, good,*" said Surfer, doing a little dance), Conrad played with his cigarette pack and kept up a steady stream of chatter, on international politics, cocoa farming, boarding school pranks and the great books of Western lit. Conrad was a mere first-semester freshman and I was already in possession of an Honours degree in philosophy and literature, and he'd pretty much read everything I had and lots that I hadn't: dollops of Trollope and heaps of Camus and the sporting novels of R. S. Surtees, all of it good use of the hundreds of hours he'd spent lounging in train stations and airports and playing hooky in English pubs.

By this point, Surfer and I were pretty much the starting B-side fly half and inside center, respectively, with Dave Civil at one flanker and Conrad at the other, though Conrad was also getting a look-see with the A-side on substitutions. The B-side had run off four or five straight wins to begin the season, and pretty much ignored the old guard on the club to make our own fun after practice and on the weekends.

Conrad had the most unusual playing style I'd ever seen, before or since. He was always around the ball, smart, great anticipation, and a very sure tackler, especially of opposing forwards twice his size. During matches, though, and even more frequently in practice, he'd just sit down in the middle of the field when he got tired. If there was a stoppage in play, or if he was simply too beat to go on, he'd just plop down cross-legged like an Indian as the action raged around him or moved down the field, leaving him there alone. Most guys would go through the motions when they were that tired, acting like they were in pursuit, or even just walking toward the breakdown with their hands on their heads, totally gassed. But Conrad had no such pretensions. Sometimes he'd get up to rejoin play within a few seconds, and sometimes he wouldn't. It was the darnedest thing.

Conrad was an excellent player, like a great artist, very instinctual in his choices and unselfconscious. He was our best loose forward, although we had several very good ones, including Dave Civil, a guy named Chicago Ed, Keith Platt, and Farwick. (In the scrum, the two flankers and eight-man are the loose forwards, since no one is binding them into place.) Back in England at Rossall School, Conrad had been selected for a representative schoolboy team that went undefeated on a tour of Singapore, Hong Kong, and Japan, where they beat the All-Tokyo Schoolboys side; even then he was always sitting down during matches (which probably stumped the very disciplined Japanese), because he was usually in such terrible condition, loving rum and Coke and butts and hating to train the way he did. His favorite activity was getting together with close friends to drink beer, grill up some burgers, get high, listen to his favorite band, The Clash, and make no physical effort whatsoever. When he ate hallucinogenic mushrooms, he'd put on an antic disposition and run wildly about, proclaiming "I'm a young lion," or else he'd don headphones and wander through the local Winn-Dixie listening to The Clash's "Lost in the Supermarket" on his portable cassette player while doing whippits from the aerosol cans in the whipped cream aisle.

Conrad had worn an earring since the age of thirteen; been beaten up by skinheads in London, had the muzzle of an automatic weapon pressed against his belly by cops searching for pot in Venezuela, and spent his first afternoon in Gainesville over a few drinks at Big Daddy's lounge, chatting with a psychopath who'd just gotten out of the state prison at Raiford. He chain-smoked Marlboros that he bought with handfuls of pennies from a coffee can, because he was always waiting for money from home, and he was so generous when he had some that his friends would give him cash for just about anything, except to buy cigarettes. Conrad was truly a child-citizen of the world, the living embodiment of easy come, easy go, and for the next two-plus years I would call him up at every hour of the day or night, in crisis or in celebration, knowing that whenever and for whatever reason I'd called, he'd always be agreeable, saying "Sure, boofoo, come over. Yes. Anytime is fine. Adiós," and how many people can say they have a friend like that?

Dusk was filtering down through the live oak that overgrew the Mansion, the coals turning red-gray in the dimness. Earlier we'd run out to Publix for a couple of T-bones and as I hauled three more cans of PBR out of the cooler, Surfer took out his little box camera and snapped a picture of Conrad holding the bloody steaks up with a triumphant smile, like he'd killed a wild steer out on Paynes Prairie and slaughtered it himself. The aroma of roasting meat wafted over the ghetto, and I popped open my beer and lay back on one shoulder in the dusty grass. Saying, in so many words, that it was incumbent upon us, the charter members of the Florida FADC, to recognize and duly enshrine the noteworthy deeds and achievements of our forefathers, I repeated for the humble assembly a tale from the annals of Ralph Stea, recently conveyed by my good pal Drew Cooper.

The starting tight end on an Acadia U championship football team, Coop was also the best rugby player on campus and my best friend. An agreeable, lantern-jawed number eight from Valois Bay on the West Island in Montreal, Coop was, over a period of several years, a perennial short-list candidate to play rugby for Canada's national team, a side traditionally dominated by athletes from British Columbia. At a provincial select side tournament that summer, Coop told me, he'd run into his pal Ralph Stea. To preface this, Coop's stories about playing for the Wanderers RFC in Montreal were the primary reason I was playing rugby, capturing at once the drama and mordant humor and pathos of the sport, and of *la comédie humaine* in general, as they often did. (Coop and I had never taken the pitch together, but he and his younger brother, Trevor, who was also a marvelous athlete, and I had played European handball at Acadia, on a squad composed mainly of Coolen's Trailer Park refugees. Shortly after Coop and I left Wolfville for good, the guys on that team represented Nova Scotia in team handball at the annual Canada Games, and Trevor was killed in an auto accident.)

While Surfer and Conrad divided up the steaks and opened another round of beers, I finished this preamble. Just a few months earlier, when Coop had been selected as eight-man for the Quebec provincial side, they'd taken part in the Eastern Nationals held in St. John's, Newfoundland. Representative teams from Quebec, Ontario, Nova Scotia, New Brunswick and Newfoundland were vying for the right to go to the national championship match and "get killed by BC," the western champs, Coop said. After the first day of competition, the traditional players' banquet was held at a posh social club on the outskirts of St. John's. Entering the hall, Coop was very much looking forward to seeing his old football teammate Ralph Stea, and fellow Acadia man Rob Murray, both of whom were playing for the Nova Scotia team.

The Ontario players in the lobby were decked out in matching blazers embroidered with the provincial insignia, neatly pressed gray flannel slacks and striped provincial ties. Coop looked upon these Upper Canada posers with a mixture of amusement and disgust, as they were "more interested in winning than getting gunned" at the players' bar. The Quebec players, at least, wore jackets and ties, which were required by rugby union organizers, though none of their outfits matched. They devoured the free food and piled into the bar. There Coop spotted Ralph Stea, attired in an obnoxious yellow and black checked suit he'd purchased at Frenchie's, the infamous used clothing store. Coop said that the suit was so loud it was screaming, and it looked like Ralph "had stolen it from Herb Tarlek," the tacky sales manager at the fictional WKRP in Cincinnati. But it was a suit, nevertheless, accessorized by an equally garish purple and green tie. Ralph's outfit made an impression, to be sure, but the pièce de résistance of his remarkable ensemble was—no shirt! It was awesome, Coop said, made even more so by the way the Ontario snobs avoided Ralph like he had a communicable disease.

Later, most of the players convened at a nightclub in downtown St. John's. Ralph was seated at a table in the middle of the room engaged in spirited conversation with a local hard guy, apparently a total stranger, when Coop and a few other Quebec players rolled in. Within a short while, they heard a major commotion from that direction and looked over to see Ralph and the guy he was drinking with in a knock 'em down, drag 'em out fistfight. Tables and chairs were overturned, beers were spilled, glasses were being smashed and pretty soon there was a wholesale brawl that involved several of the bar's regular patrons. Ralph and his opponent each landed a few shots before it degenerated into a wrestling match. Then, just as quickly as the fight had started, it stopped, and the pugilists righted their table, chairs and glasses, returned to their seats, shook hands and continued their conversation. Nobody in the place batted an eye, and the Quebec players turned back to the bar and resumed drinking.

Their empty plates flung aside, Conrad and Surfer were stretched out on the front lawn of the Mansion, staring over their crossed ankles at the fire. They laughed at the antics of the legendary Ralph

Stea, admitting their kinship with him and agreeing that we'd have to live up to the gallant history of the FADC through the boldness of our future actions (which wouldn't take very long), and then we all three resumed drinking.

Chapter 7

I Used to Work in Chicago

By late October of that first season, I was elevated to the A-side for a handful of games, playing on the wing, initially. This change of circumstances along with my Boston accent, which became more pronounced in times of stress and adrenaline, raised my profile in the club and brought me to the attention of Mark Carpenter, one of the second row forwards and the team's social secretary that year. Marcus Aurelius, as I began calling him, for he resembled that estimable Roman emperor and Stoic philosopher in manner and bearing, was a twenty-two-year-old swell from North Carolina who, along with his younger brother Noel, just then finishing a stint in the army, had gone to high school in Miami, where he had played football and wrestled.

Marcus was responsible for the UF B-side being called the Mangoes. One day at practice he was propping for us in a scrimmage against the A-side. As the forwards prepared to scrum down, Marcus yelled out, "Come on, you bunch of Mangoes!" Coach Van Blokland was refereeing, and he started calling all the scrum put-ins, lineouts, et cetera, awarded to the B-side as "Mangoes ball" and we were the Mangoes from that day forward.

Six foot one and 225 pounds, Marcus had windblown auburn

hair, parted in the middle and worn over the collar, a grand Olympian physique burnished by the sun and a pair of balky knees that resembled bags of peanuts and caused him to walk in a distinctly pigeon-toed gait. After my first A-side match, a home victory over the St. Pete Pelicans, the big second row offered me a ride in his shiny white Buick Regal, upholstered in blue leather and equipped with a massive Blaupunkt stereo that could tear your ears off at full volume.

We had beaten the Pelicans by eight or ten points, a satisfying win, and I had done all right for myself, making a couple of decent open-field tackles. Marcus and his roommate, Kenny Wells, another UF player, were hosting the post-match party at their town house out near Archer Road, and Marcus invited me along while Tom Petty sang from the stereo about cruising down Highway 441, which was less than a mile away. Petty was a Gainesville boy, Marcus said, detouring north a few blocks to show me the shotgun shack where the rock star's father, Tom Petty, Sr., still resided. When we drove by, he was standing on the porch smoking a cigarette.

Presently, we had a more important errand. Out near Butler Plaza, Marcus eased the Regal into a narrow stucco building that was open to vehicles entering from one side and exiting the other. Pablo's Tunnel was a repurposed car wash some local entrepreneur had transformed into a thriving business that was at once brilliant and wrong-headed: a drive-through liquor store. Now, mind you, I had spent most of the previous five years in Nova Scotia, where the provincial government controlled the sale of alcohol, making it unavailable for retail purchase from 5 P.M. on Saturday until late Monday morning; not to mention that I hailed from Massachusetts, where the blue laws prohibiting liquor sales on Sundays had been on the books since the Pilgrims landed at Plymouth Rock. Pablo's Tunnel, therefore, represented a veritable Shangri-la of convenience and vice to someone like me; the long-haired carhop probably sold bags of pot and hits of acid to those customers who knew the password.

Without getting out of the car, his AC blasting and Tom Petty wailing away on his guitar, Marcus pressed the button to lower his window a couple of inches, ordering a fifth of Smirnoff vodka, two bags of ice, a case of Rolling Rock, a bag of pretzels and, at my suggestion, a half gallon of cranberry juice. After the kid ran around to the various cases and cubbyholes to piece together our order, and then loaded all of it except a six-pack of beer into the trunk, Marcus paid him with a fifty-dollar bill and handed me one of the long-neck bottles of beer.

"Welcome to Florida, buddy," he said, clinking his bottle against mine.

The town house where Mark Carpenter and Kenny Wells lived had matching furniture, old rugby photos on the wall, two clean bathrooms, a well-stocked kitchen opening onto a breezeway, and a shared backyard that included a volleyball net and fire pit. It was several notches above the Mansion in style and function, and after a three-minute shower, I took a seat at the counter while Marcus poured a splash of cranberry juice into a tall glass of vodka and ice, handing it to me. Out the kitchen window I could see a few players from the UF women's rugby team beginning to arrive.

Marcus fixed himself a drink and sampled it. "These Cape Codd-ahs are pretty good," he said, imitating my accent.

Dusk arrived, and Kenny Wells stacked a few broken wooden pallets and old shutters in the pit, doused them with gasoline and lit a huge bonfire. Lubricated by vodka and puffed up with my A-side debut, I wandered over to the blaze with Surfer and Conrad and Greg Taylor, replaying moments from the game and eyeballing the chicks. My theory, formed through years of observation, is that rugby players are tolerant of people outside the mainstream because of their proximity to, and close social relations with, female rugby players, who, in the U.S. at least, are often gay by majority, or in significant numbers. We're pretty much down with the gays, blacks, Latinos, Asians, Jews, Muslims, ultra-liberal wack jobs and right-wing crazies, provided they subscribe to the creed espoused by our coach, Dr. Jon van Blokland, which we printed on club T-shirts that year: RUGBY'S NOT A GAME, IT'S A BLOODY *RELIGION*.

The University of Florida women's team featured a star forward named Miriam, who Kenny Wells and Marcus and some of the other veterans had told me about. I'd never seen her before, but I knew who she was the moment she walked into the party and stood by the keg with a red plastic cup in her hand, bathed in firelight. Miriam was Filipina, or of mixed racial heritage, twenty-two or twenty-three years old, and built, as my dad would've said, like a brick shithouse: about five foot nine and 150 solid, sexy pounds, with smooth almond-colored skin and shiny black hair cropped at the nape of her neck. She was in ROTC or the Army Reserves, as I recall, and showed up at the party in black spandex shorts and a camouflage tank top, her breasts protruding like artillery shells, and her legs and ass sculpted from hours spent at the squat rack.

Miriam was holding hands and laughing with a comely blond girl wearing rugby shorts and a tube top. In her little fatigue hat, Miriam was a Che Guevara wet dream of Amazonian proportions, and many of the Young Turks at the party that night fantasized about joining with her to spawn a race of enlightened beings who could kick a football.

It was my first experience with what would become known as lipstick lesbians, and I stood over near the fire pit gawking at them. "Look at *that*," I said.

Conrad laughed, smacking me on the arm. "They'd kill you, boofoo," he said.

After a couple more beers, Surfer gathered everyone over by the volleyball net. Like many other cadets at West Point, he'd joined the rugby team because it was one of the few sanctioned ways to get off campus, especially for first-year cadets, or plebes, as they are called. The first and third sides would play at home on a given Saturday, while the second and fourth sides traveled to another college for their matches, switching week by week. Despite the fact that the rugby club was overseen by U.S. military and visiting British officers, and West Point regulations concerning alcohol and fraternization were very strict, drinking beer and singing traditional rugby songs is so ingrained in the culture of the sport that the West Point coaching staff was inclined to look the other way when it came to post-match drink-ups.

Surfer was a natural choirmaster, and reveled in the two-part ditties that required a lead singer and responding chorus. I had an inkling of the tradition at Acadia, where I had joined in with one or two songs at the Anvil Tavern after my first match, but didn't know quite what to expect or that I would end up enjoying it so much. With a flourish of his arms, Surfer got into the middle of the circle and taught us the first song:

> I used to work in Chicago
> At the old department store
> I used to work in Chicago
> I don't work there anymore

One of the A-side flankers, who I had played with that afternoon, was a laconic, ginger-haired fellow called Chicago Ed. He had that street-smart look about him, and a keen, narrow face with blue eyes and a smattering of freckles. He was probably about 170 pounds, average height, but he possessed a don't-fuck-with-me attitude, on the field and off, that meant he was a city kid from up north. After teaching us the chorus, Surfer hit the first verse and Chicago Ed looked over at me, hoisted his bottle of Rolling Rock and laughed.

> A lady came in for a hammer
> A hammer from the s-t-o-o-o-r-e!
> A hammer she wanted
> Nailed she got
> I don't work there anymore
> O, I used to work in Chicago . . .

It went on for as many verses as you could make up: the lady wanted some dynamite, banged she got, and so on, while the beers went down like water and the boys leaned on each other's shoulders and sang at the rising moon. Outside center Steve Defraites took off his shirt (which he would do for almost any reason, as he spent a lot of time at Gainesville Gym), and Miriam kissed the blond girl and smirked at Dave Civil and Steve Smith, who had already made passes at her and been shot down.

Apparently Miriam was a little bisexual, or just a good sport, because I heard later that after most of us had piled into cars to hit a few joints downtown, she and a guy named Chuck, who used to play for UF but was now scrumhalf for the Pelicans, had ended up in Kenny Wells's bed together. Chuck managed to get Miriam top-less somehow, and they began kissing and rolling around. By repu-tation, Chuck had a certain gift from the Lord, and was doing everything he could to showcase it: *Look what I have.*

That Tuesday before practice, Surfer and Conrad and I killed our-selves laughing when Mark Carpenter told us what Miriam had said: "That's nice, Chuck, but it just doesn't do anything for me."

It was an important week of training from my perspective, and I ran hard in the fitness and hustled from drill to drill. J.T. was un-available for some reason, and I'd be playing inside center between Carlos at fly half and Steve Defraites at outside center. My first road trip for the A-side was to Jacksonville, and the starting lineup had a few new wrinkles: Conrad and Dave Civil were the flankers, and our loosehead prop, Stormin' Norman Litwack, a huge, agile man with good rugby sense and decent speed, was moving to fullback. The side was a little hodgepodge, and the older guys on the team were grumbling at some of the changes.

Jacksonville in those days was a smelly, active port with an abun-dance of giant rusty cranes and derricks, run-down corner stores, pawnshops and working-class bars, at least the parts we saw when in town for rugby. The match was very tight until late in the second half. With the score tied at 17–17, Defraites broke a tackle at mid-field, off-loaded the ball to me and I went for a run into open terri-tory. For a guy six foot three inches, 240 pounds, Stormin' Norman was pretty fast, and as a Jacksonville flanker stepped up to tackle me, I spun the ball to Norman. Barreling toward the try line, he took out the opposing fullback and wing like a bowling ball picking up a 7–10 split, thumping down in the end goal for the winning try, 21–17. (Tries were worth four points back then.)

The Jacksonville rugby bar was located at the southern end of town, a dank concrete pillbox with a rectangular bar in the center of the room, and an old Wurlitzer jukebox loaded up with Johnny Cash and Willie Nelson and The Charlie Daniels Band. The bar opened onto a open courtyard, bracketed by a rusty superstructure hung with withered grapevines. We were out there draining a free keg that the Jacksonville guys had provided, me and Marcus and Surfer and Stormin' Norman; I was wearing my favorite T-shirt, which was dark blue with white Helvetica lettering in a dense paragraph across the front. It defined the word "Yankee" in mock-dictionary style, noting that its wearer enjoyed lobster and steamed clams and stories of Southerners who had saved their Confederate money, et cetera.

We were feeling like rock stars after the match, especially me, since I'd played a small role in the winning try. Big semis rushed past on nearby I-70, and Johnny Paycheck was growling from the jukebox, telling the man to take his job and shove it. Temporarily, we had a guy on our team from Missoula, Montana; he was passing through Florida on a walkabout tour of the U.S., billeting with rugby players whenever possible and picking up B-games here and there. (He had crashed on my floor at Mrs. P's boardinghouse for a few nights, before she caught on and threw him out.) He was a stout, bearded fellow with a raucous laugh, and he was busy instructing us on how to drink beer Montana-style, gripping the beveled edge of the mugs in our teeth, and tossing it back without touching it with our hands.

Some dude in the bar heard us laughing and came outside. He was six and a half feet tall, over 250 pounds, a cement head from the backwoods of Georgia somewhere, with a neck carved from granite, massive arms and a high and tight haircut. Looming over me, he talked in a slow train of monosyllables: "What . . . is . . . rug . . . by?"

After watching us down glasses of beer Montana-style, a low-watt bulb must've gone off above this guy's head, because he leaned down to grip a full pitcher of beer in his teeth—the half gallon of Old Milwaukee plus the glass pitcher must've weighed close to ten pounds—then straightened up, the cords in his neck standing out like telephone cables, and sucked the pitcher dry.

High-fives and head butts all around. It turned out that the guy had been honorably discharged from the Marine Corps that day, after a six-year hitch. Giants have befriended me for as long as I can remember: Stormin' Norman Litwack, Drew Cooper, and Dag Fullerton at Acadia, even going back to grade school with Dave Pandelena and a kid named Jimmy Currier, a bullet-headed orphan fresh out of reform school who claimed to know the forbidden patch of woods adjacent to the Ashford playground like "the back of

[his] hand," and who smoked a cigarette at recess once, insisting that he and I "were tied in fightin'," though there was little doubt he could mop the floor with Dave Pandelena and his brother Mike, one at a time or both at once.

So it was with the ex-jarhead. He and I were side by side beneath the bower of dried out grapevines, and when the hubbub had subsided he leaned over to read my T-shirt. He laughed and said, "Check . . . this . . . out."

He took off his shirt. Running from his collarbone to his belly button was a large, garish tattoo of a Confederate soldier, wild haired, fierce of visage, mounted on a rearing charger and brandishing his sabre, with the inscription, FORGET, HELL! printed underneath.

I survive on the basis of my quick wit, though this revelation left me speechless. The guy continued to look intently at me. "You . . . have . . . to . . . bust . . . ass," he said.

The din of the bar continued around us: loud music and laughter, glasses banged down on tables and complete strangers bellowed salutations at one another. The rugby players were occupied with the keg, and the ex-jarhead looked down at me with his tangled crown of grapevines, pointed to his heart, and said, "You . . . know . . . what's . . . in . . . here—"

I nodded and drank my beer.

"—and . . . what . . . it . . . takes," the giant said.

After the keg was gone, I climbed into the Regal with Marcus, Defraites and Stormin' Norman and we raced back to Gainesville. At a bar called Dub's, I met a shapely brown-eyed girl from Illinois and the two of us went back to the Mansion. My roommate was visiting his girlfriend back home so I got the water bed that night, which had come with the apartment and was unheated. When I woke up the next morning, my kidneys felt like they'd been on ice in Pablo's Tunnel and the brown-eyed girl was nowhere in sight; mostly I was thinking about Koffler anyway, and wondering what she was up to.

Staggering into the kitchen, I poured a Gator cup full of sweet tea out of the refrigerator and took a copy of Hemingway's *Green Hills of Africa* and a kitchen chair and sat in the empty driveway to catch up on my reading. I had the shits, a groin pull, a swollen knuckle and my kidneys had thawed and now seemed to be working at twice their normal rate, as I had to piss every few minutes. But overall, I wouldn't have traded the contents of the previous twenty-four hours for a bucketful of gold coins. As U.S. discus thrower Al Oerter, a four-time Olympian, had once said, "Until you've done it once, you don't know what it is."

Chapter 8

Mister Yay

Things continued in that fashion into the winter months, with the rugby team winning the majority of its games and my role shifting between A-side substitution and B-side starter. By January, one of my favorite professors was Dr. Alistair Duckworth, the academic star of the literature side of the program. Unlike Harry, Alistair was always neat and pressed—brown or gray corduroys, checked oxford shirt and matching cardigan—with his argyle socks and penny loafers, altogether the portrait of a literary man, right down to the pipe tobacco aroma of his office. He had traces of a Highland burr in his voice, a solid, square-built, middle-sized fellow, with a round face, thinning blond hair and a pleasant demeanor. I liked his teaching method a great deal, which consisted of Socratic inquiry conducted in his soft, agreeable voice; and the course material, particularly Horace, whose *The Art of Poetry*, written in 14 BC, contained lots of practical advice for writers and rugby players: "Do not neglect the long labor of the file."

Dr. Duckworth was often found in his office on the third floor of the GPA building, even on Fridays, when Harry was well into his cups at Lillian's or the Winnjammer. One raw, cloudy afternoon, I was passing by and noticed his door ajar and rapped lightly on the molding; from inside, Dr. Duckworth said to come in.

He knocked his pipe into a little glass bowl, standing up as I entered. Duckworth gestured toward the extra chair, put aside the volume of Jane Austen's letters that he'd been reading, and smiled at the cuts and abrasions on my face.

"Hard at it, I see," said Dr. Duckworth.

At this time in his early forties, my lit crit professor had the avuncular bearing of a sitcom dad and the slight paunch of a recreational tennis player. So it was more than a little surprising when Duckworth told me he'd been a representative rugby player growing up in Scotland, having appeared on schoolboy select teams, touring sides, and first-grade clubs, most often at fly half. Unlike many ruggers who grew up overseas and learned the game as children, Duckworth had continued playing the sport after he'd gotten married, finished his Ph.D., and sought a teaching job in the U.S.; he didn't retire from rugby until he was thirty-five, after playing with a men's club that made it to the regional championship in Illinois or Ohio somewhere.

This news delighted me, and I didn't try to hide my excitement from that moment on. It ran counter to Dr. Duckworth's reputation in the department as an Old World scholar and gentleman; it would've been no less of a shock if he'd admitted that he'd robbed trains as a lad in Aberdeen. As we both giggled like schoolboys, I insisted on a rugby story and it didn't take him long to fix upon a very good one.

While he was in grad school, young Alistair picked up with a representative side touring the Middle East, playing against clubs that were scattered across the vestigial outposts of the British Empire. In northern Egypt, I think it was, there existed a local rugby club made up of British military officers and expats that were living in and around Cairo. Occasionally this team would find a game with an Australian or South African side that was passing through the region; or in this case, a team of university selects on tour. The match was scheduled for a rickety old soccer stadium in the desert near Tobruk, an athletic contest that would've gone unnoticed by the locals but for the presence of a single player on the home team:

Prince Mohammed El-Akbar, some sort of royalty and a graduate of Eton and Cambridge.

Akbar was, according to Dr. Duckworth, a glamorous and beloved figure in that part of the world, with his slick black hair, dark handsome face, and graceful manner. He was also a hell of an athlete; a sailor, horseman, cricketer and rugby player who had proven himself adept at whatever presented itself. The villagers therefore came out in droves to watch Akbar play, and when Duckworth and his teammates showed up they were surprised to see that stands had been erected and a couple of thousand Arabs were roosting there, anticipating a grand performance by their hero.

The match took on greater cultural significance as a result, and the early minutes were fraught with vicious tackling and a couple of brief fistfights. Duckworth played fly half and so did Akbar; they were both proficient in tactical kicking, using the boot to keep their opponents pinned back inside their twenty-two-meter line. Alistair said that his opposite number, though not a large man, was a powerful runner and that he had to drive his shoulder into Akbar a few times to make sure he got him on the ground.

The score was tied 7–7 in the waning minutes, with each side scoring an unconverted try, good for four points, and each place' kicker, Alistair and Akbar, making a penalty in the second half. Thereafter, play was bogged down in the forwards near midfield, and Alistair noted the referee sneaking a look at his watch to see how much time was left. Tackling was hard and desperate, as each pack of forwards was set upon keeping the ball away from the other team's star kicker.

Gripped by this drama, the crowd of Arabs began a chant that was barely audible at first, Duckworth recalled, but grew in strength as the seconds ticked away.

"Akbar. Akbar. Akbar."

The opposing fly half stood opposite him, Duckworth said, his hands on his hips and a look of supreme confidence on his face, while his forwards rucked the ball ferociously, trying to dig it loose for a final, desperate kick.

"Akbar! Akbar!"

Standing on his own side of midfield, Prince Akbar was more

than fifty yards away from the opposing goalposts. If Akbar's team produced the ball and he tried to make a run to get closer, Alistair planned to close the gap and stuff him in the tackle. Just then, Akbar's forwards stormed into a maul and were on the verge of winning the ball from the tight-loose when the chanting increased in volume, ringing down from every corner of the stadium.

"AKBAR! AKBAR! AKBAR!"

The opposing scrumhalf leaped into the pile, secured the ball, and threw a long dive pass to Prince Akbar, standing to one side on a little patch of browned-over grass. The referee had a hand in the air, whistle in his mouth, gaze fixed on the sweep hand of his watch.

"Akbar! Akbar!" whispered the crowd.

With an agile little sidestep, Prince Akbar eluded Duckworth's tackle, arched up on his left foot, let the ball tumble nose-first toward the ground and drop-kicked it with a resounding thump. All the players and the referee and the packed grandstand followed the path of the ball, mouths open, eyes wide, as it rose higher and higher into the white desert sky, aimed straight at the goalposts, nearly sixty yards away.

"As competitive as I was, I sort of wanted him to make it," Alistair said. "It was a beautiful sporting moment."

After reaching its zenith, the ball fell from the sky like a bird that had been shot, falling, falling, and just clearing the crossbar as the referee shrieked on his whistle and time expired. The three points made Prince Akbar's team the winners and the Arab crowd, praising Allah and screaming with joy, thundered down from the stands to carry their champion from the field.

"I just shook my head and laughed," said Duckworth.

After trading rugby stories with Alistair, I ran home to get my soccer boots and kit bag. Soccer had become just another way to stay fit for rugby, but that afternoon, the English Language Institute team was going on the road for a match versus an unusual opponent: the team fielded by a medium-security prison fifteen or twenty miles away. (The only other American on the team, Tim Murphy, a full-time instructor at ELI and our goalie, had arranged the match somehow.)

Soon Murphy was driving the UF van across the barren winter

landscape while the eleven or twelve other players on the team chattered away in Spanish and Arabic, oblivious to where we were going and what we'd see there. Thirty minutes later, the edifice of the prison rose up from the gloom, a series of low concrete buildings encircled by three layers of fencing, each twenty feet high and topped with curlicues of razor wire. As Murphy eased the van into the appropriate lot, the players fell silent as they stared at the bleak silhouette of the jail.

We walked in through the main gate, after Murphy had explained who we were and showed his ID. We left our kit bags in an anteroom off the dingy reception area, and then a trio of beefy corrections officers led us down a long, windowless corridor. We were dressed in our white ELI jerseys, blue shorts and stockinged feet, as we'd been told to carry our soccer boots to the first checkpoint. There we went through a metal detector, were patted down, and our boots were examined. Nobody spoke, except for a few gruff words from the COs that searched us. The kids from Latin America, who'd grown up, many of them, in a culture that accepted wrongful imprisonment and torture as a necessary part of jurisprudence, were wide-eyed and submissive. All of a sudden they appeared very young, like grade-school children sent to the principal's office.

Once we cleared security, we were led into the actual prison, the steel door clanging shut behind us. We were being treated to a pre-game meal in the prison dining hall, a large, brightly lit room lined with steel tables that were bolted to the floor. An area had been set aside for us, and we passed through the chow line ahead of the seventy or eighty prisoners who were having lunch at the same time. The food wasn't bad for a prison, but nobody had much of an appetite. I ate an orange and a peanut butter sandwich and some cookies; ninety minutes of soccer with only two substitutes was going to take some effort, and I had no idea what sort of team they were going to put out against us, or what the refereeing would be like.

During the first part of the meal, the orange jumpsuited prisoners eyed us coldly, talking among themselves. Obviously, they'd known we were coming and were sizing us up. But when Enrique, our stylish young striker, a kid about twenty years old from Venezuela, got up to refill his glass with fruit punch, a few Cuban guys walked over to speak to him and a couple more ELI players joined in the conversation. The prison didn't have any murderers or habitually violent offenders, we'd been told, but there were some rough customers in there: tattooed hulks that were pumping a lot of iron, weaselly looking junkies, older guys with ratty teeth and greasy hair and more than a few young street punks.

After just a few minutes we were celebrities; they didn't get many visiting sports teams, the inmates said, and a few of our Latin players were athletic-looking dudes who might've been stars with the Pumas or Tricolores. Once the ELI kids saw they were welcome, a good portion of their machismo returned and they spoke loudly and rapidly in Spanish to the Cuban inmates who had approached them, shaking hands and smiling with their perfect, upper-class teeth.

Soon it was time for the match. We were separated from the population, and again led down a blank corridor that emptied into a paved quadrangle. Following a CO across to another building, we were directed into an empty concrete storeroom that would serve as our clubhouse, though we had no extra gear besides our cleats, which we were now allowed to put on. Tim Murphy was our player-coach, sort of, a long-haired, singer-songwriter type who played guitar in class and had zero experience with soccer until forming the ELI team a couple of years earlier. He said a few perfunctory words about playing hard and representing the school, et cetera, but most of the Latin kids were gazing at the bare concrete walls or staring down at the floor. No one knew what to expect.

A whistle blew outside, and an inmate in a makeshift soccer uniform, consisting of ALACHUA COUNTY written in a felt-tip pen across the front of his T-shirt and a crooked number on the back, stuck his head in the room saying it was time to warm up. We got to our feet and ran out the door, along a short passageway and onto the field.

It wasn't a bad playing surface; maybe a few yards shorter and narrower than a regulation soccer field but with decent grass, and official-looking goals and line markings. A couple of hundred inmates sat close to the field in a makeshift grandstand, watching us intently. Guys were nervous in the pregame warm-up, shooting wide, kicking it over the bar and complaining, with arms thrust out in the typical Latin manner, when passes didn't arrive where or when they were supposed to. During this period I retrieved an errant ball near midfield and stopped for a moment to watch our opponents. They were mostly in their twenties and early thirties, with a few middle-aged guys sprinkled in, but ragged and unskillful; not one of them that I saw could trap and control a bounding ball. It would be an easy match.

The referee was a gray-haired Irishman I knew from playing matches in Gainesville. He made a little notation on a pad of paper, shrieked on his whistle and the game began. I was the starting right midfielder. Our striker, Enrique, scored on a short half volley in the opening minute or so, and again right after that, dribbling between and around three defenders. He was a good-looking kid who wore his shiny black hair in a kind of pompadour; I called him the Venezuelan Elvis to make the other guys laugh. One of our wings scored on a direct kick, and Enrique put another ball in the net on a fancy banana shot that curved around their fullback, easily beating the goalie. It was a laugher, and soon the best players on our team began crowding the left side of the pitch when we had possession, intent on freeing Mr. Yay for a run down the open side of the field. (Most of them pronounced the "J" in my name as "Y".)

I had two good, open chances before the half. On a pass across the top of the area from Enrique, I dribbled in and took a low shot that glanced off the right post and bounced away. I was obstructed on another play when I entered the penalty area to chest-trap a ball; the referee awarded a penalty kick and Enrique, who was the captain, waved me over to take it. Back at Acadia, I had practiced these regularly, with one of our fullbacks, a sturdy young farmer named Phil Moxsom, good-naturedly agreeing to play goalie. I usually went to the low right-hand corner, and going back to the old summer league in Methuen had made several of them in a row. But with a 6–0 lead and absolutely no pressure, I sent this one over the crossbar and into the dusty reaches of the park, the referee blowing his whistle for half time.

I went down and stood at the end of our bench, frustrated with how I was playing. There were more people watching this match than had attended our varsity soccer games at Acadia, and as the only native-born member of the ELI team (besides Murphy), I wanted to score a goal in front of all these jailbirds. But I was pressing too hard—crowding my defender, getting Enrique all crossed up, hogging the balls to the right side—when I should've just flowed into the open space and let the ball come to me.

While I was muttering to myself, one of the inmates climbed down from the stands and walked over. Apparently they had all been patted down and searched, because the COs let him through. He was about my height, a year or two older, with close-cropped dark hair and brown eyes and a compact build; if not for the orange jumpsuit he could have been a fellow student greeting me on the Plaza of the Dirtbags back in Gainesville.

"You from Lawrence?" he asked, naming the town adjacent to where I'd grown up.

His name was Mike, and he said he knew I was from the Boston area when he heard me calling for the ball: "Hey, play it ovah him! Put the ball in the ayah." But he narrowed it down ever further when I yelled "mingia" after missing an open shot; pronounced *ming-ya*, a foul piece of Italian profanity used often in Methuen and Lawrence, "mingia" is an all-purpose word expressing chagrin, anger, joy or surprise depending on the emphasis and circumstances.

"I speak 'Lawrence,' too," Mike said.

Mike was from the Tower Hill neighborhood and had graduated from Lawrence High two years before I left for Acadia. He knew a couple guys whose names I'd heard playing hockey, and said he'd been working odd jobs back in Lawrence and trying to get on the fire department or the DPW. With the economy so bad, he'd agreed to drive down to Florida to pick up a load of cocaine for some dude who hung around the Wonder Bar. He got pinched with the coke in Orlando, and was six months into a five-year sentence for intent to distribute. For a second it occurred to me that everyone in jail usually says they're innocent.

"That sucks," I said. It felt like I was talking to a guy I went to high school with. We knew all the same places: the 400 Lounge, Lawton's-by-the-Sea, the Tally Ho. "Maybe you'll get out early for good behavior, or something."

The referee called over to us: it was time to start the second half.

Mike looked glum. "It's a federal beef," he said. "I gotta do the five years."

Enrique ran past and clapped me on the arm and I started onto the field. Then I turned back so I could shake hands with Mike.

"I just wanted to talk to someone from back home," he said. "Good luck."

Chapter 9

The First Noel

I had heard that Mark Carpenter's brother Noel would be enrolling at UF as soon as he was discharged from the army, and that he was strong-minded, opinionated, cagey and a little wild. In late January he turned up, wearing his boonie hat and driving a brand-new Mercury Cougar. Noel had just finished his hitch as a sergeant in the 82nd Airborne, 307th Medical Battalion, which is stationed in Fort Bragg, North Carolina. He was a narrow, blond-haired, wiry twenty-two-year-old with a nuclear reactor's worth of energy, smart and funny and daring, with a measure of Conrad's and Dave Civil's cheerful nihilism and a mathematical intellect that, when he was sober, worked three or four moves ahead of everyone else and led to some fabulously elaborate schemes. If by that winter I felt like I'd already earned my baccalaureate in bacchanalia, with Noel Carpenter as the new headmaster we'd all soon be deep into postgraduate work in madcap antics and modern misadventures.

My first recollection of Noel comes from one night after rugby practice at Ricky's bar, a cool, funky, atmospheric place on the university golf course that Humphrey Bogart would've felt at home in. Ricky's was dotted with potted palms, mismatched wicker furniture, an ornate zinc bar and French doors that overlooked the darkened fairways of the golf course. Noel had spent the previous summer with the 307th up at West Point, and he and Surfer struck up a lively conversation about it. Before long, they were going around Ricky's with some kind of phony raffle that only hot-looking coeds were eligible to sign up for—the prize was a round of free drinks that Noel had talked some rube into paying for. Noel and Surfer chatted up the skirts as easily as Dr. Dolittle talked to chipmunks, and pretty soon the entire bar was at Noel's command, looking at their swizzle sticks or whatever he was using for tickets, and praying they'd be chosen.

I was sitting in an alcove having a couple drinks with Chicago Ed, a quiet, low-key guy who used his brooding silences to attract the sympathy of good-looking women. We watched as Noel and Surfer ran around the bar, talking a blue streak. Obviously there was new blood on the team, a manic force that had taken over, and a lot of the younger guys were caught up in it. Finally, Chicago Ed threw down a twenty-dollar bill to cover our tab and stood up, glancing around the bar.

"Guess I'll go call up an old hole," he said, stifling a yawn.

After that night, Surfer, Noel and I began to hang around together almost all the time. Conrad, Civil and Greg Taylor rented a house at 9 NW Twenty-Fourth Street, and we formed a pretty tight alliance with them through FADC and backyard barbecues on Sunday afternoon. It was like a battle of the bands: with their blond hair and shining white teeth, Noel and Surfer made our little group like a dangerous version of The Beach Boys. (I was like their dark-haired cousin who stood in the back, playing a tambourine.) Conrad's gleeful decadence, Dave Civil's bad-boy-next-door philandering and Greg Taylor's anarchic physicality turned those guys into the Rolling Stones of North Florida rugby. Party invitations began streaming in from all quarters, and we developed a nearly foolproof method of gaining entrance to semiprivate gigs, a bit of business that Noel worked out with his brother Mark and Steve Defraites.

The first time this method was put to good use was after a home game versus Iron Horse. Six of us were crammed into Mark's Buick Regal and there was a convoy of vehicles filled with rugby players behind that, including Keith Platt and several guys in the bed of his pickup truck, drinking beer. Someone said there was a party over at graduate student housing, a collection of town houses a block away from Florida Field, where the Gators played football. Immediately, Mark threw the Regal into a U-turn, indicating with his hand that the cars following us should do the same. Now, most people would blanch at twenty rugby players coming into their apartment en masse, particularly the male inhabitants, who would perceive our arrival as a threat, and with good reason. Therefore, the newly developed Carpenter-Defraites Ruse was in effect.

Noel saw a few of us as noncoms or squad leaders, and the rest as grunts, so certain aspects of the plan were on a need-to-know basis; some guys had active parts to play, and others were handed a beer and told to keep out of the way until they were summoned. On this occasion, Mark and Steve Defraites went around to the sliding glass door in the rear of the town house, while Noel and I headed up the walkway to the front door. Surfer was crouched nearby in the bushes, watching for the signal and keeping the other guys quiet. At the prearranged time, Mark and Defraites slipped in the back way and we came through the front door: Noel immediately yelled across the crowd and his brother answered, giving the impression that we knew someone there and had received an invitation. Mark began talking to the hostess, while Noel and I met Defraites in the middle of the living room and shook his hand like we were his long-lost cousins. At the same time, Surfer began inserting the rest of the boys, shuttling them through the front door in twos and threes. It was a simple, ingenious strategy, and almost always worked.

Once inside the party, we had a pretty set routine. Surfer and I would commandeer the stereo; Platt and Defraites would dominate the keg; and the Carpenters would scan the room for hot-looking women. Once the rugby players had infiltrated, Noel would give Surfer and me the high sign and we'd put The Doors' "L.A. Woman" on the turntable. By then, everyone on the team would have a beer and we'd form a circle in the living room, nodding our heads and snapping our fingers to the beat of the music. During the intro, Steve Defraites or Surfer would dart into the middle of the cleared space, freestyle a couple of dance moves and take the lead in the sing-along.

At the beginning of each verse, articles of clothing would be discarded. Male onlookers left the room, glared from the periphery or just got into the spirit of the thing and sang along. (At one party, a skinny non-rugger took off his shirt and dropped to the carpet and started doing push-ups but everyone ignored him.) As crazy as it sounds, a lot of girls were intrigued by this performance and edged closer, slugging their drinks and giggling. And the later it was, the better we sounded.

By the time Jim Morrison had reached the "mojo rising" part of the song, fifteen or sixteen rugby players would be down to just their sneakers and socks, huddling in the middle of some stranger's living room and crooning into their plastic cups. We would scream along with Morrison and toss droplets of beer from our fingertips, gradually rising from the floor as the last verse reached its crescendo.

Always quick to show off his muscles, Steve Defraites would start jumping around, knocking over lamps and upsetting end tables. It was a real shit show, but the University of Florida was like the wild west back then, and we met plenty of girls by violating Jim Morrison's copyright.

Next, Surfer or Noel would extract a roll of aluminum foil from a kitchen drawer while I put Springsteen's *Greetings from Asbury Park* or Tom Waits on the stereo. With the showmanship of nightclub magicians, Noel and Surfer would make elaborate foil hats for themselves and all the girls in attendance: Tutankhamun's headdress, Apache war bonnets, berets, fezzes, replicas of the Eiffel Tower and Taj Mahal; even, one time, a tin foil tuxedo that would've made a matador's suit of lights appear drab by comparison. These guys had serious military training, and the efficiency of their creations would often wear away the last bit of social reserve at a party, sending it into unknown territory.

I remember standing in the kitchen that night wearing an aluminum foil fedora, and chatting with a pretty redhead who had a sheet of foil fitted over her good-sized breasts and a crinkled silver bone in her hair, like a disco cavewoman. We were getting along famously, discussing the state of world affairs, and so on. I had been leaning against the kitchen counter with Kenny Alabiso, our starting loosehead prop, and the redhead and her friend, a chunky blonde, had been looking at us from across room when Kenny waved them over. By our metric, picking up even a moderately nice-looking girl after midnight was like bowling a perfect game: everything had to come together just right, and then you chalked it up to luck. I was doing some kind of pirate riff and the redhead was laughing at everything I said, until I stuck my foot in my mouth and called her a wench.

"What did you just call me?" the girl asked, drawing away.

I explained, quite reasonably, that "wench" had its origins in Middle English, by way of Old English, and that it was originally "wencel," or child, from "woncel," tottering, like a child learning to walk; and the term was, in effect, a harmless colloquialism, dating to about 1350 AD, and that I was a professional and not to worry about it. A healthy wench, a country lass, that sort of thing. Kenny nodded, a serious look on his face, like we were two etymologists who had discussed this usage beforehand.

But it was too late: the redhead turned and walked away, taking the chunky blonde with her. "You don't know when to quit, do you?" said Alabiso, punching me on the arm. "And take off that stupid fuckin' hat."

Kenny Alabiso was a good sort. Originally from Jacksonville, Alabiso used to chaff the underclassmen he played high school football with, calling them all Wee Wee because he couldn't remember their names. Naturally, Surfer and Noel and I turned this around on him, since we were in charge of the team roster and took it upon ourselves to assign everyone goofy nicknames. Thus, some obscure rookie became "Step Child"; Keith Platt was "the Epitome" (of American violence) one season and "Brown Man" the next, due to his habit of dressing monochromatically; and Mark Carpenter was "Axis." He thought this moniker stemmed from his heroic appearance, but it was more of a geological reference: Mark believed that the world revolved around him. And as hard as Kenny Alabiso tried to shuck the name, passing it to someone, anyone else, he became known forever as Wee Wee.

A trio of sorority girls entered the kitchen, looking for something to mix with the handle of vodka they were carrying. Wee Wee started a conversation with a little brunette but "Statesboro Blues" was blasting from the stereo and it was difficult to hear anything. The girl closest to me, a smooth-looking babe with a petite, trim

body and fascinating blue-green eyes, responded to Wee Wee's remarks by putting a hand up vertically in front of her mouth, and
saying, "White?"

Even in my befuddled state, this gesture struck me as odd. Nudging Wee Wee, I couldn't help pointing out that the normal reaction
to his comment would've been cupping a hand to her *ear*, and saying *"What?"*

Wee Wee's philosophy for picking up girls was to "go ugly early,
and cut one out of the herd." These three were pretty cute, and just
the way they were hanging around, twirling fingers in their hair
and whispering to each other, they appeared to be interested.

The smooth-looking girl said something that was lost in the din.
I put my hand over my mouth and said, "White?"

"White?" the girl said, covering her mouth again.

Wee Wee began to crack up. With my beer against my chest, I
shouted over the music that the proper expression was "What?" and
that making a kind of funnel with your hand and placing it by your
ear would result in the other person's reply hitting its mark.

The three girls looked at each other. "White?" they all said. I put
my hand up to my mouth again. "White?" I said.

The girls looked at Wee Wee for an explanation. Raising his big,
hairy paw, he mimicked their wide-eyed expressions, and said,
"White?" Again, the girls retreated and we were left alone by the
stove.

Around 2 A.M., these parties would reach their final, critical stage,
again with Noel and sometimes Mark and Surfer as the catalyst.
Under the best circumstances, Noel would enlist one or more of our
gullible hostesses in his endeavors, but even if that didn't occur he'd
forge ahead with his late-night culinary enthusiasms, pulling out
mixing bowls and waffle irons and muffin tins, greasing up a skillet
or two, and loading the counters with everything in the fridge and
cabinets that struck his fancy: cartons of eggs, loaves of bread, slabs
of bacon, sausage links, ham slices, pancake mix and, inevitably, a
bottle of artificially flavored maple syrup in the shape of a portly
black woman with a bandanna tied around her head, just the sort of
racist stereotype, I'd point out, that corporate America has always
thrived upon.

By now, rugby players made up the largest percentage of those who remained at the party and they'd line up against the wall and kibitz as Noel and Surfer wielded oven mitts, fired up the stove and, like a couple of spastic fry cooks, began preparing a feast made from a total stranger's weekly allotment of comestibles. Although a massive breakfast was often the first and only item on the menu, one of our players, Rob Kaplan, a hard-nosed center (he'd been team MVP as a running back at Miami Killian Senior High), had a peculiar affinity for luncheon meats. Kap used to make special runs to Publix to stock up on rare roast beef, Black Forest ham, honey-glazed turkey breast, German liverwurst and an array of other delicacies nestled in those flimsy plastic bags. Gourmet deli meats were like a fetish with Kap.

Broad shouldered with a narrow waist and thick legs, Kaplan had a mane of reddish-brown hair and pale white skin dotted with freckles that was stretched over his veiny musculature. He was a nice Jewish kid from Miami, but looked like an Irishman right off the boat: I gave him the nickname "O'Shaughnessy" and on Saint Patrick's Day, in a little Irish pub I discovered in a strip mall, we convinced a bunch of girls from Orlando that he was my cousin visiting from Belfast. They all crowded around, asking Kap what he thought of our TV shows, and whether he'd ever seen an alligator, or the Daytona 500. It was the same with "Boca Scott" MacDonald, our new scrumhalf—put a cowboy hat on him and he looked like Texas, even though he'd grown up in Boca Raton.

Most of the time it went like clockwork, with Noel cooking up a twelve-egg omelet amid a few wisecracks, and Kaplan putting away a Dagwood sandwich for the ages, all shits and giggles, like the children's story "Stone Soup," where the charming old hobo puts a rock in a kettle of boiling water, cajoles one passerby after another to toss in a few carrots or leg of mutton and goes away whistling at the end, with a full belly and the stone in his pocket. We were the guys that cooked you breakfast, the mercenaries of fun, sure to liven up any get-together—the dudes who got naked at the drop of a hat and sang rowdy songs. But occasionally things went a little awry.

A few weeks after the party at the town house, we engineered a similar entrance at an apartment in the same neighborhood. Mark wasn't around, but Noel and Surfer and I were in attendance, while Steve Defraites and his brother Scott, who sometimes filled in at wing or fullback and later became a TV weatherman, decided to start preparing breakfast a little earlier than usual, catching us off guard. Apparently the hostess took offense and soon all five or six of us were being routed out of the house, first by an irate young woman and then a squad of her male neighbors, the eggs broken into a bowl and a big sheet of aluminum foil draped over the kitchen table.

We were leaving without much protest when one of our escorts made a smart-ass comment. The Defraites brothers had a dark side, especially when they were together and had been drinking. Going through the door, Steve turned and threw a heavy punch that landed square on the guy's forehead, knocking him back into the apartment. When the guy's buddy jumped through the doorway to retaliate, Scott Defraites leaped up from where he'd been huddled against the near wall and cold-cocked him. A melee ensued.

The brawl spilled onto the front lawn. There were a half dozen of us, including a few good-sized kids who liked to fight, and apparently my services were not required. I have no recollection of this, but Steve Defraites got a kick out of telling everyone later that I was going around to the various skirmishes with a beer in my hand, squatting on my heels if the guys were wrestling on the ground, and saying, "Well I'm a *writer* and there's really no need to—" and "As a *writer*, I understand that people can disagree without—" Steve may have suffered a hard-knocks childhood and his mean streak came through sometimes, but he and I found each other amusing. And it wouldn't be long until his nose for trouble saved me from a dangerous predicament.

But that night ended up okay, with just a few bruises and skinned knuckles as we packed into the cars and drove off to Skeeter's for our usual late breakfast. That spring we really came into our own, après rugby wise, making chaotic celebrations into a recurring thematic presentation: Noel Carpenter and Surfer John Hearin present their Rugby Theater of the Absurd. At Saturday afternoon parties, at home and on the road, we perfected the elephant walk; in this traditional rugby promenade, each player pulls his shorts and underwear down to his ankles, bends over at the waist, and extends one hand ahead and reaches back through his legs with the other. Every man in the troupe links hands with the man in front and behind, and together they form a shuffling conga line that wends here and there among the startled, delighted, bemused or offended onlookers.

One fine Saturday, we were at a high-end party in north Gainesville with one of our newest players, Matt Allen, a towheaded prankster from central Florida, at the head of the column. The only guy with a free hand and an unobstructed view, the intrepid rookie toured us through various well-appointed rooms and was heading for the front door with the intention of walking across NW Thirteenth Street, only to have it open of its own accord to reveal two cops, a male and a female, both of whom couldn't keep a straight face. (At another party, titled Christmas in April, a few weeks later, a pair of Gainesville cops knocked on the door to number nine several times, informing us that we had to quiet down. After work, they changed into their civilian clothes and came back to join the festivities.)

One night at a party following a match against the Tampa Bay Rugby Club, Steve Defraites got into a strip-off with a scrawny visiting player. Above the waist, Defraites was built like an Olympic weightlifter, and as raunchy music played from the stereo, he shook his head condescendingly at the sight of his opponent's chicken-breasted physique. But when the other guy's pants and underwear came off, Defraites realized that he was at a monumental disadvantage, grabbing his clothes and refusing to continue as his skinny rival practically jumped rope with his ancestral endowment.

We were on the road in St. Pete when Noel got into an argument with a local girl and called her an unprintable name several times over, which got us tossed out of the Pelican's bar. In a show of solidarity, a guy named Chuck, St. Pete's scrumhalf who'd also played at UF, marched back inside and took all his team's trophies from a shelf over the bar. A few weeks later in Fort Lauderdale, our fly half, Carlos Ballbe, whose dad was a retired racecar driver from Buenos Aires, set the course record at one of those little go-kart joints. When the kid manning the attraction wanted to know how he did it,

Carlos said, "Don't touch zee brakes" as he sailed out through the little gate.

After a match in Tallahassee, we had another rookie follow Steve Smith around and report back what he said to girls, because he was a fantastic pervert and got laid almost as much as Surfer, which was a considerable achievement. Up in Atlanta, we had rendezvoused at a prearranged time on the morning after our game for the convoy back to Gainesville. One of our players, an earnest, gangly second-row forward named Alan Hicks, was a few minutes late. We called him by the name of his hometown, Eau Gallie, a little burg on the central coast, which was pronounced *Oh Golly*, which fit him to a tee.

Someone scribbled a note on a paper bag that said, "Eau Gallie, we have left, good luck," weighing it down with a rock; and though Hicks got dropped off by some girl just as we pulled away, he got stranded anyway because Wee Wee thought it would be a shame to waste such a heartfelt message.

The sun was shining brightly as the days grew ever warmer, and we were winning a mess of rugby games. Our starting props were Wee Wee and Martin England, the thirty-year-old New Zealander who was studying for his Ph.D. in astronomy and, with his full beard and bandy legs, resembled the Tasmanian devil. Conrad and Civil were the flankers, two undersized guys that tackled everything in sight. Boca Scott could play scrumhalf, number eight, center, or fullback. At fly half, Carlos Ballbe, though slightly built, was strong as hell and could kick a football like Akbar. Steve Defraites and O'Shaughnessy were knocking people over in the centers and Surfer was our utility man, playing several different positions. I wasn't getting any more games on the wing because Greg Taylor, the former wrestler from Maryland, was the fastest white guy any of us had ever seen; and on the other side of the field, Mike Siskin, who was bigger and wider than Greg, had been a championship hurdler. We were shaping up as a formidable side, and although spots for me in the first fifteen were becoming increasingly rare, I knew I belonged out there with the rest of the guys, somewhere.

Chapter 10

Ballad of the Hillsborough County Jail

I didn't have a car my first several months in Gainesville, thus my most frequent means of transportation around town and on short rugby trips was via "the Egg," Surfer's godawful 1969 Volkswagen Fastback. "Fastback" was a misnomer. It was a robin's-egg blue, standard transmission, two-door piece of junk, a rusty decrepit machine with a removable backseat, holes in the floor through which you could watch the street rushing beneath you, no air-conditioning, and a passenger-side window that didn't roll down. The Egg had nearly two hundred thousand miles on the odometer, and when you were riding in it, you felt like you were inside a cheap wind-up toy that could fall apart any second. Surfer would park at the top of a little rise so he could slide into neutral and jump-start the engine with the assistance of gravity and a few well-chosen curse words. The car was an object of derision, even among rugby players, most of who owned nothing more elaborate than a bicycle and should have been envious. But the Egg got us to practice, home matches, and downtown to the Winnjammer and Harmonica Joe's, where we liked to do our drinking.

The best way to keep rugby players out of trouble was to schedule a lot of rugby games. One weekend that spring we had an open date, which allowed for an FADC meeting—we usually skipped them when we had to play on Saturday. Noel was in Fayetteville, North Carolina, visiting his girlfriend, Kathy (he called it Fayette-Nam), and Surfer hosted the FADC at his apartment complex, a dilapidated set of attached town houses known as Landmine.

It was a brilliant, seasonably warm afternoon in late March, perfect North Florida weather, the sky absent of clouds with a breeze rustling the palms. We chipped in for a keg, and around 4 P.M. a dozen or so rugby players congregated on the pool deck, reggae music coming from the windows of Surfer's apartment. After a couple hours, Conrad and Civil drifted off, and a few other guys left a while later to prepare for their evening activities. Surfer, Steve Defraites, Ken "Burr" Farrington and I sat beneath one of the palm trees, wondering what there was to do around town that night. I suggested we go visit Dave Barnes, an old Acadia buddy of mine who had recently gotten married, and was coaching high school football over in Tampa. I hadn't seen Barnesy for a couple of years, but we were pretty tight. He was our light heavyweight on the wrestling team, going at under 220 pounds, with the 235-pound Terry Tapak, one of the charter members of the FADC, wrestling heavyweights over 220.

Barnesy only weighed about 185 pounds, a scruffy, amiable, quick-witted fellow with dirty blond hair. Getting your ass kicked is a fairly common occurrence when asked to wrestle guys twenty-five or thirty pounds heavier than you, especially at the college level, but Barnesy did it cheerfully, once in a blue moon squeezing out a point for the team. He'd stagger off the mat, drop onto the stool panting and struggling for breath, then look up with a mischievous glint in his eye and say, "Make room in the van. He'll be too embarrassed to go back to Frederickton after that one."

Against all reason, we decided that visiting Barnesy in Tampa, over a hundred miles away, was a good idea. It never occurred to us, while we removed the backseat from Surfer's car and positioned Burr and Defraites on a couple of old boat cushions on either side of the keg, that going on an FADC road trip was a dubious concept: like a product that combined shoe polish and dog food, or a brightly colored children's hand grenade. What could go wrong?

We tottered out of Gainesville at dusk, with Defraites and Burr nipping at the keg from the hose and Dylan's "You're Gonna Make Me Lonesome When You Go" blasting from the Egg's single speaker. Surfer drove and I rode shotgun, monitoring the radio for good songs and keeping him alert. Defraites and Burr were talking among themselves in the back, like two kids on a family outing, except the beer dripping out of the spigot was already pooling at their feet. Every so often, they'd take a piece of cardboard and push the spillage toward one of the holes in the floor, keeping the reservoir from getting too deep.

Around 10:30 P.M. we stopped at a highway rest area and Burr and Defraites, pretty ripped by this point, were clutching at each other as they rampaged around the little convenience store. While I was at the register, the old gent on duty cast a glance out the window and said, "Y'all better be careful tonight. The highway patrol's just in here. It's been quiet, and they got nothin' else to do, their own selves."

Outside by the car, Surfer confessed that he was too tired to drive. In the backseat, Burr and Defraites were passing the hose from the keg, laughing in a sharp crazy tone like barking seals. I'd been away from Massachusetts for so long that my driver's license had expired, but neither of those guys was in any condition to drive. Reluctantly I took the keys. By this time, the shine was off the idea I'd concocted back at Landmine. We were two hours out of Gainesville, and nearly an hour away from Tampa; I hadn't seen Barnesy for quite a while, and hadn't bothered to call and tell him we were coming. There was no choice but to keep going and hope for the best.

I started up the car, grinding it into gear as we pulled away. Intermittently, a huge semi went highballing in the other direction, headed for Jacksonville or Atlanta; otherwise I-75 was deserted, a ribbon of blue in the moonlight. Surfer was asleep in minutes, his head pressed against the doorjamb, snoring lightly. The other passengers were quiet, but I could hear the bubbling in the hose as they kept up their assault on the keg. I moved the Egg into the center lane, coaxed it up to fifty-five miles per hour, and headed straight for the coast. The clock on the dash said 11:00 P.M.

On a forlorn stretch of highway, I saw headlights behind me, just a speck on the horizon that slowly drew closer. After a few minutes, the car was approximately one hundred yards back and holding steady. I switched to the inner lane, allowing the other car room to pass but it moved over to the right-hand lane, keeping the same distance. I looked down at the gauges: I was five miles below the speed limit, and driving within the lane markings. Just as I nudged Surfer, the police lights went on behind us.

"Surf. Wake up," I said. "The cops."

He was difficult to rouse. Moving into the breakdown lane and rolling to a stop, I shoved him with both hands. "Surf, we gotta switch seats," I said. "I don't have a license."

"Huh? What is it?" In the rotating lights of the police car, Surfer's face was bruised-looking from the door panel and marked by half-conscious surprise. "What happened? Were we in an accident?"

"The cops. We just got pulled over. Here, switch seats."

Surfer and I had played beside one another in a couple dozen rugby matches by then, and I usually knew what he was going to do. But he was groggy with interrupted sleep, and as I tried to slip underneath and allow him to climb over me into the driver's seat, we both went low, knocking us back where we started. A couple of seconds went by, the powerful beam of the highway patrol's spotlight illuminating the dust motes in the cab. On the second go-round, each of us attempted to go over the top and I got my leg caught against the stick shift. Finally we managed to switch sides of the car, just before the highway patrolman knocked on the window with the butt of his flashlight.

Surfer rolled down the window. "Yes, Officer?" he asked.

"Turn off the engine, sir," said the crew-cutted young patrolman. "Step out of the car, please."

Surfer climbed out, and was led to the rear of the Egg. Two deputy sheriffs in their late thirties or early forties met him back there. Apparently they had been riding with the highway patrolman, as there was only one cruiser behind us. In the backseat, Burr and Defraites had thrown an old sweatshirt over the keg and were leaning on it like it was an end table or something. But whenever they moved their feet, you could hear a splashing sound, and the entire car reeked of beer.

A few minutes later, the young highway patrolman stuck his

head in the open door, and said, "Jay, could you step to the rear of the car, please?"

We were on a long, flat, dun-colored stretch of highway, the stars gleaming overhead, with a low mist creeping through the trees, which stood in a line about fifty yards away. I got out and joined the deputies in the breakdown lane, going over beside Surfer, who had his hands manacled behind his back. One of the deputies did the same to me.

"I'm placing you both under arrest," said the highway patrolman, taking my expired driver's license. Then he read us our Miranda rights, which we were familiar with from television.

He was a clean-cut, pleasant fellow, with an athletic build and firm jaw. A small metal plate over his breast pocket said his name was B. J. THOMAS. *Like the singer*, I thought.

"Do you know why I pulled you over?" he asked.

Surfer shook his head. "No idea," he said.

"You've got a taillight out," said Officer Thomas. He looked over at the two deputies, tall and grim beneath their wide-brimmed hats. "Go call this in," he said.

The deputies ambled back to the patrol car. When they were out of earshot, Officer Thomas shined the flashlight into the car, and then snapped it off.

"You guys on some kind of sports team?" he asked.

When I told him we were rugby players, Officer Thomas said that he'd played football at the University of South Florida and that it was our lucky night. "I know you were the one driving," he said to me, "but I'm not going to give you the Breathalyzer, or the field sobriety test." He looked over at Burr and Defraites, who resembled wax dummies in the glare of the lights. "You weren't driving fast, and I only stopped you because of that taillight. Since I have these two deputies with me, I'm going to have to arrest you, though."

Officer Thomas gazed at the wall of trees. "Jay, I'm going to charge you with driving in the state of Florida with an expired out-of-state license, and John, you'll be charged with allowing an unlicensed driver to operate your vehicle. These are misdemeanors, and they won't affect your insurance rates, I don't think, or your safe driving records."

There was the crackle of radio static, and then the deputies went to each side of the Egg to ask Burr and Defraites for their IDs. For a moment, Surfer and I were alone on the pavement, with the faint lights of Tampa-St. Pete visible on the horizon.

"This guy is cutting us a major break," said Surfer.

"I gotta take a major piss," I said.

It was embarrassing, but I told Officer Thomas about my dilemma and he removed the handcuffs but then cuffed me again in front, directing me over to the guardrail. When I came back, Surfer and I were informed that, to avoid a towing charge, we needed to produce a sober, licensed driver to follow us in the Egg to the Hillsborough County Sheriff's Department.

It was inching closer to midnight, and we were two and a half hours from Gainesville—none of our rugby buddies was venturing out from there at the present hour. I hadn't seen Dave Barnes since the summer after I graduated from Acadia, or even called him; his phone number was in a letter that was folded in half and sticking out of my back pocket. There were no pay phones in sight, so Officer Thomas did us another favor. He took the letter from my pocket, retreated to his patrol car and radioed Barnesy's number to his dispatcher. The dispatcher called Barnesy to explain the situation, and my old buddy agreed to have his wife take him out to the middle of nowhere so he could drive a stranger's car to the county jail. I knew he would; Barnesy was loyal.

He was an odd duck. Even in Wolfville, or Wolfburg, as our wrestling teammate Jay Buckler, from Massapequa, Long Island, called it (Buck didn't really know where he was upon his arrival as a six-foot, 126-pound freshman, telling his parents in an initial phone call that he was in "Wolfburg, Canada," a name that stuck with the generation of athletes to follow), a town filled with eccentrics, Barnesy was a true original. He used to attend classes with his tiny golden Lab puppy, Samson, sticking his head out the neck of his snorkel coat. Although it was a college town, there wasn't much interracial dating, and for more than a year, Barnesy, who was almost colorless he was so pale skinned, with a blocky head like Samson's and the same light yellow fur, went out with a lovely girl named Betty White.

"Betty White, ain't," Barnesy would say, and, "Once you go black, you never go back." Betty would laugh and shove him away, and then they'd embrace one another and kiss for two minutes straight, in front of the president's house on Main Street or on the dance floor at the gym. It was a great thing to see.

We waited an hour for Barnesy to roll out of bed and come find us, and twice more I had to ask Officer Thomas to cuff me in front, so I could take another piss. At length a pair of headlights went by in the other direction, veered off at the next exit, and came sweeping back around, easing to the shoulder thirty yards in front of the Egg. Barnesy soon emerged, in a pair of red pajama bottoms, rawhide slippers, an old T-shirt, and a ratty-looking shearling vest that predated his Acadia days. (Whenever he saw a T-shirt or baseball cap of mine that he liked, Barnesy would chuckle and say, "That won't be making the trip back to Mass.")

His hair was matted to one side and his face was peppered with stubble; he'd just been hired to coach football at a high school in Tampa and was due on the field at 6 A.M., when his team began spring practices. In the spotlight from the patrol car, which cleaved the darkness for a hundred yards or more, I could see Barnesy's wife, whom I'd never met, as she slid behind the wheel of their car. I'd been told she was a few years older than Barnesy, and her face, revealed in the unforgiving light, was pale and furious. She gunned the engine, and zoomed off.

Barnesy ducked his head into the Egg as he passed, where Defraites and Burr were still seated on either side of the keg, "Interesting strategy," he said.

Officer Thomas explained that Barnesy would drive Surfer's car to the Hillsborough County Sheriff's Department, where he could inquire about our bail arrangements. Everything was agreed upon, and after Surfer and I were placed in the cruiser, still handcuffed, Officer Thomas drove off toward the halo of light above Tampa. As we passed by, I caught a glimpse of Barnesy taking a drink from the keg and shaking hands with Defraites and Burr, whom he'd never met.

When we arrived at the sheriff's department, a gaunt, three-story brick building illuminated by klieg lights, we said our good-byes to

B. J. Thomas, who pulled a sharp U-turn and went back to his patrol route. Barnesy and the Egg would arrive shortly, but Surfer and I were led shuffling into the glare of the station house by the two deputies, who were not as obliging now that our protector had departed. The booking officer, a lumpy, sallow-faced man with a creased forehead, sat at a tall desk enclosed by Plexiglas. The handcuffs were removed, and we were asked for our IDs again. Though I hadn't taken a drink since Gainesville, in the chill of the air-conditioning and beneath the fluorescent lights, all at once I felt inebriated. Steve Defraites had come in behind us, and after a minute of deliberation, the booking officer said our bail was forty-five dollars apiece. Surfer and I had less than twenty bucks between us, and Steve left to hunt down an ATM, which were a novelty back then, few and far between. A deputy working somewhere behind the desk uttered a comment about my northern heritage, and he and the booking officer shared a laugh. Then Surfer and I were directed through a heavy steel door into the bowels of the sheriff's department. Our IDs were not returned to us.

We were led along a cinder block hallway where another deputy, an enormous, round-shouldered man with a cannonball for a head, took out a ring of keys and unlocked the door to one of the cells. Apparently it was the drunk tank, because as soon as the door opened, we were assailed by a chorus of loud voices, including a squirrely, middle-aged black man, just one of six or seven prisoners already shoehorned into the tight, smelly, windowless room.

"Twenty-seven goddamn dollars," said the black man. "I was walkin' down the street, mindin' my own bizness, and now I need twenty-seven *goddamn* dollars to get outta this heah place." He smacked his fist into an open palm. "I don't have it. That's the thing of it. Twenty-seven goddamn dollars is what I gotta get."

Because of the cramped seating, I went to one side of the cell and Surfer to the other. I took up a position on the bench next to a thin, droopy man in his late forties with a receding hairline and a battered sport jacket. He was the only other white guy they had locked up, and in a voice containing traces of a Middle European accent, he asked me where I was from and what I had done to end up there beside him. I told him and he laughed, saying that he would surely make bail and be released ahead of me. I asked him what he'd been arrested for, and the continental gentleman laughed again.

"I shot my wife," he said.

We sat there for an hour, tired and dirty and crowded together, with the one guy nattering on about the twenty-seven goddamn dollars like it was a mysterious equation that could be solved through a public vetting. It was clear after only a short while that there's little consideration in a drunk tank about what your fellow detainees might view as worthy topics of conversation, as well as a dearth of sympathy, insight, or the romance of imprisonment.

Finally, there was the sound of a key in the lock and the deputy with the cannonball head peered inside and said my name. I jumped up, laughing at the European guy and then shot a glance over at Surfer. "See ya on the outside, Baby Face," I said.

But as soon as the deputy locked the door behind us, he unlocked another one across the hall and told me to enter. It was a tiny cell, about ten feet deep and four feet wide, with a narrow bench attached to the right-hand wall and a little shelf above it. I asked the deputy what was going on, but he locked me in the cell without offering a reply.

Not sure when I'd make bail, I took the photo of Darlyne out of my wallet and placed it on the shelf. I had been awake for about twenty hours, gotten drunk and sobered up, and notions of wrongful imprisonment and my own stoic detachment from it began to occupy my thoughts. Jail wouldn't be so bad if only I had brought a harmonica. Flopping onto the concrete bench, I played an imaginary one, accompanying myself on an old jailhouse ditty: "Nobody knows what troubles I seen. Nobody knows what sorrow . . ."

After a few minutes, the key thudded in the lock again and hope returned. I'd been in jail a little over an hour, and it felt like I was on Devil's Island. But I was thwarted a second time when the deputy led me down another corridor, away from the booking area, and ushered me onto an old service elevator. Another officer was waiting on board, a solemn black man with powerful-looking shoulders and thick wrists; he wore a corrections uniform, which consisted of a white shirt, small gold badge, and dark trousers. The CO pushed the button to go upstairs, which was a bad sign since the way out of the building was on the first floor, where we were now.

Arriving on the second floor we passed through a heavy-gauge steel door that had to be opened from the inside, and entered a small rectangular space lined with corkboard that started halfway up the walls. Three additional corrections officers were there, which brought the total to five, and I was surprised to see two other prisoners, both good-sized black men, neither of whom had been at the booking desk or in the drunk tank with us.

"Strip down," said one of the COs. A minute later, the three of us stood in a line, naked. "Bend over and spread 'em," the CO said.

While crouched in this humiliating position, I swiveled my head toward the prisoner on my left, and whispered, "Is this standard procedure?"

His eyes fixed straight head, the man said, "For me it is."

"But I'm here for a traffic violation."

My neighbor winced. "Then they definitely fuckin' with you," he said.

After getting dressed, we were taken out through the far door. An awful feeling of having my constitutional rights and my dignity violated began to well up in me: I knew that either somebody had made an error in my paperwork, or there was some kind of weird Civil War payback afoot. So far nothing had been explained to me, but I'd already figured out that asking a lot of questions and complaining wouldn't help. *Everyone in jail is innocent.* Besides, deep down, I knew what it was: the two deputies had bitched that the highway patrol had given us preferential treatment and I was from Massachusetts. You didn't have to be a rocket scientist to realize that Surfer, a native Southerner, was not in the lineup with us and, presumably, still wearing his clothes. With any luck, the sheriff's office had had its fun and now I was going to be released.

Halfway down the corridor one of the COs unlocked a steel door, motioned me inside, and opened another one beyond that, sending me into a large, brightly lit room with bunk beds along each wall and a common area running down the center. It smelled of bleach and old sweat. This was the county lockup, with more than twenty inmates serving anywhere from a weekend (until their arraign-ments on Monday morning), to thirty days or more, for simple as-sault, vagrancy, child support violations, and other insults to society. The doors clanged shut behind me, and the room fell silent.

Now I was really in the shit. For one thing, there weren't any other white guys in the dormitory and it was a good bet I was the only inmate who hailed from north of the Mason-Dixon Line. Guys in wife beater T-shirts and dungarees eyed me from the far end of the room, where it appeared that some kind of card game was going on. It was two o'clock in the morning, and it didn't look like anyone had been sleeping, or even trying to.

As casually as I could manage, I walked to a set of bunk beds about halfway down the right side of the dorm. They were sawed off, with the top bunk at chest level; this was one of the few unoccupied ones, made up with a coarse blanket and lumpy pillow. It appeared to be unclaimed. No sooner had I hopped onto the top bunk, lying on my back with my head nearly touching the wall, when one of the card players got up and sauntered over. *Here we go,* I thought.

He was a medium-sized fellow wearing a bandanna tied around his head like a kerchief and a cutoff denim work shirt, about twenty-six or twenty-seven years old, with close-set yellowish eyes and a raised tattoo on his bicep. "Gimme any money or cigarettes you got," he said, looming over the bunk.

"I don't have any."

"I said: Gimme your money and your cigarettes."

I remained matter of fact about the situation—and truthful. "I don't smoke, and if I had any money, I would've made bail."

Again the man retreated, this time to discuss the situation with the other card players. Before this deliberative body had reached a con-sensus, there was a rattle at the door and one of the COs walked in. I stuck my hands beneath my out-thrust legs, crossing my fingers.

"Michael Anderson," the CO said. "Which one of you is Michael Anderson?"

I glanced around the dormitory, wondering who it was, and then the CO looked down at something in his hand. "Michael Atkinson," he said. "No, I'm sorry. Jay Michael Atkinson."

Michael is my middle name, a Catholic name, after the archangel of God. It sure felt like he was up there looking after me as I sprang from the bunk and followed the CO into the corridor. I never looked back: so long, county jail, the twenty-seven goddamn dollars, and the mysterious gentleman who claimed to have shot his wife. On the brief elevator ride, I looked over at my escort and said, "I hope I never have to do that again."

"See that you don't," he said, gesturing me toward the front desk.

A deputy handed me my expired license, and I walked out the front door. Outside it was still dark, and Barnesy and Surfer hailed me from a clump of trees bordering the parking lot. It turned out that Defraites had come back with our bail money about thirty minutes after we'd been booked. Around the time I was getting strip-searched, they processed Surfer and released him. I was in jail almost two hours longer, during which Barnesy and Defraites had succeeded in draining the keg, right there in the sheriff department's parking lot. Burr was passed out.

Definitely sober now, Surfer drove us to Barnesy's place, a neat little ranch in St. Pete with a decent-looking yard and a built-in swimming pool. We crashed on the living room floor until daylight, when Barnesy had to get up for football practice. The four of us went around to the backyard to take a dip in the pool, and when Barnesy was ready he came out to say good-bye. With his wife glaring at us from a window, he embraced me and then drew back to reveal the Gator rugby T-shirt he had pilfered from my bag.

"This won't be making the trip back to Gainesville," he said. Then he shook my hand. I haven't seen or heard from him since, but Barnesy was always funny like that.

Chapter 11

The Pioneers of Parkour

There's rugby as it's played on the field, with a certifiable starting time and a definitive conclusion, eighty minutes full out; and then there's the element of rugby that continues, day and night, in every setting, when rugby players congregate. There's always a pecking order, even among close friends on the same team, and guys are always jockeying for position, testing each other and themselves: who can eat the most chicken wings, dance with the prettiest girl, et cetera. You either go hard, or go home.

An original member of the Gainesville FADC, Greg Taylor was our fleet-footed winger and a try-scoring maestro. Even by rugby standards, which are outrageous, Greg was one of a kind; an interesting, thoughtful guy with an unpredictability that bordered on Dadaism. He was the son of a career air force officer, Colonel Henry C. Taylor, who among other notable achievements trained the chimpanzee Ham to travel to outer space; served a combat tour in Vietnam; and worked seven years for joint services at the Pentagon. Narrow in the hips and strong as a wire fence, Greg Taylor was a varsity tennis player and a wrestling tri-captain who went undefeated his senior year at Friendly High in Fort Washington, Maryland. At Florida, he came across as a polite, reserved fellow, almost scholarly in his detachment, with an ironic, understated way of speaking. (Whenever and wherever we met, Greg Taylor always greeted me the same way: "Hey, man.") We had many long, involved conversations at FADC, usually while being hectored by Conrad, who would interject comments like "Bollocks" and "You would each do well to read a few more books," and it was there that I dubbed Greg the "Closet Psycho," which was later shortened to just plain Psycho.

Every rugby club has someone named Psycho, a Sully or two, and there's typically a Duke, King, Prince, or Atlas; place markers like Harvard Bob (and his older brother, Syracuse Tom), Chicago Ed, and the like; as well as the bearers of several other popular nicknames, many of them derivative of, or related to, various comestibles, including Animal, Meat, Crab, Vegetable (or Veggie, as we called Chris Roehm at UF, the first sighting of an actual vegetarian in out midst), Burgers, Chicken, Cheesehead, the Tuna, Stingray, Halibut (the immortal Kevin West from Amoskeag RFC, whose younger brother Rick was the slowest runner any of us had ever seen, thus nicknamed "the Blur"); Pork Chop, Short Ribs, Short Bus, X-man, the Flying Refrigerator, Scotty the Body, and my own moniker in these latter years, Angry Vegan.

Greg Taylor first became known as Psycho because he was a different guy with a buzz on. When he wrestled, Psycho and his fellow captains believed that doing what no one else would do was the most accurate measure of one's intrinsic worth, or if not quite that, the measure of how fucking crazy you were. One afternoon at the Landmine apartments, Psycho was coming out to the pool area with a beer, and one of the guys was sitting in a lawn chair directly in his path. Without breaking stride, Greg capped the beer with his thumb and dived over our surprised teammate, executing a quick tuck-and-roll on the other side and springing up from the grass to continue ambling along like nothing extraordinary had occurred. A trend was born.

Soon the Closet Psycho was jumping and diving off everything in sight, and usually after running in a long, spectacular try or two in the match that afternoon, due to his electrifying speed. One trick that Greg mastered, and that Civil, Conrad, Surfer and I picked up on, was the table dive. Oftentimes, the after-match drink-ups were held in American Legion Halls, antiquated social clubs and other seedy bars that were delighted to host such a mob of afternoon drinkers, at least initially. A lot of these places featured the sort of collapsible tables found in middle school cafeterias, which were sometimes covered in tablecloths in an attempt to give these joints a homier atmosphere. One Saturday in Winter Park, Greg Taylor took a quick, three-step start and launched himself headfirst onto a row of two or three tables laid end to end, sliding on his belly like he was on a sheet of ice. The key to this maneuver was to relax as you picked up speed, since the bunched up tablecloth acted as an accelerant, and there was no hope of braking, anyway. At the very end of the table, you grabbed the edge with your hands to soften your crash onto the floor, doing a little half twist in the air as you fell. Carlos Ballbe sometimes flipped right over, landing on his feet like a cat and walking away to a smattering of applause from the regulars.

After a little table diving to loosen things up after a match in Polk County, Steve Defraites, big surprise, went shirtless on the dance floor, humping away with Conrad and Steve Smith, while Surfer and Noel tangoed past and several other guys jumped around and hollered along with Roy Orbison on the jukebox. I was standing at the bar overlooking this scene, when a meaty, red-faced man beside me turned to his drinking companion and said, "We got a bunch of them Vaseline boys here, and I don't like it."

I was going to reply but kept silent as Greg Taylor hopped on the bar, a tall, polished wooden fortress that was nicked and stained and dented by ten thousand such afternoons. A half dozen of our players materialized in the throng, forming a gauntlet at the terminus of the bar, each with his hands locked on the wrists of the man opposite. As Roy Orbison sang in his plaintive falsetto, Greg ran along the bar, flung himself toward the ceiling, executed a front flip about eight feet above the dance floor and landed in the network of interlaced arms, his legs stuck out straight and arms fallen neatly by his sides.

The other middle-aged guy at the bar, having witnessed this, turned back to the red-faced man and said, "I don't know, Clete. It looks like fun to me."

We didn't have any matches over spring break and I flew People's Express back home, returning at the end of the week by car. My dad had purchased a 1971 Chevrolet Monte Carlo from an elderly woman he knew: it was in mint condition, very low mileage and repainted its original sky blue, with a black Landau roof. My dad had been given a company car that year and told me I could take the Monte back to school; it rode like a dream, and with a powerful 350-cubic-inch engine, it had a lot of balls. I loved that car.

With the end of the spring season drawing closer, Dave Civil and Conrad and two of his pals visiting from South America got the idea of taking a ride out to the nearest beach, on the Gulf side. Soon we were in the Monte, roaring along a county two-lane toward Cedar Key, about fifty miles away. Nobody was on the road, and verdant grasslands dotted over with cows whizzed past on both sides. You could go seventy miles an hour as easily as you could go forty in that car, and without even realizing it I was flying down that old concrete highway like we were racing on the circuit.

Civil was in the passenger seat, the manure-scented air rushing in the windows and an old Bob Marley song trailing behind us. Not saying a word to me (though somehow I knew what he was going to do), Civil got up from the seat onto the edge of the window, his entire upper body outside of the car. Then Civil, who was barefoot, put his hands on the flat of the roof and lifted himself up, his feet curled over the door frame, three-quarters of his body disappearing above my line of sight. Without being told, I nudged the Monte past eighty miles per hour.

Out of the corner of my eye, I saw Civil's feet edging closer to the windshield, and then, in one smooth motion, he'd left his position on the door and was crouched on the hood of the car. As the speedometer topped ninety miles an hour, and we shot toward the horizon, Civil began duck walking forward, moving closer to the center while inching toward the front bumper.

Civil was like one of those barnstorming wing walkers from the 1920s. The only sound was the air whipping in the windows, and the heavy thrum of the car's engine; the radio, which was pretty loud, had somehow faded away, out of consciousness. It was like my hands and feet and what I was thinking were intricately connected to Civil's ideas, as well as the tiny leanings of his body into the onrushing wind. An eerie sense of transference, like automatic writing, had settled over the affair, and when I pressed on the accelerator, topping out at 110 miles per hour, Civil looked back and grinned at me.

I brought our speed down gradually; Dave retreated, looming larger in the windshield, and then reversed his movements around the passenger-side mirror, and back through the window onto the front seat. We were going sixty again; the cow pastures rematerializing from the blurry diorama on either side. The music came back in a rush—The Band singing "The Night They Drove Old Dixie Down." Conrad laughed; someone uttered an exclamation in Spanish; Dave leaned over to turn up the radio; and we zoomed toward the ocean, which none of us had seen in weeks.

You only had to wait a little while, and something you'd seen would be outdone by a new trick or derivation that you thought you'd never see. In the last week or two before the Gator Invitational tournament, we hosted a party at the VFW out on Waldo Road. It was imperative at a place like UF that if you lost the match, as we had that day to Tallahassee, you were expected to do whatever it took to win the party. Our ace in the hole, besides a willingness to get naked at the slightest provocation, was Psycho; and at the VFW that evening, word was being passed around that he had something in mind that would definitely put this shindig in the win column.

The VFW was a quaint, two-story cottage located in a grove of trees. Atop the front entrance was a little A-frame pediment, making it approximately thirty feet from the apex to the sidewalk. Around 11 P.M., the crowd became agitated when Psycho suddenly appeared up there, with his halo of curly brown hair and patchy Sandinista beard.

Lots of rugby players in Florida had witnessed Greg Taylor and some of his teammates execute table dives, fence dives and other collaborative field exercises, including the time Noel and Surfer found some old high school cheerleader outfits in Tampa and surprised everyone at the party by running out onto the dance floor wearing the miniskirts and shaking their pom-poms. *Rah-rah, sis boom bah, let's win one for Old Cross-dressing High!* But when Greg turned up at that height, a cluster of Tallahassee guys hooted and waved their hankies; not even a psycho was going to leap into a cradle of forearms from thirty feet in the air. And who would be willing to risk a fractured arm or dislocated shoulder in trying to catch him?

Within seconds, I was part of a double line of guys on the front walk that included Mark Carpenter, Wee Wee, Noel, Surfer, Rob "the Groper" Spadafora, Civil, Steve Smith, and Steve Defraites. Gazing upward, I reached over and crossed my wrists, locking hands with Mark. Psycho angled forward, settling his gaze on us. Those assembled on the sparse lawn of the VFW held their collective breath, and not a plastic cup rattled anywhere.

Psycho frowned. We were standing on a bunch of paving stones, and he waved us to the side, onto the edge of the grass. He may have been crazy, but he wasn't stupid. Greg said later that he didn't know if we'd be able to catch him, but he was certain we were going to try. Once we were in position, he toppled forward, extending straight out before his feet left the roof, so he'd fall parallel to the ground. His body was aligned properly, but the trick was to stay relaxed while in the air. Liquor helped with that.

Eight of us gaped upward, our hands locked, shoulders relaxed and knees bent, anticipating the impact. I'm not a physicist, but 175 pounds falling a distance of thirty feet created a force that couldn't be resisted: he smashed through our grips, knocking all of us to the ground like bowling pins. Greg told me afterward that it was the only dive he ever attempted where he hit the ground, but we'd succeeded in breaking his fall sufficiently that his only injuries were having the wind knocked out of him, and a few minor cuts and bruises.

Guys risked breaking a forearm or dislocating an elbow because of the things that Greg Taylor did on the rugby field: he was fast, fearless and had a knack for getting into the try zone. And, even more important, he would jump from heights of thirty feet without a moment's reflection because he trusted us; and he felt that way because every time he had to sidestep with the ball, cut inside and run into a stiff tackle, one of us, or two or three of us, were there in support. He leaped, and we caught him. Non-ruggers need not apply.

Chapter 12

The Party at the Star Garage

The last rugby event on the schedule that year was the Gator Invitational tournament, played on two hard, flat pitches in front of Butler Plaza, a shopping mall located across town from our usual venue, Norman Field. It's not easy to get a bunch of college rugby players to plan something months in advance, but somehow the tournament came off as scheduled, with a dozen teams, including clubs that drove down from Atlanta and New York, even as far away as Dartmouth College in Hanover, New Hampshire. A team from Cornell delighted everyone at the tournament when they showed up a half hour before their opening match, crammed into the back of a U-Haul like refugees, with the captain and vice captain enjoying the relative comfort of the front seat as driver and shotgun.

Upon this occasion, with half a dozen matches being played by each team, several of the Mangoes, myself included, were A-side selections for at least a couple of games, receiving a baptism by fire against tough clubs like the Atlanta Renegades and Pensacola. We didn't win, but we learned.

Dedicated rugby players, those who truly love the sport, at least here in the U.S., do a lot more than just turn up for the matches: afterward, they scour the parks those matches are played in, removing every beer can, discarded wad of tape, and any other scrap of refuse left behind, because they understand that the reputation of the game, and all those who play it, is at stake. Unlike lacrosse and soccer, or even nonsports like Frisbee and Throlf, rugby cannot afford to leave a blot on the social register. Say what you will about rugby players—their outlandish drinking and mating habits; indifferent fashion sense; excessive (though creative) use of profanity; benign neglect of non-rugby commitments that fall on Saturday, including the weddings, baptisms and birthdays of close friends and relatives; and a visible disdain for top-down systems of authority, such as municipal government, school systems, and Little League (even the cops and firemen who play rugby, and their numbers are legion, share this trait)—they leave behind a spotless venue when they finish playing.

No one is exempt from cleanup duty. As a rugby player, no matter what your station in life, high or low, poor or exalted, you are never really a member of a class, not the intelligentsia or the professional class, certainly; you don't even really belong to a group as clearly demarcated as union carpenters or plumbers, law enforcement, or schoolteachers and municipal workers. You are none of these—just a rugby player, pure and simple. In that way, rugby is the most egalitarian of collectives, transcending education, income and social standing; beyond even race, gender and religion. Ask any rugby player, and he or she will tell you that, amid the hurly-burly of the game, teammates are devoid of any significant characteristic beyond the color of the "strip," or team jersey.

Tidying up after a match at Norman Field was fifteen minutes' work for a half-dozen guys, but with twelve teams involved in the Gator Invitational, the chewed-up greensward fronting Butler Plaza looked like it had been intentionally strewn with debris. Overflowing trash cans stood at regular intervals, and the ground was littered with beer bottles, sweat-sopped T-shirts and socks, half-eaten sandwiches, bloody head wrappings, an occasional soiled jockstrap, even a ratty tuxedo jacket. It resembled the abandoned encampment of a retreating army, most likely the French.

Eventually we got the park returned to its natural state, knowing that we'd be back in the morning to play the second round, fouling the lot all over again. Leaving Butler Plaza in the pink glow of twilight, Surfer and Noel and Wee Wee and I fetched our kit bags and headed across the field to the cars. At the edge of the parking lot, Noel discovered a cooler that one of the teams had left behind. It contained a few beers and a resealable plastic bag stuffed with a large number of little black capsules. Wee Wee remarked that he was pretty sure the cooler belonged to one of the clubs from New York.

Noel tossed the beers to Surfer and me, upended the cooler to dump out the leftover ice, and pocketed the bag of capsules. "Fortunes of war," he said.

Throwing a party for a dozen rugby teams was a logistical challenge, especially since our club had a minuscule budget and a widespread reputation for over-the-top celebrations, win or lose. Someone on the team had booked a cavernous space downtown called the Star Garage, and Noel drove us there around seven o'clock.

The Star Garage, located on SE First Avenue, is a one-and-a-half-story redbrick building with a masonry front and a large, painted façade. Originally the Crawford and Davis livery stable, it later served as one of Gainesville's earliest automobile dealerships, known as Poole-Gable Motors. Just as we arrived, one of the huge doors of the facility was opened from inside and a beer truck, studded with taps on both sides, drove straight into the garage.

"I've never seen *that* before," said Noel.

There was a scruffy-looking band playing in the corner but the rest of the space, a large, bare concrete floor divided by iron pillars, was empty but for a few early arrivals. Noel had been a medic in the army, and took it upon himself to dispense the bag of pills he'd found in a medicinal fashion: whoever had an injury, or even complained of being tired, was given a prescribed amount—chosen randomly, of course. A British team that was participating in the tournament sent an emissary to inquire about this new development. When he asked what the pills were, Noel said they were ampheta-beans, otherwise known as black beauties. Noel enlisted Rob Spadafora to help distribute the beans, after he deputized him by administering the Hippocratic oath, whereby the Groper agreed to, first and foremost, do no harm while handing them out to all the women in attendance.

Pretty soon half the people in the joint, which encompassed more than three hundred rugby players, fans, girlfriends and curiosity seekers, were talking as fast as auctioneers and jumping around to the cacophony of the band. Probably the guys from New York were pissed off that their weekend supply of ruggers' little helper had been exhausted before the second day of the tournament, where they'd no doubt planned to gain a chemical advantage over their hungover opponents. But Noel had decided this was a more democratic method of distribution, thereby leveling the playing field when the actual competition resumed on Sunday morning. Besides, there hadn't been that many people elated by their own prospects on the selling floor of Poole-Gable Motors since the new Studebakers had arrived in '32. For the rest of the weekend, whenever one of the Brits saw Noel, he'd say, "Hey, mate. Do you have any more of those *beans*?"

My energy level has always run high, especially at rugby parties, and Noel and Surfer and I went around fueled by whatever kind of beer was in that truck. At one point, with the band cranking away at a song that lasted about ten minutes, a couple of guys from the University of Miami Rugby Club, the long-haired brothers, Darnell and Hammond Hunckey, were in the midst of an ecstatic dance of some sort when they seized a trash can and heaved it through one of the plate-glass windows. A large jagged sheet of glass fell to the sidewalk out front, startling passersby, and not long after that the beer truck driver shut off his taps, climbed into the cab, and drove out through the old livery stable doors. He was chased quite a ways down SE First Avenue by an energetic crowd of Brits, who finally left off running, and diverted themselves into a nearby barroom. Noel and Surfer and I laughed, stepping out through the giant hole in the window onto the sidewalk. We figured we'd hit Lillian's Music Store for a drink, and then call it a night.

We didn't run into Harry Crews at Lillian's, my first visit since the night I almost got shot there. Harry was a celebrity, locally and nationally, and Noel and Surfer and my other rugby friends got a kick out of meeting him and going out for a few drinks now and then. Occasionally we'd drop by Lillian's, or the Winnjammer, an old working-class bar that was one of Harry's favorite spots and where he'd sometimes invite us to meet him after class. Usually I'd take a seat beside Mike Costello, the Vietnam vet, and watch some of the loudmouths from the master's program take advantage of Harry's generosity: ordering trays of raw oysters and pitchers of beer, putting it all on Harry's tab. I often stayed close to Costello, a quiet, steady guy who only talked when he had something to say, and when he left the Winnjammer, I'd leave, too.

Harry was an inspirational teacher when he was off the booze: tough, assured, exacting and unassailable, but supremely patient at the same time, always willing to reread and comment upon a story that he'd already looked at half a dozen times—something that I now know, as a writing teacher myself, is one of the most indispensable but difficult aspects of the profession, since a writer's early stories are rarely any good and almost never finished. Harry used to say, when he was in the mood for handing out compliments, which wasn't very often, that I had an original voice; I merely had to learn how to write stories, which is a pretty tall order, now that I look back at it. For months, I worked on one called "A Small Penance," about a young priest, a former tough guy and brawler, who returns to his home parish in an attempt to right a few wrongs. In one passage, I describe the priest after an unexpected encounter with an old drinking buddy who is trying to hit him up for some money. The priest rebuffs the man, thereby rejecting his old life and, in a paradoxical way, for the first time embracing Christ as his risen Lord and Savior.

We were sitting in Harry's office, with the handwritten pages of my story beside him (I wouldn't learn how to type until the following year) and without consulting the manuscript, Harry recited one of the final lines in the story, when the priest walks away from his old friend toward the rectory and his evening prayers: *His image flickered like an old newsreel, as the light held him briefly between the trees.*

After he spoke the words, Harry cut his eyes over to the window, gazing out at the blue enamel of the sky. He seemed to be considering a topic of some importance. "It's a fine sentence," he said, "but it ain't a story."

I wanted to write my stories fast, just so Harry would read them.

And I looked forward to Thursday nights all week, if only to hear what he'd have to say about other students' work, about what we should read and about the hard, desperate struggle to get on in this life. Harry was certainly no optimist, but there was a hint of exultation in his Bacon County stoicism, in his bearing, and his weekly lectures to us, and I would rush from Norman Field in my dirty rugby kit to hear him talk about what he called "the thing."

He'd perch on the edge of the desk, his eyes closed or gazing at a spot on the wall over our heads, and say, "The thing. [Without having it explained, we knew he meant writing, and the writer's life.] That's the *thing*. To have the passion for the thing, and to remain true to it, in the face of all that's coming. Because it's coming: the heat, the grief."

It was the same with rugby. There were always a hundred reasons not to practice: homework, a lingering groin injury, early appearances at happy hour, and a recently acquired phone number of a bosomy waitress from Dirty Nelly's. Rugby matches were fun; rugby practices were torture. In the tackling drills, with no protective equipment beyond a mouthpiece and jockstrap, you'd have to throw yourself at guys like Sergio, the 240-pound former linebacker, or Platt, who flew at you like a refrigerator dropped from an airplane. On Thursday nights, so close to the weekend matches, a lot of the contact would be replaced by fitness: two-mile threshold runs, a nasty impromptu steeplechase over hedges and hydrants where we'd chase Surfer and Greg Taylor through the neighborhood surrounding Norman Field, only to have Van Blokland arrange us into lines of four or five players upon our return. We'd sprint the length of the field passing the ball down the line and back; any dropped passes and your whole line would stop in place, bang out twenty-five push-ups, then continue the sprint.

After practice one Thursday night, I bagged up my gear and ran across campus to the fiction-writing seminar. I had just dropped into my chair, sweating profusely, when Harry announced that he was canceling class, so we could attend a poetry reading that was being held across campus.

The other people in the class began gathering their things, but I remained seated, my arms folded across my chest. I must have cleared my throat or something, because Harry shot a look at me, and said, *"What?"*

"I think our time would be better spent in here than listening to some fucking poet," I said.

A few feet away, Mike Costello emitted a little sound with his tongue against his teeth. Around the room, the other students froze in various attitudes; challenges to Harry's authority were a rare event. "You probably don't know much about poetry, because you're such a tough guy," said Harry, with a tinge of sarcasm.

I knew I was in for it now, and that I probably had it coming. Harry fixed his cold blue gaze on me, asking if I was familiar with the work of Siegfried Sassoon, who had covered some hard stuff in his poetry.

I had heard of Sassoon when I was at Acadia, but hadn't read his work. (Much later, I would become a devoted admirer.) Sassoon was a decorated World War I trench warfare survivor who won Britain's Military Cross for dragging a wounded man back to safety under enemy fire. Nicknamed "Mad Jack" by his fellow Royal Welch Fusiliers for his repeated heroics, Sassoon was a dedicated sportsman as a young man and, in addition to his wartime poetry, the author of semiautobiographical works like *Memoirs of a Fox-Hunting Man*, which I now reread every year.

Furious with my own ignorance, I admitted to Harry that I didn't know anything about Sassoon.

"I've made my point," said Harry, dismissing me with a gesture.

The spring rugby season ended with both the A-side and the Mangoes having won several more games than they'd lost, and the annual breakup party was scheduled for late May at Crescent Beach. We had the place pretty much to ourselves, and after one of the guys drove his car out there to provide music, we started throwing around a Frisbee, drinking beer, body surfing and playing foursquare. Normally a little kid's game, foursquare morphed into an intense competition lasting all afternoon. A square with twelve-foot sides was drawn in the wet sand, and that, in turn, was divided into four equal compartments, with a single player occupying each one. We used one of those red playground balls, which the server, positioned in the first square, put into play with the heel of his hand. It was like four-way tennis with only a line in the sand for a net; you had to play the ball back, into any of the other three squares, after letting it bounce once.

When any of the players missed a shot, he rejoined the line of guys waiting to get back into the game. After my first round, I figured out how to play and, passing Steve Defraites on my way to the back of the line, said, "Most of the day, son. Most of the day," inferring I'd be in control of the game from then on.

Twenty guys, more or less, were involved in the foursquare tournament. When I reentered a few minutes later, I looked at whoever was across from me, garnered his attention on the sly, and indicated that I'd set him up to eliminate the player to his left. After two or three goes at this, I shifted allegiances, made another surreptitious nod, and got my former coconspirator knocked out. I had good hand-eye coordination and footwork, and was occasionally called upon to make a difficult shot when another player wised up, or became enamored of the double cross. Like everything else we did, this was rugby under an assumed name: skill, guile and improvisation.

My strategy was effective, since different opponents came and went frequently, and most of the other guys were standing around in the hot sun guzzling beer. I'd stay alive for ten or fifteen minutes at a time, and when I was finally knocked out, Defraites would shake his head and laugh as I walked to the end of the line, saying, "Most of the day."

That night, the whole lot of us packed into a single room at a cheap beachside motel. Defraites was the only player on the team crazy enough to bring along his girlfriend, a short, curvy brunette named Suzy. Guys were flaked out on the pulled-apart mattress and box spring, or whatever floor space they could find. Sometime after 3 A.M., when we were pretty much done partying, Suzy went into the bathroom to change into her pajamas. Moments later, she was confronted with the sight of the usually conservative Jim Thul, stark naked and drunk as a lord, seated in an armchair, which had been placed on top of the bed, wearing a paper crown from Burger King and a pair of mirrored sunglasses.

"Good evening, miss," J.T. said. "I hope your stay is a pleasant one."

When the laughter ebbed away, and a red-faced Suzy had chosen a spot on the floor as close to Defraites as possible, the lights went out and everyone settled down. Occasionally a titter erupted from somewhere in the darkness, and then it would be quiet again. After a few minutes of silence, when it appeared that guys were falling asleep, from my spot on the floor, I said, "Uncle Surfer, tell us a story," and the room erupted in laughter again.

The day after the rugby party, I stopped into GPA to see Harry. Classes were finished for the semester, and the halls were deserted. I found him in the creative writing lounge, and in the middle of his rap about falling off the wagon (he hadn't taken a drink in a couple of months, he said), Harry reached over and handed me a copy of his novella, *The Enthusiast*. One of the best pieces of fiction he's ever written, Harry's tale of the crazed lawyer and fitness freak Duffy Deeter had just been published in a limited edition of two hundred books. When I opened the leaf, I saw his autograph and the hand-inked Roman numeral "XXX," indicating that I'd been given volume number thirty.

"Take it," said Harry. "Keep it out of the hands of women and children."

I was so flabbergasted by the gesture that I neglected to thank him, although it wasn't the last time I'd be on the receiving end of Harry's thoughtful, generous side. A week or so before I was going to leave for home, he told me that a new magazine, *The Gainesville Observer*, had contacted him, asking if he would recommend a piece of student work for publication in their inaugural edition. Harry had taken the liberty, he said, of providing them with a copy of something I'd written for class, a story called "The First Day," about a little kid's frightening debut at school. He said that a lovely young blonde from the magazine would be calling me for some biographical information. Perhaps I could arrange to meet her at Lillian's or the Copper Monkey to be interviewed, he said with a wink.

When I left GPA, dusk was falling and I unlocked my bicycle from the rack and went across the plaza, huge shadows thronging amid the trees. Turning east, I navigated the sparse evening traffic, cutting across an empty lot to the 7-Eleven. When I rode up to the pay phone, I began digging in my backpack for the story that was going to be published, fumbling for some change at the same time. Dropping a coin in the slot, I dialed my home number back in Methuen, Massachusetts.

The dime fell back to the return slot when my mother accepted the collect call. The phone was located in a dingy corner of the parking lot, next to the Dumpster. I was straddling the bike, attempting to locate a passage in the story that would give my mother and father a sense of what it was about.

I was so preoccupied I didn't notice the shabby figure that rose up by the fence and was approaching through the trash-strewn lot. It was a man in late thirties, dressed in ragged clothes, his face moldy with drink. He grabbed the handlebars of the bike when he got close, jerking me toward him, and nearly ripping the phone out of my hand.

"Whoa," I said, righting myself.

"Gimme some money," the man said. He reeked of liquor and sour clothing.

I asked my mom to hang on for a minute, cupping the phone against my chest. Yanking the bike out of his hands, I told the pan-handler that I was a student and didn't have any money. "I don't want any trouble," I said.

The tiny voice of my mother echoed in my chest cavity, asking me what was wrong. The man scowled at me, retreating a few steps. Then he turned back for a second, waving his arm. "I been to 'Nam. Where you been? You've done shit," he said.

The guy staggered away, and I looked down at the loose sheaf of papers in my hand. It was something to think about.

Chapter 13

The Bunker

That summer I went home to work for the town picking up trash, while playing for my old soccer team, the Wanderers FC. At the end of August, having saved a little over a thousand dollars, I drove the Monte back to Gainesville, and Surfer and I moved into Noel's brand-new condominium near Archer Road. The units were made of scored brown concrete, with a head-high stone wall in front of each one, like a machine gun emplacement. Upon seeing it for the first time, I called our place the Bunker, and the name stuck, though Surfer and I could appreciate a clean, well-lighted place to go home to.

Surfer and I shared a room because Noel's girlfriend, Kathy, would be coming to live with us that fall. Noel had the master bedroom, of course, and soon purchased a king-sized bed and other amenities with money he had saved in the army. (Surfer and I had little twin beds that looked like they'd been salvaged from a 1960s TV show.) Setting up our headquarters, I made Surfer laugh by referring to it as "Noel's gulag." But compared to the hovels we'd been living in, this was like staying at the Ritz.

My new roommates, who were entrepreneurial in their scheming, set the tone for the Bunker on the afternoon we moved in. After unloading boxes and crates of books and other items from the

Monte, I went for a run through the neighborhood to get my bear-
ings, showered, and was lounging with a book of Flannery
O'Connor's stories. Noel had unpacked a set of tools, and he and
Surfer were outside, on the lawn behind our row of condos, engaged in some kind of technical activity I could only guess at. During this time, Surfer came in to fetch a pair of wire cutters and I
noticed that his shorts and bare legs were streaked with reddish
brown dirt from the yard. He had an insane gleam in his eye, but so
did the huckster in the story I was reading, an itinerant who had
fixed an old woman's car and then pledged his love for the woman's
idiot daughter. So I paid little heed to these dubious goings-on, and
reentered the world of O'Connor.

Occasionally a loud banging and resultant profanity erupted
from the backyard, but the automobile in the story had not been
driven in quite some time, and these noises failed to interrupt my
reading. I also heard digging, like someone was tunneling beneath
the house, but dismissed those notions, as well. At some length,
Noel popped in to say that my assistance was required, and with a
sense of irritation I tossed the book aside and followed him out to
the backyard. In the story, the con artist, Mr. Shiftlet, was abandon-
ing the girl at a lunch counter, absconding with the newly renovated
automobile.

I was surprised by what I saw out behind the condo. A freshly
dug trench, eighteen inches deep and just over a foot wide, ran from
the concrete footing of the Bunker roughly thirty feet to a spot on
the lawn between the first row of units, where we lived, and the
second row. At the point where the trench ended, Noel and Surfer
had dug out around a cable television box, having fed a length of their
own cable along the trench from our unit to the metal box.

"Hey, Mr. Shiftlet," I said to Noel, laughing as I figured out what
they were doing.

Noel took his battery-powered drill and augered a hole through
ten inches of poured concrete, going at a slight angle from just below the level of the grass (they had removed several squares of sod
to make digging the trench easier) to a point above the baseboard in
Noel's room. While Surfer ran inside to tack the cable along the wall
and attach it to our TV, Noel cut the main cable a few feet away from

the junction box and, using a splitter the size of a cigarette pack, spliced the fugitive cable into the box.

At that moment, Surfer appeared in the window. "We have lift-off," he said.

Before he buried the cable and replaced the sod to hide this feat of engineering, Noel had a small job for me. He was certain that he was getting a feed from the cable's main line, and fairly sure he'd spliced in far enough from the junction box to avoid detection when the cable technicians added new subscribers, or performed routine checks. But he needed to verify that local customers had only suffered a temporary disruption in service when he'd severed the cable, otherwise the company would send a repairman out to inspect the line.

"You're a writer," Noel said. "Come up with a story."

Surfer had joined us on the back lawn. "Yeah, Jack-o, invent a character: 'the guy who was watching the ball game when the cable went out.'"

Noel and Surfer remained squatting by the junction box, shovels at the ready, as I went off, reluctantly, to knock on a stranger's door. But what I was about to do was informed—"shaped" is a better word—by what I'd been reading. Mr. Shiftlet needed that car and was willing to accept, at least temporarily, the company of the retarded girl, just as we, I suppose, as poor college students, needed free cable and were willing to dig holes and fool our neighbors to acquire it.

I rapped on the slider of the first unit I came to. A minute later, a frowsy-looking woman heaved upon the glass door. "Sorry to bother you, ma'am," I said, "but did your cable just go out for a second, and then come back on again?"

The woman replied that the very thing I described had just occurred moments ago. Satisfied with this, I was heading back inside when Noel waved me over to the next row of condos, just to make sure. An unshaven, middle-aged fellow came blinking to the door, his stained T-shirt askew and the hair on the back of his head mashed flat. Sure enough, the man said, he had been watching a movie and the TV had gone white with snow. Before he could fiddle with it, his program came back on.

"Mine, too," I said, shaking my head. "I was watching this show about a guy who promises to marry a girl, and then steals her mother's car."

Returning the way I had come, I gave Surfer and Noel the thumbs-up. They got busy refilling the trench and replacing the sod, patting it down with their hands, and I went back to my reading.

Practice resumed a few nights later, and Coach Van Blokland took to running us even harder than the year before. Surfer and Noel had been through army basic training (and would each join the Marines the following spring and go through basic again, at Quantico) and said that Van Blokland, though much more personable than the drill instructors they'd known, was just as coldhearted when it came to laying on the fitness. Rugby is at once aerobic and anaerobic, requiring superior endurance and bursts of strength, and Van Blokland had us sprinting around Norman Field like commandos, our limbs heavy as lead, breathing in tortured gasps. It was also unbearably hot. September is part of midsummer in North Florida, and I dreaded those early season workouts, with 95 percent humidity and not even the hint of a breeze to cool you off. I'd be sweating in rivulets just putting on my boots.

Scrimmaging live, fifteen on fifteen, was easy compared to straight fitness, and we'd all start grinning when Van Blokland keened on his whistle and began dividing us into two teams. More than sixty guys were out for practice that first week. As returning players, the coach chose us first in the practice games and occasionally stopped the action to work on set pieces like penalty plays and lineouts, things we'd need during the season. He'd put his arm around your shoulder for a moment, telling you what to do in a given situation, and you basked in the mute admiration of all the new guys while catching your breath at the same time.

At the first session, Van Blokland informed us of some new rules affecting Florida rugby and, consequently, how A-side selections would be altered somewhat. Though we'd still compete in the club division, playing against established men's teams like Orlando, Boca Raton, Iron Horse, Tallahassee, Fort Lauderdale, et al (they were stocked with larger, more experienced players than a typical college side, which hastened our development, both individually and as a cohesive unit), we would field a particular sort of team against our archrival, Florida State, as well as the U of Miami, Central Florida, and a handful of other college sides. Only full-time matriculating students were eligible to play in these games (thankfully, graduate students were allowed to compete, at least for the time being), and our record against the other schools would determine whether we were invited to participate in the NCAA tournament. Just one team from Florida, the overall collegiate champion, would play in the Eastern Rugby Union playoffs scheduled for Princeton University that spring. So we'd finally put out a side composed of all the young guns on the team, at least during certain matches.

Two weeks into the semester, we found a promising new bar, Harmonica Joe's, located on East University Avenue. Actually, it was Noel who discovered it, stopping in for a beer one night after rugby practice. Harmonica Joe's occupied a former retail space on the downtown strip, an old shoe store circa 1940, by the looks of it, with plate-glass windows, a recessed entranceway, and battered wooden floors. It was twice as deep as it was wide, with a gallery overlooking the main room, a marble-topped bar running along the left-hand wall, and a makeshift stage raised about six inches off the floor. Harmonica Joe's turned out to be a lively place on weekends, packed to the wainscoting with pretty coeds and featuring live entertainment, in particular the nameless house band, which played just about every Saturday night that year.

Surfer called them the World's Ugliest Band, and their groupies, both of them, were among Gainesville's least desirable prospects. The guys in the band were a tubercular lot, hollow cheeks and spindly legs, their scratchy-looking beards crawling halfway down their necks. The bass player wore thick glasses and was badly in need of a diet and exercise program, and the lead singer, a potbellied fellow in his mid-thirties with thinning black hair, often appeared onstage wearing a cardigan sweater, of all things. They only played covers, but the band was tight and they were gifted mimics, re-creating the tone and timbre of Van Morrison, Dr. John, the Eagles, and classic Stones, as well as older, funkier groups, like Archie Bell & the Drells, Wilson Pickett, and Paul Revere & the Raiders, among others.

One of their signature numbers was Otis Redding's "(Sittin' on)

The Dock of the Bay." After the chorus, there's a lengthy whistling solo, and as talented as these guys were, not a man jack among them could whistle worth a damn. So when they came to that part, they'd simply play an instrumental version of the passage, and then launch into the next verse. One night we were at the bar, and Noel, who could've been a professional whistler if there was any call for it, put the index finger of each hand into his mouth and rendered the part in key, and at the proper volume to reach the ears of the band. Up onstage they laughed, bowing to him in homage.

From then on, Noel became a small but indispensable part of the act, with the lead singer looking for him between sets to arrange his cameo. Noel was at his messianic peak that year; even on a campus with more than thirty thousand students, where future NFL stars like Cris Collinsworth walked around mostly anonymous, it was amazing how many people called out to Noel and felt like they knew him. Neither Surfer nor I were wallflowers, each quick-witted and outgoing enough to hold down a barstool, but we were often astounded at some of the things that occurred when Noel was around.

On a Saturday night that fall, we drove out to a wealthy section of town where a swank, invitation-only soiree was being thrown for the varsity swim team. The place was an immaculate, Spanish-style hacienda with a colossal pool in the backyard, strung with paper lanterns and other decorations. Florida's varsity swim team is an NCAA powerhouse, often stocked with Olympic athletes and prospects, and as we mounted the lawn, tall, perfectly built, attractive young people were arranged poolside like an Abercrombie & Fitch advertisement. Suddenly one of them called out to Noel, and several others erupted in greetings and laughter: *"He's here!"* they cried, high-fiving one another. Noel was wearing one of those guayabera shirts and entered the party with his arms raised over his head, like a Panamanian dictator.

Trailing along behind, Surfer and I just looked at each other and shrugged. "I don't know exactly what's going on, but it's gonna be a good night," Surfer said.

Karen Koffler was there, along with her water polo teammates. After some introductions, she and I spent a half hour talking privately, our sandals off and feet dangling in the pool. A sophomore now, Karen was dating the Gators' star running back, and I'd been seeing a girl named Darcy, a varsity gymnast. I kept wondering that night, and many other times when I was lying awake at the Bunker, why something always seemed to pop up at the last minute, blocking Koffler and me from each other. It seemed like cosmic interference: I'd be making a beeline for her, and suddenly an obstacle would appear, like a missed phone call or a 225-pound Gator tailback. Still, we had an easy rapport, and as Karen leaned against me, giggling at something I said, a beaded tendril of her hair rocked against my chest and I inhaled her scent, fresh and wholesome, like the smell of bread baking.

Right after midterm, I got my first A-side start of the season, against Orlando at their home field. It was a club match, but a few regulars, including J.T., weren't available, and Dave Civil and I were going to start at fly half and inside center, respectively. (Civil was an odd choice over Surfer at fly half since he usually played flanker.) Coach Van Blokland's mother, a demure, handsome woman in her seventies, was visiting from Britain and attended the match, escorted by Dr. Mel Fried, a UF medical professor and the club's faculty adviser. While we listened to last-minute instructions from Van Blokland, his mother and Mel Fried settled into a couple of lawn chairs in the shade of an oak tree.

The Orlando backline was composed of a particular sort of athlete seen throughout North Florida: raw-boned former defensive backs, nearly all of them fair-skinned, a shade under six feet tall and around 185 pounds, with shag haircuts—except for one of their wings, known as Pops, a tall, sturdy black man of indeterminate age who, even back then, had a smattering of gray in his hair. Pops was a hard runner, and he was still there, playing for Orlando, when I returned with the Vandals twenty-five years later.

Loosening up, I was more nervous than I'd ever been prior to a rugby game: Civil and I had never played together at these positions, and he'd be distributing the ball to me. Besides that, Orlando had beaten us the previous spring; it was not going to be an easy match. As we got ready to kick off, I pulled up a couple blades of grass from a tuft between my feet, made the sign of the cross, kissed my fingertips and threw the grass aside. I'd repeat that same action hundreds of times just before the ball was kicked, across that season and preceding every game I'd play in on five continents over the next thirty years.

Immediately we were on our heels, as Orlando pressed the attack in short, bruising runs, the ball left on the ground for the next man to gather up and bash into our defense. Nothing tires you out quicker in a rugby game than going backward, and it took a series of stout tackles by our props, Wee Wee and Martin England, to keep the opposition from scoring right away. That season, we lacked a bona-fide first-string hooker, the player in the middle of the scrum's front row, responsible for heeling the ball back so our scrumhalf could put it in play. Therefore, when Martin buried one of their flankers in a tackle and we were awarded a scrum, the ball didn't emerge cleanly at the back and our momentum stalled. Just as our half of the scrum threatened to disintegrate, Gully MacFadden, our new scrumhalf from Edinburgh, Scotland, picked the ball out of the churning boots and made a quick dive pass to Civil.

Normally, our backline would've been arranged at steep intervals, approximately seven yards apart with each player in the line set five yards deeper than the next, so he could get a running start and take the pass at full speed. But Orlando had pushed our scrum backward and we were flat-footed, each standing only a yard or two deeper than the previous man as we fretted over the ball coming out. Even in this lousy situation, if I could transfer the ball quickly there was a chance that Steve Defraites, positioned to my left, could exploit a seam in Orlando's defense, which was also flat and creeping up on us.

Civil took the pass from MacFadden standing still. With their flanker right on him, Civil made a hasty, alley-oop-style pass to me from several yards away. It was too high and as I jumped for it, extending my arms, I could see the blur of my opposite number streaking toward me. Reaching up like that, my ribs were exposed, and as I grasped the ball out of the air and heard Defraites calling for it, Orlando's inside center drove his shoulder into my rib cage, just below my heart. Pivoting in midair, I was able to off-load the ball to Defraites who caught it at a dead run. But my opposite number kept churning his legs, driving through the tackle. As my feet went out from under me, the defender used his weight to drill me into the ground, my breath escaping in a great whoosh.

From my position on the ground, I saw Defraites make a nifty, twenty-meter break through their line, but he got tied up before he could get it to Psycho, and we didn't score despite my acrobatic pass. The Orlando guy rolled off me and as I struggled to my feet, a blade of pain knifed in between my ribs with each breath. I pressed my left elbow against the spot, and limped toward the breakdown point.

We played horribly after that, and I was the worst of all. It hurt just to move, and if I attempted to tackle anyone in the open field, the white-hot space in my rib cage seemed to widen, and an electric jolt of pain rushed in. Back then, teams were only allowed two substitutions for injury, and we'd already used one, in the first minute when somebody had his forehead gashed open by a cleat. I kept thinking it was just a bruise, and would improve as the game went on. It didn't. My opposite number scored two tries, and we lost the match by twelve or fifteen points.

Afterward, standing in the parking lot with a bag of ice pressed against my ribs, I stared into space as Van Blokland addressed the team. He was a jovial, laid-back guy, coaching the sport of his youth just for the fun of it, and I don't remember any other time when he seemed upset after we'd lost a match.

"My dear old mum," he said, referring to the gray-haired woman over by the fence, "who's seen more rugby matches than you've had hot suppers, said our side lacked aggression." Van Blokland started to say more, but clamped his jaw shut. Then he added: "See you Tuesday."

The next day at the campus infirmary I found out that I had suffered a costochondral separation, or displaced rib cartilage, commonly referred to as broken ribs. In a week or two I'd be able to do some light jogging, but no contact was allowed until after Thanksgiving, by which time there'd only be a couple of games left in the fall season. Noel and Mark's father, Gus, owned a company that provided municipal holiday decorations for a big section of Dade County, and Surfer and I'd been invited to stay at the Carpenters' home in Miami, where we'd work around the clock for twelve dollars an hour. It was an opportunity to make six or seven hundred dollars in just a few days, hanging those giant plastic candy canes from hundreds of utility poles. But with a broken rib I couldn't lift anything over my head or even climb a ladder, so I had to make other plans for the holiday.

After being kicked out of the dorms, Conrad was renting at Landmine and dating a lovely blond girl named April, who liked to go around barefoot and wore flowers in her hair. Neither of them was leaving Gainesville over Thanksgiving, and Conrad bought a pony keg and spent the entire day preparing a turkey in a special woodburning smoker. My new girlfriend, Darcy, wore a light blue cotton sundress patterned with tiny flowers, and I picked my best rugby T-shirt from a pile of clothes under my bed. We sat by the pool until dusk, listening to Elvis Costello and The Clash, until Darcy and I said our good-byes and she drove us to the Bunker.

I was stuffed from dinner and when Darcy went into the bathroom, I took off all my clothes and stretched out on Noel's bed. I must've dozed because when I looked up, a single candle illuminated the room and Darcy, completely naked, was at the foot of the bed, one arm raised like she was saluting the judges at a competition. With that, she kicked into a handstand on top of the mattress, walking around its lower half as easily as I navigated on two legs. Her body was a symmetrical array of beautiful parts, taut planes of flesh and diamonds of muscle, her back and buttocks toward me, dappled in candlelight. Her hair, dangling over her face, brushed my shins, my knees and my thighs as she moved up toward me.

It was like being presented with an upside-down mannequin, perfectly proportionate and still, her tiny feet held together and pointed at the ceiling. Then, with a single exhale, Darcy performed a maneuver that must have thrown a scare into the Russians: she dropped into a pike position, and then completely inverted; she was facing me now, her hands still holding her off the bed, legs out straight to either side in a straddle split. She used her arm strength to walk up halfway, her legs completely horizontal, and caught me in herself. The knurl of her toes lowered to the edges of the bed, she raised her hands in the air and began to undulate her hips in a manner that I had not seen before.

Chapter 14

In the Front Row

Five minutes after I'd quit the rugby team for good, Coach Van Blokland found me wandering the Norman Hall parking lot in my
cleats, swearing under my breath and spitting on the strip of as-
phalt between the cars. I hadn't made any formal announcement or
declaration, other than a couple of terse words to Surfer as I left the
field. But a shepherd knows his flock, and spying me in this unchar-
acteristic posture, Van Blokland waded among the Fiats and Mus-
tangs and Jaguars to find out what was wrong.

After a couple of weeks off due to my rib injury, then a solid week
of practice, I was fit to play again but had been passed over in selections for the match on Saturday. On most clubs, selections are done
by committee, usually on Thursday after practice. Committee membership varies by team, but is often composed of the A-side captain,
sometimes the B-side captain as well, and at least one or two veteran players considered a lock for the first side. On many rugby
teams, the head coach is part of the committee, and, in some in-
stances, he or she is the sole selector. At UF, Van Blokland had decided not to be a member of the committee, for whatever reason, but
would listen to the discussion and occasionally offer an opinion.

Selection committees are notoriously political: persuasive guys who are adept at voting in their closest friends (who often belong on the second side); old warhorses who get chosen out of habit, rather than a standard of usefulness; as well as questionable self-selections; punitive or compensatory choices; and a particularly divisive habit, occurring at every level, from the most humble club side to the national team, of selecting star players who haven't attended practice that week, choosing them over steady, hardworking types who have; and of granting a place on the A-side to an outsider not yet affiliated with the club—a dubious recruiting technique that alienates your in-house fullback or scrumhalf or whoever, as well as his supporters.

None of these scenarios applied to me, at least in this case. I'd been a sporadic choice at inside center, either when J.T. was out or injured, or when we were playing a college side, and Boca Scott MacDonald, who was twenty pounds heavier and much faster than me, was needed somewhere else in the lineup. But I'd played enough A-side matches to feel the sting when I was eligible to be selected and was left off the panel altogether—fifteen starters, and four reserves, two each in the backs and the forwards. The trouble, as I saw it, lay in the fact that J.T. was a key selector and we played the same position: I was never going to find a steady place in the team so long as that remained the status quo.

In the parking lot, I mumbled a bit of this while Van Blokland listened politely. As usual, he was wearing a pair of white canvas shorts, a light-colored polo shirt, a dark sweater tied around his neck, along with white socks and sneakers. His face was tanned and lean, with abundant crow's-feet radiating from his clear blue eyes when he smiled, which was often. His sandy hair was thinning a little on top and he was quick with a word of encouragement, or a salty colloquialism, if things weren't going well. He was a subscriber to that eat-drink-and-be-merry-for-tomorrow-we-die insouciance common in rugby circles, and we all liked him.

After I spoke my piece, Van Blokland commiserated, referring to my "bête noire" without mentioning J.T. by name, and stating that the team needed me. He also mentioned that the sooner I "got it sorted out" the better, whatever that meant. Still, it was a nice gesture and as I stood there with my head bent, nodding at the pavement, he whomped me on the ass and sauntered away.

That night, at the Sin Sity Saloon, where we usually drank after practice, a few guys shook my hand without saying anything. Our faculty adviser, Dr. Mel Fried, was at a table with Van Blokland and a few other guys, and he called me over, indicating that he'd like to meet me by the bar for a private chat.

Mel was in his late fifties, a gray-haired, pouch-eyed gent, with an avuncular, reassuring way about him, like an old country doctor in a TV western. He wasn't athletic-looking, or a dashing bon vivant like Van Blokland, just a friendly older dude who needed a hobby, I guess. Years later, I learned that Dr. Fried was a well-respected professor and researcher at UF's medical school, and had been awarded the Croix de Guerre for meritorious service on behalf of France during World War II. But to us he was just plain old Mel, ubiquitous, cheerful and totally lacking in rugby acumen.

Stopping here and there to shoot the breeze, I made my way to the bar. Mel was drinking Scotch, and insisted on buying me a beer though I didn't feel like drinking. An air of conspiracy hung over our little corner of the room, as guys laughed and joked all around.

"We've got to get you on the field," Mel said. "I've been thinking about it, and I have an idea."

Just then, Spad came over to the bar with Carlos, who was going on at some length, in that staccato, south-of-the-border voice, about the trouble he was having with his then-girlfriend, now his wife.

"When I was with Katie, it was the best," Carlos said, waving his hands in the air. "And then, when I wasn't with Katie"—the motor-mouthed Argentine searched his internal Spanish-to-English dictionary for just the right expression—"Oh, Spad, it was the *worst.*"

When they walked away, Mel leaned in closer. "A position change. That's what you need," he said. "You just need to be in the right place out there."

I had to admit, this notion intrigued me. But when Mel revealed that the perfect spot for me was at flanker, I knew he was wrong. To excel at flanker, you have to be a sure tackler, especially in the open field, and that wasn't one of my strengths. You also had to be fit and hard and fast, with great instincts for the game, and knowing where the ball was headed (and what you were going to do when you acquired it) had to come without a moment's thought. Civil and Conrad and Farwick were excellent loose forwards: they'd all been playing for a long while, and had a knack for it. All told, I had a little less than two years in the sport and though I could feel some things becoming more natural, I had to think about what to do—I didn't yet have the experience to cut loose and just *play*.

Later that night, alone in our room (Surfer was staying at his girl-friend Maria's a lot), it occurred to me that for the first time in more than a dozen years, I had no teammates to call my own, just a bunch of friends that I *used* to play rugby with. It made me feel lonely, coupled with the fact that, nearing the completion of my degree, I lacked a job and didn't even really want one, in the conventional sense. In fact, my emerging ambition in life was to become a rugby-playing vagabond and writer—to live by my wits, and see a good part of the world.

When I'd recovered from my burst of anger and petulance (and had missed a couple of training sessions, constantly glancing at the clock between 5:30 and 8 P.M.), I admitted to myself that J.T. was right. He was the better inside center and, most of the time, de-served the Λ side selection. Evaluating my skills with a dispassion-ate eye, I concluded that I was a "good field-no hit" sort of athlete; with excellent coordination and agility, but absolutely no speed (I was quick, but that's not the same as being fast); strong for my weight but incapable of bowling anyone over; and born with an ability to read a game, figuring out what will happen next.

But I didn't have enough natural talent to change the direction, or flow, of the action in front of me. I was a jack of all athletic trades and master of none: rugby, soccer, ice hockey, wrestling, team hand-ball, street hockey, you name it—and a classic late bloomer. On the rugby field, I had pretty good hands, quick reflexes and could kick the ball short distances with the right touch, though I was incapable of the booming up-and-unders that our fullback, Tom Grasse, and Carlos made routinely.

I knew that I would benefit from being a little nastier out there—but I noticed that when I was thoroughly warmed up and did a couple of nice things early, I could handle my end. I loved the fi-nesse aspect of the game, and could execute a few skills gracefully: making sharp, accurate, what Van Blokland called "sympathetic" passes; doing something heads up with tapped, loose or rolling balls, which usually meant falling on them and getting right back up, though sometimes I'd scoop one up in stride, catching the opposition flat-footed. Once, at Norman Field against Tallahassee, I made a little pop kick at a dead run, barely clearing the heads of the onrushing defense, and Steve Defraites ran between their centers, picked up the ball on a soft, perfect bounce into his hands, and scored an easy try.

On any team I ever played on, in every sport, I was a spear-carrier. Never the star. But I played. Ask anyone: I was there. I had my moments in big games, and important competitions, even at Acadia. And to be remembered by those guys, to be someone they could count on, that was worth something to me. It was worth a lot, if you want to know the truth.

I skipped the last game of the fall season, mooning around the Bunker until the boys got back from Winter Park. A few days later, I flew home for Christmas, arriving back in Gainesville a week after New Year's. By this time, nearing the completion of my degree, I could see that the rugby team was going to make a run at the league title and I didn't want to miss it. We had practice on Tuesday night and I laced up my boots and went onto Norman Field without any fanfare, except when I jogged past Van Blokland, he leaned over and smacked me on the ass.

Soon I was back playing inside center for the Mangoes, with Noel on the wing and Surfer at fly half, and we won our first match of the season quite easily. That evening, Noel made plans to meet us at Harmonica Joe's around eleven o'clock. When Surfer and I arrived at quarter past nine, the place was jumping. After being home for Christmas, I'd fallen back into a lot of Massachusetts slang, even a sort of jargon peculiar to my group of friends. This included the name Jack-o, which we used as a catchall, like "buddy" or "chief"; applied derisively, "Jack-o" often referred to a stranger exercising piss-poor judgment or buffoonery, as in "Jack-o left his girlfriend alone by the pool, and Civil just took her for a ride on his motorcycle." Surfer and I were at the bar drinking vodka-cranberries, the crowd pressing in on all sides and the World's Ugliest Band wailing away at "Ramblin' Man."

The bartender was a tall, dark-haired guy in his early thirties with heavy eyebrows and a pinched, unfriendly look about him. We were pounding drinks, and at regular intervals, when we needed another round, I'd shout over the din, "Hey Jack-o, two more Cape Coddahs," and the bartender, overwhelmed by the demands being placed on him, would scowl at us as he reached for the vodka bottle.

At some point, Noel showed up, beaming from ear to ear and looking for trouble. He came over, gave me a playful shove, and asked what we were drinking.

"Hey Jack-o," Noel said to the bartender. "Three more of these."

The barman glowered at us. "Listen, you assholes: if you call me Jack-o again, I'm going to have you thrown out," he said.

We laughed and Noel threw a twenty on the bar and the guy went back to mixing drinks. A couple minutes later, a frat boy appeared beside us, trying to flag down the bartender. Not a very patient guy, he was groaning to himself and shaking his head at the bartender's inattention.

Frat boy turned to me. "Hey, what's the bartender's name?"

"Call him Jack-o," I said. "He loves it."

As soon as the frat boy opened his mouth, the bartender signaled the guys working the door and one of the muscle heads came over and tossed the guy out, no questions asked. Then Noel got called up onstage to whistle his part for the band, and I just looked at Surfer and laughed.

Harmonica Joe's was a great spot on Saturday nights, but Conrad's headquarters during the week was a place called Dirty Nelly's on NW Thirteenth Street, a couple of blocks north of campus. It was a dark underground warren located beneath a print framing shop and a FedEx outlet, with a menu that contained just four items: pitchers of beer, oysters on the half shell, Buffalo wings and scorching hot Buffalo wings. Conrad would stop in around noon with his book bag, maybe read for an hour before it got crowded, and then sit there drinking beer and eating wings with Civil or Steve Smith or whoever came by, until it was time for rugby practice. He was the mayor of Dirty Nelly's.

I had broken up with Darcy, who had exhausted her repertoire of floor routines, and me, in the process. Occasionally, I'd stop into

Dirty Nelly's to see this waitress I knew, a buxom gal from Fort Walton Beach who wore Gator tank tops and Dolfin shorts beneath her little change apron, and Conrad and I would philosophize on various topics of interest. Though not a very large fellow, Conrad would soak up two or three pitchers of beer in the course of an afternoon, along with a couple dozen oysters, and twenty or thirty extra-hot wings. The tab could easily run over a hundred bucks, but the weird thing about Dirty Nelly's was that, around 5:15 P.M. or so, when Conrad had to shove off for rugby, the place would be so busy he couldn't get anyone to tally up the bill, or take his money. Conrad would ask one bartender, then another, and they'd nod, agree with him that something had to be done about the situation, tell him just a minute, but they rarely produced anything. It was the most benign case of habitual chew-and-screw that I'd ever heard of.

Walking from Dirty Nelly's to practice one day, Conrad noted that the team was auditioning various players at hooker, now that Andrew Hallman had returned to England. To begin the season, Conrad had played a game there, and Martin England, our resident Kiwi, could hook in a pinch, but each of those guys was more useful at his normal position, flanker and tighthead prop, respectively. Conrad said that I had the temperament to play hooker, and that I should give it a try.

That week during practice the A-side was scrimmaging live against the B-side, just as they had been that first day, a year and a half earlier, when I walked up and met Dave Farwick. The B-side hooker, a guy we called Scholarship, was getting a shot with the A-side pack during this drill, and they were looking for someone to play hooker for the B-side. (Scholarship had once bragged that he'd been given a full ride to play for Life Chiropractic College in Atlanta, the most celebrated rugby program on the East Coast, which was preposterous, since he'd never once cracked UF's A-side. This boast was made at our annual breakup party the year before, at Crescent Beach, following which I tooled on him in foursquare. I taunted him so much over his lack of agility that it almost came to blows.) I'd been running lines with the backs, and when I came over for a drink of water, I said that I'd fill in at B-side hooker.

Van Blokland said sure, that would be great, and I tossed the water bottle aside and stepped into the hole that Scholarship had left in the B-side pack, right in the middle of the front row. With those three or four steps, I crossed the threshold into a new life. Spad and Rory McCann, a broad-shouldered, ruddy fellow with light brown hair, were the B-side props. They showed me how to take my binds—where to grip them around the backs of their shoulders to create a wall across the front of the scrum—and then the second row and back row added themselves behind us. The two packs were a yard apart, and with a call from Gully MacFadden, the A-side scrumhalf, we inched up closer to our opponents, and the two sets of forwards came together with a solid thump.

I have a clear recollection of my first-ever scrum, just as I have of my first ride on a bicycle. Spad was light for a prop forward, somewhere around 190 pounds, but he was strong and tenacious and had a good, tight bind on my jersey (and a solid grip on the skin underneath. I would have reddish-purple bruises in the shape of handprints just beyond and beneath my rear deltoid muscles, every fall and spring weekend for the next twenty-five years). Spad was at tighthead prop, to my right-hand side, and, as I later learned, was critical to my stability and safety in the scrum. His legs were a yard apart, his hips just below the line of his shoulders as we set into the opposition from a crouched position, creating, with the proper technique, a solid platform for the execution of the hooker's duties.

Though the physical pressure on a hooker comes from all sides—the second and back rows pushing from behind, your props squeezing your upper torso until it feels like your lungs are going to burst like party balloons, and the implacable, ton-plus weight of the opposing scrum, pressing in and down on you—for some strange reason I felt comfortable in the front row from the beginning. As a wrestler, I'd been in tight, uncomfortable positions before (I had to first overcome intense claustrophobia, on the wrestling mat and in scrums), and through playing soccer and as an ice hockey goalie I had learned to use my feet with a decent amount of touch, allowing me to control the direction of the ball. It was a natural fit.

On most clubs, the B-side is there to provide token opposition for the first team during practice. When we set into that first scrum, our instructions were to hold our ground, but not to push or strike at the ball. Initially, we did as we were told. But I've never accepted the role of cannon fodder in any sport; as a matter of fact, I'd made teams in high school and at Acadia by going all out in practice, hustling and scrapping until the coaches took notice. As an athlete, you're supposed to be competitive all the time, and in everything you do. So when Scholarship, hooking for the A-side, fumbled after that first put-in with his right leg extended stiffly, kicking the ball too hard out the side of the tunnel the way it came in, I decided that I wasn't going to submit to a passive role in this, or any other, drill. Rugby is not a passive activity, and it had already become clear to me, playing against J.T. in practice, that if you did things half-assed, you got your ass handed to you. And I could also tell from the position I was in, with my arms bound to the outside shoulder of each prop, my nose just two feet or so off the ground, that if I made less than a full effort and we got shoved backward at an awkward angle, I could get seriously fucked up.

When the two packs relented for a minute and stood up, allowing Martin to give Scholarship a brief lesson on striking the ball, I took careful note of the demonstration. As we prepared to set in again, I tapped Spad on his far shoulder with my right hand, causing him to turn his head to the left. His face was just inches away, and I gave my head a slight shake: *No more fucking around.*

The scrums collided again. My head angled to the left, I could see Gully's boots and orange practice socks, the ball dangling near his ankles as he prepared to roll it into the tunnel.

"Ready, steady: *now,*" he said, putting the ball in.

I snaked my right foot out, intercepting the put-in, and with a little roll of my out-step (opposite of one's instep), I directed the ball into our half of the scrum. Then Spad yelled, "Push," and we marched forward a yard or so, having won possession.

"Up," shouted one of the players on the other side. We stopped pushing, and the two packs came apart.

"What the fuck was that?" asked someone in the A-side pack.

"I don't know. Jay stole it."

"Well, try it again. Fuck me."

We practiced scrummaging for another thirty or forty minutes, during which I stole a half-dozen A-side put-ins (these are called tightheads, and are like found money to a rugby team; you're expected to win your own ball, but any that you steal are considered a bonus), and began learning how to strike at my own put-ins with just the right touch, using a little English to heel the ball to our eight-man's feet at the back of the scrum. I even got a few scrums with the A-side pack when Martin told me and Scholarship to trade places for a few minutes. (I stole even more of his ball with Staley, the B-side scrumhalf, handling the put-ins.)

Scholarship was furious, muttering that Wee Wee and Martin weren't trying hard enough, et cetera, but I just went back to the other side and spat on the ground, winking at Rory and Spad. Somehow it all came easily to me.

That weekend I played B-side hooker, marking the first in hundreds of matches where I'd play that position and the last time I'd play any other, with very few exceptions. We traveled to Orlando, and the Mangoes won 32–8. I can remember the try I scored quite distinctly, since it was my first one in anything other than a practice game or scrimmage. Our centers made a break down the left sideline and I outran the other forwards, sensing that the ball would work its way back to the middle of the field. You're always trying to . overload one side, getting a three-on-two or a two-on-one as you drive closer to the opposition's try line. Our backs were even up against their wing and fullback, and by hustling downfield, more like a loose forward than a member of the tight five, who are often big and slow, I was the extra man we needed.

Our wing passed the ball inside to Boca Scott, and as he barreled into their fullback, taking on the tackler at full speed, Boca turned his hips at the last second and off-loaded the ball to me. Sprinting for the goal line, I took a quick look over my shoulder and realized I was alone; the nearest defender not lying on the ground was back at midfield, and I tucked the ball against my chest and went flat out for the line.

I ran in between the goalposts to center our kick after the try, skidding down on my hip and grounding the ball for the four points. The referee came flying in after me, his right arm raised, signaling the try as he blew a long shrill note on his whistle.

Chapter 15

The Sin Sity Saloon

There are two kinds of bars in this world, and they are equally beloved by rugby players. The first sort, exemplified by Harmonica Joe's, Lillian's Music Store and other Gainesville nightspots, were the type of places that rugby players have traditionally gone to look for women. These are often freewheeling, funky joints, with sturdy furnishings, rowdy music and a raucous atmosphere. You'll find rugby players there as early as 9 P.M., and onward into the wee hours. But these are not rugby bars, per se.

You can find a good rugby bar in every major city in the U.S., and many of the smaller ones. They are the rough cousins of joints like Harmonica Joe's and Lillian's; dives mostly, little blue-collar men's bars tucked away in alleys or strip malls, with balky neon signs above the cash register advertising MILLER HIGH LIFE and PABST BLUE RIBBON; crooked, mismatched stools; little wire racks hung with Squirrel peanuts, Sen-Sen and fried pork rinds; usually a pool table or two, and a jukebox containing at least one song by Tony Bennett or Don Ho; as well as half a dozen cranky old regulars, with sparse, stringy hair and nicotine stains between their fore and middle fingers. There's the stench of old cigar smoke and spilled beer, and when you come inside, no one knows your name.

Many of these places enjoy a second life as rugby bars, a veritable Tuesday-Thursday-Saturday renaissance that brings in new blood and a respectable bump in the weekly receipts; a return of boisterous talk and braggadocio to old dark greasy rooms weighted down by history, and the heartache of lost loves and missed opportunities. Although there is oftentimes physical damage inflicted on these antiquated pleasure dens, they are nevertheless the staging ground for a slew of memorable capers, wild notions, barroom romances that sometimes lead to marriage and the resultant population growth, and several other legitimate societal benefits. Not least among these was the Hammond Lounge near Cleveland Circle in Boston, a favorite of the Old Gold Rugby Football Club; downtown Boston's Bell in Hand and the Black Rose, where we would drink after matches when I played for the Boston RFC; Gritty McDuff's in Portland, Maine; the original Irish Pub, now called the Wild Rover, on Kosciuszko Street in Manchester, New Hampshire, Amoskeag RFC's unofficial headquarters; the Poacher in Burlington, Ontario; Aunt Charley's in Atlanta, Georgia; and many other authentic rugby bars where I've had a few pints and thrown a few wild punches. Compared to these hallowed halls, *O fern bar, where is thy victory? O fancy brewpub, where is thy sting?*

One night in Boston I was traveling across the plaza at Faneuil Hall with a couple of teammates from the Boston Rugby Club when we ran into a leggy brunette and her two girlfriends. They were on their way to the Black Rose and promised to save a few extra seats, allowing us to duck into Houlihan's for a quick one. The brunette said she had several other friends coming, and we'd have to share a couple of tables, since the bar was sure to be crowded.

The other party turned out to be half a dozen Boston Bruins and their coach, Terry O'Reilly, who were out celebrating after beating the Rangers at the Garden. Hockey players and rugby players, being cut from the same homespun cloth, mingle quite easily, and I found myself seated between O'Reilly and Bruins defenseman Al Pedersen. Back at Acadia I'd dated a swimmer from Alberta, and Pedersen, who was from the Edmonton area, knew the girl and her family. Pedersen started buying the drinks, and my teammates and I felt compelled to match his largesse, slugging down Guinness and listening to an Irish band reel off a bunch of foot stompers.

After last call we reconvened outside, where the Bruins had filled the trunk of a limousine with ice and beer. It was a foggy night and we were drinking in the street when we heard the tip-tupping of hooves on the cobblestones; out of the mist emerged a mounted Boston police officer, horse and rider appearing against the historical backdrop of Quincy Market like an apparition out of the city's past. Steam arose from the horse's neck as the cop scrutinized us from on high. Recognizing several of the Bruins, he tipped his cap, reared up on the horse and cantered off into the fog. It was like being a prince of the city.

Among the hundreds of rugby bars worthy of the appellation that I've visited, here in North America and on four other continents, one in particular leaps to mind: the Sin Sity Saloon, in Gainesville, Florida. Located in a nondescript retail hodge-podge on SW Thirty-fourth Street, Sin Sity Saloon had a plate-glass façade, painted halfway up a dirty beige color, to shield the goings-on inside from the wandering eyes of housewives and children. The homemade sign, just a piece of wood painted black, was done up with white Victorian lettering, to make it appear western, I suppose, though it also featured one of those impossibly pneumatic motorcycle babes, depicted in white silhouette and sprawled suggestively across the seat of a Harley-Davidson. It was a classy joint.

In order to transform an ordinary dump into a bona fide rugby bar, you needed a good front man, an emissary of sorts, and Kenny Alabiso, aka Wee Wee, fulfilled that role admirably while we were in Gainesville. He was five foot eleven, 190 pounds, a former defensive tackle, wrestler and javelin-discus-shot-put man from Orange Park High School, in a suburb of Jacksonville. With his dark good looks, sideburns and bear-claw handshake, Wee Wee had a strong, regular guy aura about him that saloonkeepers and little old ladies cottoned to; he'd go into a place like Sin Sity Saloon on Monday evening, have a beer with the proprietor, and the next night we'd all be in there, gunning down dollar drafts and appropriating the pool table.

Affable though he was, the key to Wee Wee's triumph was the

mathematical fact that he could deliver forty or fifty guys who liked to drink into a moribund establishment twice during the week and on Saturday afternoons. He was an eloquent fellow, and had no trouble convincing Sin Sity Saloon's owner of the net gain from shooters, mixed drinks, cheeseburgers, fries, pizza and the jukebox, even if the bar sold us two kegs a week at cost. It was a win-win.

I went into Sin Sity a couple of times after practice, and then we were on the road for A- and B-side matches against our archrivals, Florida State. Our A-side had beaten FSU at home in the fall by a score of 10–9, and both our club and theirs had swept the other college sides in the state. Because of the new league format, FSU had been told by the Florida Rugby Union that if they defeated us that spring, on their home field, they would be the collegiate champs. As such, FSU would have the honor of representing the state at the Eastern Rugby Union collegiate championships scheduled for mid-April in New Jersey.

I drove up to Tallahassee in the backseat of Boca Scott's convertible, looking forward to my second match as the B-side hooker. Boca chose a picturesque route up through northern Florida, towns like High Springs and Live Oak drifting by, grazing land stretched to the horizon on both sides, divided by rows of trees and the occasional cattle fence. For some reason Boca had a strong enmity toward those bovine creatures and when he found himself in a densely populated bit of rangeland, he'd lean on the horn and yell, "Stupid fucking cows," and then remark to us in a much lower tone that they were indeed the dumbest animals God had ever created. It was funny, because even though Boca had just shouted this opinion at the top of his voice, he'd turn and whisper to us like he didn't want the cows to hear.

Playing for the B-side against FSU, I scored my second try in as many games, and we won the match by a dozen points. Once again, I got out of a scrum quickly and ran into a gap, taking the ball in from twenty-five meters without getting touched. In the scrums, I won all my own ball and two or three tightheads, and I was getting the hang of throwing the ball in the lineouts. In the modern game, the hooker usually has two main responsibilities: producing a clean ball from the set scrums, and from his own lineouts. (In rugby's early years, the wings picked up the ball when it went out of play and threw it back in.) After an opposing player has either kicked the ball, or been tackled out of bounds with the ball in his possession, the defending team is awarded the lineout. A gauntlet of up to seven players from each team lines up opposite where the ball went out of bounds, with a space between the two teams that's a yard wide. Using either a hand signal or a verbal call, the hooker throws the ball down the middle of the tunnel to a prearranged spot, and the designated jumper, usually a second row forward well over six feet tall, goes up to snag the ball on the fly. From there, the forwards mass around the ball, driving it upfield as the scrumhalf shouts out instructions.

I'd grown up playing tackle football in my backyard and on neighbors' lawns, often tiny postage stamp–sized lots where the longest pass traveled just thirty or forty feet. I had pretty good hand-eye coordination and could throw a tight spiral within that distance to a hypothetical location, eight or nine feet in the air, fast and in a straight line. (Years later, when I played with second row Tim Moser, a former U.S. Eagle and my teammate on the Boston RFC and Amoskeag, he'd say that if I could win all my own put-ins and throw accurate lineouts, he'd be willing to carry me on his back the rest of the time.)

Though I already knew that I wasn't a bang-it-up-in-there type of player like Rob Kaplan or Defraites, I found out that I could squeeze into tight places in the scrums and rucks and mauls, keep my cool and win possession. I also discovered that I had a nose for the ball in those situations, and would dig it out of pileups like a hyperactive gopher, making it available to the larger forwards or to our scrumhalf. I had carved out a place for myself on the field: a position that suited my abilities.

Noel also scored a try in the B-side match. It was a nifty run down the wing, followed by a pop kick over the defender's head. In the sort of move that you tried in practice all the time but never seemed to work in a game, Noel ran around the flat-footed Seminole player and caught his own kick, racing thirty yards for a try. Unfortunately, when he grounded the ball, FSU's fullback piled on late, a blatant cheap shot that separated Noel's shoulder. There was a lot of pushing and shoving in the try zone afterward. Florida and Florida State are vicious rivals, a historic ill will that extends to the schools' rugby teams.

There was more of that after the A-side match. FSU prevailed 10–9, in a chippy game that included a few fistfights. Things got even uglier after the match, when the Seminole players learned that their margin of victory wasn't enough to make them champions. The clubs were dead even for the year, and a one-game playoff was scheduled for Norman Field in early April. So players on both teams were disgruntled, our guys because they had lost by a point, and FSU because they had to play us again, in Gainesville. (Originally they thought they were the champs on the strength of their margin of victory against common opponents, and were pissed off when advised otherwise.) The teams were changing into their sneakers and T-shirts on the same patch of grass after the game, and a few uncharitable sentiments were expressed on both sides. We couldn't stand them, and they hated us just as much.

As it turned out, I received my first A-side selection at hooker the next day. We were slated to play the University of Minnesota on Tuesday evening, under the lights at Norman Field. It was unusual to host a match during the week, but a lot of northern colleges were on spring break, and we were more interested in playing a touring side from Duluth than enduring another one of Van Blokland's practices. Apparently, the selection committee had seen enough of Scholarship on the A-side, and I got a call on Sunday telling me I'd be starting. (As it turned out, I never played another game with the Mangoes, which was a bittersweet development.)

Van Blokland imported a union referee, a fussy, balding fellow we called Eisenhower, and the visiting Minnesotans treated us to a hard-nosed, fast-paced match. The other team had a rugged pack of forwards, as well as good tactical kicking that pinned us deep in our own end for the opening ten or fifteen minutes. They wore maroon jerseys with matching socks and white shorts, and their backline included a stud at inside center who resembled Steve Defraites and had the same punishing style with the ball in his hands: straight ahead, knees high, accompanied by a wild look in his eyes. I was forced to tackle him when they ran a crash play back into the forwards, and he came in so hard I went flat on my back, barely managing to hold on. The whistle blew, and he helped me to my feet and smacked me on the back.

Touring sides usually get drunk every night, and clubs that visited Florida, especially from above the Mason-Dixon Line, were not accustomed to the weather, which was humid and could reach into the high seventies, even after dark. Minnesota was still under a foot of snow, and all our opponents had done before their tour was practice in the gym a few times. Eventually we wore them down, running in a pair of second half tries to win, 22–10.

We arrived at Sin Sity Saloon later than usual for a Tuesday night, and in much greater numbers. More than sixty players plus coaches, friends and ardent female fans, known as rugger huggers, crowded into the bar around nine thirty. The Minnesota guys were a sociable lot—several of them remarked that they admired our playing style when both teams shook hands after the match—and immediately began shooting pool and drinking with us.

Sin Sity Saloon was sparely decorated: a few cloudy mirrors etched with portraits of motorcycles, nearly all of them Harleys. The floor, sloping toward the rear, was covered in a threadbare carpet that had worn away around the pool table and in front of the bar, exposing the splintered plywood underneath. A dozen flimsy tables were arranged haphazardly around the room, and the bar, parallel to the right-hand wall as you entered, was a tall, oaken monstrosity with a thick brass rail at ankle height along its length. Before Wee Wee had talked management into a deal for the rugby club, Sin Sity was a down-at-the-heels biker bar, and there was a banner on the wall advertising Bike Week, which was held every April in Daytona Beach.

A dozen or so customers were in the bar when we arrived, including a few hard hats and five or six long-haired guys in studded leather jackets. They were members of a local biker gang, not the Hell's Angels or Devil's Disciples, but a lesser incarnation, with their colors, or affiliation, splayed rocker-style across the backs of their jackets. When the rugby players began to stream in, yelling to one another and laughing, these guys didn't look too happy. Gangs are all about turf, and we were on theirs and not paying any attention to

them. A few of the bikers were shooting pool, mangy-looking characters with jailhouse tattoos and broken teeth, and when they saw
how many people were coming in and that it was a loud, rowdy
bunch, they let the pool cues clatter down onto the tables and
stomped out.

A few of the bikers remained after we had filled up the joint. Two
of them were at the bar: a guy sitting on a stool who was passed out
drunk, and his buddy who stood nearby, gray hair falling to his
shoulders, ratty jeans, black leather boots and his colors. Unsteady
on his feet, this guy was drinking beer from a heavy glass mug, occasionally turning around, his elbows on the bar, to glare at the
raucous bunch of collegians that had taken over the place.

That night, I had done a decent job on the field, considering that
A-side games moved at a faster pace than the Mangoes, and there
was more pressure and urgency in the scrums and the tight-loose. I
had retained all my own ball working with MacFadden at scrumhalf, and poached two of theirs; I won more than 50 percent of my
lineouts, which in the days before other players could bind onto the
jumper and boost him into the air was an acceptable result. Although I had failed to score a try, I wound up with the ball in my
hands on four or five occasions, and we successfully retained and
recycled it, going forward in the attack. So I was feeling pretty good
about myself, maybe even a little cocky, and didn't object when
Noel offered to buy me a drink.

The bartender was a short, fat man with a boiled face and hair
sprouting from his ears. He was wiping down the bar when Noel
and I walked up, one on either side of the two bikers, it was getting
so crowded. Noel leaned over and whistled in a short blast to get
the bartender's attention. Next to him, the sleepy drunk groaned
from somewhere in a fever dream, and while the guy with the hairy
ears popped open our beers, Noel swiveled around to look at the
comatose biker. There was a mischievous gleam in his eye that I'd
witnessed before.

We had a player on our team named Dave Blackwell, the only legitimate fraternity guy who stuck with rugby when I was at UF. He
was a tall second row with a thatch of brown hair and nice teeth.
Blackwell's nickname was "Three Shirts," because you could always

predict what kind of night we were going to have by what he was wearing; Blackwell preferred the layered look, in coiffeur and haberdashery, with, perhaps, a dark blue polo shirt beneath a robin's-egg polo, and a white dress shirt arrayed over all that, especially if he was excited about his prospects for the evening. At the time, this style was all the rage among a certain class of people that included the UF Greek community, and, one supposed, the landed gentry.

The passed-out biker sported his own version of Dave Blackwell's layers: a filthy T-shirt, the neckline yellow with dried perspiration; a tattered gray hoodie; a dingy jean jacket over that, topped by a leather vest emblazoned with the gang's colors. His hair, like a rat's nest in winter, was a grayish-white tangle that obscured his rather hawkish face, occasionally fluffing outward when he snorted into his own armpit. Gazing at this, Noel took one of those slender little cocktail straws from a glass atop the bar, winked at me, and used it to tickle the guy's neck, then looked away. The biker flopped around a little, complaining in a somnambulistic manner, and then settled back down. Noel repeated the maneuver; the guy started up, thumping his forehead against the bar, but didn't quite regain his senses.

I grimaced at Noel and shook my head, but that peculiar *fuck it* light was in his eyes and I knew from experience that there was nothing to be done about it. I tried to be nonchalant, glancing away, but it was like ignoring a car accident; in Latin, it's *concupiscentia oculorum,* or "gluttony of the eyes." With his back to the bar, Noel reached over again and began inserting the cocktail straw into the mass of dirty hair, guiding it like a scientific probe.

Now that widespread social upheaval was imminent, I couldn't move or speak and the action within the barroom remained inert for another moment, like a historical diorama. Then Noel's probe reached something solid and the biker erupted in a snarl, batting at his own head with one of the fingerless leather gloves he was wearing.

"What the fuck are you doing?" asked the biker standing beside me.

"I'm not doing anything," I said.

Attracted by the commotion, the little red-faced bartender came over to us. Even in crummy little dives, passing out drunk on the bar was frowned upon. Until then, the bartender was pretending he hadn't noticed, probably because the bikers were regular customers. In fact, every time I'd been in there bikers appeared to make up the lion's share of Sin Sity's clientele—at least until Wee Wee came along with his siren's song of weekday patronage and a voracious team appetite. You could tell from the frantic eye traffic going back and forth between the fat little bartender and the last standing gang member that the saloon's institutional loyalty was being called into question.

After a moment's hesitation, the bartender came down on the side of commerce. "Get him out of here," he said, pointing at the biker who had been asleep.

Noel emitted the cackle of an agent provocateur, turning away with his beer. The guy next to me helped the other biker to his feet. "You're lucky," he said to me.

"What now?" I asked.

The biker was a lanky, diseased-looking fellow with an oversize Adam's apple and extra long arms. He had a ragged mane of gray hair that fell to his shoulders, and in his right hand he still clutched the thick glass mug, which had a foamy inch of beer remaining in it.

"You're lucky you're with your fraternity brothers," he said. "Why don't you come outside?"

To a rugby player (with the possible exception of Three Shirts Blackwell), this was a pointed insult. It was like being called a Bolshevik by Senator McCarthy. "This ain't no fraternity," I said. "Why don't you get a fucking job?"

Somehow, Jack-o thought I was the one who was pestering his friend, though I was standing next to him the entire time. For once I was innocent of the charges, but had the distinct impression, and not for the first time in my life, that the biker was going to blame me for his friend's troubles, because of geographical proximity and my 165-pound frame. He cocked back the mug he had in his hand, so I reached over quickly and grabbed him by the wrist. He started punching me, short left hands that became ineffective when I stepped inside his reach, getting his lousy breath right in the face. I grabbed a fistful of his hair, thrust my right hip into his midsection, and tossed him onto the floor. He was reaching down his leg for something, but before he could retrieve it I kicked him hard just above the elbow, sending him onto his side.

Before I could follow up, a solid wave of bodies crashed over me—Mark Carpenter, Steve Defraites and Rob Kaplan—landing on the biker while delivering a fusillade of meaty punches from various angles.

With the biker on the ground and Marcus and Steve kneeling on his chest, I tried to give him another good boot but Mark caught my foot in midair and flipped me onto my back like a rag doll. Then he smashed the guy between the eyes with a fist the size of a Christmas ham.

The bartender and a good-sized flunky came around to break up the fight. But when the biker got to his feet, he still had the mug in his hand. Rearing back as if he was going to throw it at me, his motion stopped abruptly when Kaplan rushed forward and unloaded on the guy, a right hand that flashed out like a lightning bolt. I knew the guy meant to brain me with the mug, and when he reeled from Kaplan's punch, I cracked him again for good measure, sending him back against the bar.

Traditionally, the motorcycle gang had served as unofficial bouncers at Sin Sity, therefore nobody was working the door that night. Steve Defraites and his Minnesota twin, who had been drinking together, grabbed the ornery biker under the arms and gave him the bum's rush through the exit into the parking lot. Sleepy and Dopey and the rest of the gang had already departed, but this one dude was persistent. He fell against a parked car, reaching into his boot for whatever he was going for when he started in with me.

It was a knife. Apparently the scabbard was sewn into his boot top, because Jack-o produced it in one smooth motion now that he had his hands free. It had a wicked five-inch blade, glinting beneath the streetlight as he waved it around.

Defraites and the Minnesota guy went straight for him. Arriving first by a split second, the Minnesota guy put a judo hold on the biker's arm, twisting the knife from his grasp while Defraites took a couple of running steps and delivered a punch to the biker's forehead that put him on his back. Defraites picked up the knife and cut the biker's hand with it, making only a slight wound, and then bent the blade in half against the pavement and threw it down the sewer. I watched from the doorway without much sympathy for the biker, who would've sunk that knife into my guts if he'd had the chance. Everything was in black and white, the good guys and the bad guys, no gray area whatsoever. If I got anything from the experience, it was that the world was a scary place and it was good to have friends.

At closing time, Dave Civil emerged from the saloon with a blonde who had followed the rugby team down from Duluth. They finally located the girl's car, and just as Civil took her keys to unlock the driver's side, the shaggy-haired biker, his face pulped from the beating he'd taken, sat up from the pavement.

Only half paying attention, Civil held the door for the blonde, closed it after her, and looked down at the biker. "Kill you," the guy said, throwing a feeble combination of punches at the air.

Civil used his foot to gently push the biker to the ground. "Easy, fella," he said. "You've had a tough night."

Chapter 16

The Electric Conrad Mushroom Test

I was walking along the corridor between the English department proper and the creative writing suite when Harry Crews loomed up in a doorway. Having finished my coursework for the master's degree, I was concentrating on my thesis, a short story collection titled *A Small Penance, and Other Stories*. Harry had me grinding out the revisions on this modest quartet of fictional tales in the same manner that Van Blokland pushed me through the interval training on Tuesday nights. Both were known to induce queasiness. In fact, Harry used to say that real writers got so tired of reworking their manuscripts that their first action upon sitting down at the typewriter was to throw up in the wastebasket.

I asked Harry how he was doing and he said fine, coming back with a boisterous, "How 'bout you OWNSEF?" an expression out of his native South Georgia that I loved. The writing program was in the midst of the three-day Florida Writer's Conference, an annual seminar for aspiring writers that drew a few big names to campus as featured readers. Grad students in the writing program, for the most part, were expected to be seen and not heard: manning the welcome desk in the lobby, filling out name badges for the attendees, perhaps even fetching the celebrity writers from the airport and driving them to their hotel.

Throughout the weekend, participants signed up for colloquiums on various topics—Writing the Mystery Novel, How to Start a Literary Magazine, et cetera—some of them interesting, many of them not. I had just come from a one-on-one tutorial with a prominent novelist that had been held in a glorified broom closet, space was at such a premium. He was a long-faced, somber man with unsympathetic eyes and a downturned mouth that looked as if it rarely did much laughing. Other conference participants were waiting outside the door, and when it was time for my appointment I entered the room like a man about to endure a root canal. A few weeks earlier, I'd been asked to submit a brief sample of my work, so that one of the visiting writers could read it and provide commentary. I wasn't too keen on this exercise, but Harry had encouraged it.

The novelist was fairly well known, although I hadn't read any of his books. On the desk in front of him was a stack of manuscripts a couple of inches thick. When I sat down and told this fellow my name, he shuffled through the papers for my writing sample, which had been sent to him in advance. In person, the novelist had an affect of world-weariness and cynicism, like an Italian ski racer or Albert Camus, though it seemed to me that his attitude masked a lack of confidence—in dealing with people, and in himself. He pulled out my manuscript, frowning like it was a lab report that stated I wouldn't be around much longer, then cleared his throat and leveled his gaze on me.

I don't recall a single detail of what he said (in marked contrast to Harry's many throwaway comments, which remain indelible thirty years after they were uttered), but the gist of his critique was that I should find another line of work—one that I was more suited for. The people in my story were, for the most part, ordinary working stiffs with high school educations and substandard vocabularies. Wasn't I overemphasizing their plight? (I believe he meant to say importance, but managed to check himself.)

It was obvious that my characters—the sort that I cared enough about to try and invent—were not this guy's people. With his Harvard credential and grimly serious novels, perhaps seven or eight by that time, he had little affinity for a young parish priest from a humble background, or a third-shift ice-rink manager with a drinking problem. Of course, reading them over now, my stories weren't any good; they were a student's early work, scribbled in a notebook between rugby games and late-night elephant walks across Thirteenth Street. But I doubt that many of the stories submitted for celebrity mentoring were much better, and after talking to people afterward, I discovered I wasn't the only writer who'd seen an expression of cruelty spread over this man's face as he summarized their work. It occurred to me afterward that his disdain wasn't based so much on content as it was on notions of class; I wasn't one of *his* people, either.

Largely absent from my experience at Acadia, distinctions based on one's pedigree were something I'd become acquainted with a decade later, when, upon accumulating some useful life experience, I reentered academia and began teaching in earnest. I'd been spared most of that kind of prejudice at UF, since it was a state college filled with public school kids, and because, strange as it sounds, Harry and I had a fair amount in common. Still, it was a little daunting, even for a blue-collar jock like me, to be told, basically, that you have little aptitude for what you've chosen to do with your life. So I felt a mingling of excitement and horror when Harry stopped me to say I'd been selected to read my work in front of everyone, including the visiting celebrities, at the conference's final event.

Apparently, the department chair, flushed by all the attention the program was getting, had asked Harry to pick a couple of students to read at the closing ceremonies. Harry chose me and a guy from Louisiana, a good ol' boy that he often drank with and who chauffeured Harry around. (I even knew what the other student would read, a scene from his Civil War novel-in-progress; I knew because he read the same three pages every time there was an event.)

I didn't mention to Harry that I'd just been kicked around by my so-called mentor; that would've been a sign of weakness. But I did express a modicum of trepidation over what I possibly could've written that was worthy of such a distinguished assembly, and reminded Harry that I'd never read my work aloud, except in his class, in front of the same ten or twelve people.

Harry didn't have much patience for these misgivings. "Just read the thing," he said.

That night I fretted over which two or three pages I'd read. Surfer came in around eleven o'clock to get a few things to take to Maria's, and I told him about it. This sort of task was so far removed from his experience in aerospace engineering that all he could do was shrug. "Read the thing about your grandfather," he said. "That's pretty good."

The next day, I worked for a couple of hours at the conference welcome desk, telling retired schoolteachers and other attendees where the bathrooms were located. I was treated to a free lunch that wasn't too bad, and in the late afternoon I went across the Plaza with another grad student, Randy Rutsky, to have a few pops at the Copper Monkey. Rutsky was studying for his Ph.D. in American literature and often audited Harry's class, just to see how the other half lived. A tall, quiet fellow with a lurking wit, Rutsky always encouraged my writing, offering thoughtful critiques in the workshop and more than a little cheerleading outside of it. As it got closer to six o'clock, when we'd have to go back across the street, Rutsky bought me a shot of Jack Daniel's.

"You play rugby every week," he said. "That's harder than reading a story."

Among the headliners for the conference were the novelist Susan Shreve and the poet Donald Justice, as well as the snobby Ivy Leaguer. Shreve was a well-published author, and Justice, who would soon be coming to teach at UF, was a Pulitzer Prize–winning writer. But the big kahuna was Czesław Miłosz, the Lithuanian-born poet, translator and critic who had been part of the resistance movement in Poland during World War II, as a writer and publisher. Miłosz had received the Nobel Prize for literature not long before the UF writer's conference, which had everyone buzzing.

The final symposium was held in a large room adjacent to the English department offices. That afternoon, Randy Rutsky, a few other grad students and I had set up more than a hundred folding chairs, arranged in front of a podium emblazoned with the University of Florida seal. By six thirty, nearly all of the chairs were taken, except for a couple of rows to the left of the dais, which conference goers assumed were reserved for the visiting writers, UF administrators, and other dignitaries.

Some gasbag from the department got up there and welcomed the assembly, delivering a speech about literature as the breadfruit of humanity, et cetera. He introduced the panel of writers, gushing over Miłosz like a teenage girl over a preengagement ring, and finally sat down when the vice provost or somebody began glancing at his watch. Rutsky and I were busy scribbling notes on a piece of paper shoved back and forth: *Wants to bang Miłosz. First writer he's ever seen. Nobel cherry busted*, and so on.

The Ivy Leaguer, wearing the required item of pretentious clothing, a Greek fisherman's hat, regaled the audience with an expertly limned, referential piece of literary wizardry that demonstrated how smart he was, and lacked any hint of what life was really like. I could only take so much of *the brule of a lavender sky* and *the ethereal glow of poached eggs in the morning light*, scribbling to Rutsky that I wanted another drink. After more fawning by one of the UF professors, Donald Justice shared two poems that I really enjoyed; owlish-looking, with black-framed glasses and thinning hair, Justice, who'd been widely praised for his *Selected Poems*, came across as a modest fellow who'd labored at the craft for many years. The retired orthodontists and schoolmarms and tweed jackets clapped politely when Justice thanked the audience and sat back down.

A brief intermission ensued, while I poked around in my backpack at the stories I was carrying, still unsure what I'd read. None of them seemed up to snuff, but before I could settle on one, the president of the university walked to the podium to introduce Czesław Miłosz. Everyone in the room stood up and clapped.

I'd never seen a Nobel Prize winner before, or since, except on television or in a newspaper photograph. Miłosz was not a very large man, though sturdy-looking for seventy-one, with a strong, fleshy face, bristly upturned eyebrows and a high-crowned head of graying hair. (If he were a rugby player, he would've undoubtedly been a prop forward, those stalwarts of the scrum.) Just the way he said "Good evening," with a kind of Slavic finality, inspired us all with confidence in what he was going to say. Miłosz's talk, incorporating his personal recollections and a few of his poems, was understated, and bursting with an obvious kindness. He'd seen a lot of terrible things in his life, particularly from under the boot heels of totalitarianism: first the Nazis, and then the communists. But he'd maintained his sense of optimism, of belief in his own future and that of his fellow man, a good lesson for a young writer like me. During a brief Q&A after his remarks, a woman in the audience wanted to know what Miłosz thought of himself, and he responded by saying he was a poet, which only meant he was a lover of things in the world.

After sustained applause for Miłosz, Harry got up to introduce the other grad student and me, and the guy from Louisiana read his tried-and-true scene about a former Confederate soldier, years after the war, coughing up pieces of a bandanna that had gotten into his lungs when he was shot in the chest while wearing it. My classmate, a wiry, compact fellow, was supposed to be an ex–bull rider, and was a little full of what he used to ride. I don't know if he ever finished the book it was supposed to go in, but he sure wrote the hell out of those three pages.

His oratory was like a murmuring brook as I sat there, pawing in my bag for whatever I was going to read. When the other student was finished, there was a slight problem with the microphone and I stood aside for a minute, a sheaf of pages in my hand and lines of sweat running down my back. A fellow in work clothes was summoned and I'm thinking, *This is perfect, it's one of my people,* and the janitor stepped through a knot of Ph.D.s and fixed the microphone in about four seconds, and it was my turn to read.

Czesław Miłosz stared at me intently, his eyebrows standing up on his forehead like a pair of inquisitive caterpillars. A bit unnerved by this, I dropped a couple of pages on the floor and several people laughed. Just as I stood up, the door at the far end of the room swung open and in walked a line of new arrivals: Surfer, Noel, Spad, Greg Taylor, Civil in an oxford shirt, Steve Smith, Wee Wee, more than a dozen guys in all; and somewhere among them, Karen Koffler, in a pair of beige clam-diggers and a white, off-the-shoulder jersey, accessorized by the same kind of dangling gold earrings that Conrad was wearing. They excused themselves to get past Miłosz (I could imagine Conrad saying "Pardon me, boofoo"), filing in like children at a school pageant, their faces shining, hair neatly combed, until they were all seated and Smitty thrust out his tongue at me and laughed.

Looking down at the pages in my hand, I put aside the slick little story that had appeared in *The Gainesville Observer*. Instead, I took out something I'd only begun working on a few days earlier: "All that he knew about his grandfather was that he died in 1963, and near the end he called the telephone the radio because he was remembering the war. He had been dead for ten years . . ."

It was a just a fragment, part of a story, a thing that I'd been spinning out in my head for a while and had only recently set down on paper. The idea was kicked off by a remark I'd overheard at the dinner table when I was a kid. But it showed that the past was always chasing me, and sometimes I merely had to slow down and let it catch up and I'd have something to write about.

When I finished reading, there was a respectable burst of applause, though it hardly registered as I gathered my stuff and abandoned the podium. Somebody got up to dismiss the assembly and as I went down the aisle, Conrad and Steve Smith and the rest of my friends rose from their chairs to give me a few punches on the arm and high-fives. While I stood there, blushing and stammering, Koffler slipped in between the rugby players and slung her arms around my neck, kissing me on the cheek.

"That was beautiful," she said.

Karen Koffler was rooming with two other girls in a neat little cottage just a few blocks east of Norman Hall. Two days after the conference, we dined al fresco in her backyard: roasted chicken with fresh vegetables, a bottle of white wine, and classical music playing from a radio perched in the kitchen window. Koffler looked fetching in a white cotton dress, her legs long and tanned, and her scent like driftwood and ocean breezes. She laughed often in a slightly husky tone, and over dinner she reached for my hand every few minutes and I felt its warm press against the veins in my wrist.

Washing the dishes together, I felt more at ease with Koffler than I had anywhere in Gainesville, even at the Bunker. She had broken up with the football player, but I was dating someone new by then, an operating room nurse I'd met at Big Daddy's lounge. Loretta was a slim, dark-haired girl with luminous green eyes and abundant freckles; she was a friend of my teammate Barry Fisher and his girl-friend, Sally, who introduced us. Sally said that when Loretta saw me in the bar, she didn't care so much that I wanted to be a writer. But after finding out I was a rugby player, she splashed on a little of Sally's perfume and asked to meet me. We didn't see much of each other during the week because Loretta worked double shifts at the local hospital, but I was determined to show her a good time on the weekends.

My date with Koffler was preempted when her roommates came home unexpectedly. Suzanne and Simone were attractive, fair-haired girls from nice Southern families, well mannered and sociable, though not as easygoing as Koffler. Before long, I was on the horn to the Bunker, arranging for Surfer and Noel to meet us at the Winnjammer, only a few blocks away. Noel was on his best behavior and the night began in promising fashion, with drinks going around and everyone talking and laughing. But somewhere after a few vodka-cranberries, I became a little rambunctious. Karen and Suzanne were natural beauties, no elaborate hairstyles, expensive jewelry, or other trappings of the country club set. They were lithe and athletic and often dressed like tomboys. Simone was pretty, too, but more artificial looking: designer handbag, gold jewelry, her light brown hair in a fancy updo. She resembled a rich young housewife in a John Cheever story.

I was beside Simone at the bar and she was turned the other way, listening to what Noel was saying, which gave me the opportunity to examine her shoulders, the line of her neck, and the matte of her complexion without being discovered. In the cast of yellowish light from over the bar, I detected that her face, nearly as smooth and tanned as those of her roommates, was the result of expertly applied foundation, blush, and finisher: a mirage courtesy of Saks Fifth Avenue and Fabergé. Simone was still angled toward Noel, but he was looking in my direction; as I slowly reached out my hand, approaching Simone's mouth, Noel's expression changed from mirthful to puzzled and on to horrified, no doubt mirroring my own facial transformation the night he stuck the cocktail straw in the biker's ear.

Before Noel could intervene, I touched Simone's lips, removing a smear of her bright red lipstick with my thumb. It was so thick I could have used a putty knife.

"*Ugh.* What are you doing?" Simone asked.

"You're a nice-looking girl," I said. "You don't need all that stuff."

The girls departed shortly thereafter, Koffler's brief, sad smile hovering in the doorway just before they disappeared into the night. Up to that point, it seemed like Koffler and I were finally going to get together, though I had managed to jinx it again.

Noel and Surfer and I remained at the bar, drinking vodka and staring at our reflections in the pier glass. "Let's go somewhere," I said.

"Let's go to the mall, so you can push some old ladies down the escalator," said Noel, while Surfer shook his head in further admonishment.

The next evening, I was back in the same neighborhood. Once again, Boca Scott had volunteered as director of the Gator Invitational rugby tournament, our last competition before the playoff game against FSU. He needed help with things like preparing the fields, et cetera, and right after practice, several of the guys attended a meeting at Boca's house. He lived on the south side of town, out beyond Norman Hall in a neighborhood of seedy bungalows that was considered the wrong side of the tracks. It was a run-down, blue-collar area, and most of us, who had grown up in like circumstances, felt at home there. Boca Scott had further extended the sense of bonhomie clinging to the event by tapping a pony keg.

Nine of us were sprawled across the legless couch and moth-eaten chairs in the gloomy front room of the house. Holding a clipboard, Boca Scott passed out a mimeographed agenda, expressing his determination to address each of the items prior to the social deterioration that attended all rugby club functions, sooner rather than later. He was wearing one of those foam-billed UF ball caps, with a fighting Gator on the front and an adjustable, mesh-backed rear portion. Glaring at us till the hubbub died down, Boca donned his reading glasses and assumed a serious, almost funereal demeanor.

Conrad was late, as usual. He rattled up to the front porch on his decrepit bicycle, some kind of dented metal contraption under his arm as he glided to a stop out front. Watching him through the window, I realized that he was a rugby-playing version of the Little Tramp, a whimsical, Chaplinesque figure who tottered around under the power of his own weird logic, entertaining himself first and foremost, and the rest of us merely as a by-product. He was bare chested, a string of puka shells around his neck, dressed in a baggy pair of pants and broken down work boots. Conrad had a sort of physical genius reminiscent of vaudeville, as he balanced the bicycle temporarily, juggled the metal urn to the other hand, nearly lost the bike, caught the tumbling urn in his free hand and repeated the entire process.

The urn was a Rube Goldberg samovar for making tea, sporting various spouts and valves, a banged-up, moldering little device that looked like it had been rescued from a garbage heap. It contained a horrid-smelling wild mushroom tea that Conrad had brewed up; it was thick and gooey like molasses, and tasted like a rancid mixture of boiled oak leaves and somebody's old rugby boot. Boca Scott had a dozen or so plastic Gator cups lying around, and the vast majority of the guys shook themselves an evil-looking cocktail of cold beer and the mushroom tea, and then resettled in the dusty front room for the meeting.

Boca Scott ticked off the items and we followed along, sipping our drinks and occasionally making a wisecrack. Pretty soon Steve Smith and Spad arrived, toting an additional case of beer. It didn't take long, maybe twenty minutes, before the effects of Conrad's tea began to kick in; it was a potent brew, and many of us were on empty stomachs after a hard workout and susceptible to anything new entering our bloodstreams, particularly the essence of wild mushrooms grown from a lump of cow shit.

Somewhere between item number six on Boca's agenda, the dearth of public sanitary facilities at Butler Plaza, and the next item, arranging for an ambulance to stand by, the room fell into a profound silence. Shadows had crept in, overspreading the room with a dark gray net, and about the only things that retained coloration were Boca Scott's ball cap and the disks of his eyeglasses, catching the reflected light from the kitchen.

A ball of mortal excitement began turning in my chest. After a moment or two, when a separate reality began to dawn on us, Surfer pointed at Boca Scott, and said, "He looks like Charlie Pell," naming the UF football team's head coach, a middle-aged man wearing a Gator ball cap and hoisting a clipboard who was on national television every week. Everyone laughed, and Steve Smith passed around some beers and a few guys went back to the kitchen for another cup of Conrad's tea. The official portion of the evening adjourned soon after, and Spad turned up the Grateful Dead on the stereo.

Before long, we had migrated onto the front porch, drinking up most of the beer in short order, and then clomped down the stairs into the street. It's an old section of town, antique streetlights and wide thoroughfares, edging up to the bar district on one side and downtown on the other. There were no dreamy landscapes or ghostly apparitions like you see in the movies, or obtuse mathematical formulas superimposed on the ether, like they'd been written in the sky with a grease pencil. A shower had passed over and, looking up the street, the objects on either side, fire hydrants and mailboxes and abandoned tricycles, were clear and their shadows were sharply defined; the pavement gleamed from the rain and the light, and you felt like anything could happen, good or evil, and it did, just by gazing at that street, and you took that mental image away from it, if nothing else.

It was like we were the first men on earth, yet we had a long history together, and the shabby little houses, gray and dark and set back from the roadway, were familiar to us, as if we'd lived in them during some other era and had known each other then. We were friends and neighbors; we had been children on that street; we'd grown up together and worked together and now our own children were on easy terms with one another. It was our world, a complete world, and we loved it so.

We went up one empty street and down another for what seemed like a considerable amount of time, hauling along what was left of the beer. The terror and awesome potential of everything ordinary became clear: trees grass flowers televisions cars ponds fields fences and trash cans, lots of trash cans. A tiny cornfield situated on an empty lot that Conrad wanted to explore became the cornfield of terror. Some lit-up trailers belonging to the power company became the illuminated NASA trailers of terror. Surfer went over a chain-link fence and tried to start up a front-end loader to "clear the AO," the area of operations, but when he pushed the right button and the heavy equipment started up with a prehistoric bellow he turned it off, jumped down, and ran away.

There were quite a few little bars in the vicinity that didn't bother advertising in the Yellow Pages. An old trolley car propped up on cinder blocks turned out to be a funky little juke joint; you climbed up on a metal step to get in, and the place had some kind of suspension system that allowed it to give beneath the weight of the dancers. It was smoky and dark inside, with only a string of Christmas lights illuminating the tiny bar that served tall boys and shots of bourbon and gin. A trio of musicians was crowded onto a little stage and the gyrating couples, maybe five or six of them, were like hoofers from an earlier time: the men in flashy zoot suits and fedoras, their lady friends wearing tight gold lamé dresses or poodle skirts. Sweating freely, the guys mopped at their faces with large white handkerchiefs and the women twisted and shimmied while the *thump-THUMP-thump* of the music rattled the bric-a-brac lining the walls.

It took a minute to realize we were the only white people in the joint, wearing our rugby shorts and sunglasses and baseball hats. The bartender flashed a smile at us, popping the tops off a mess of longnecks. The trio filled the crowded little room with their music, which got down into our lungs and pounded along with our heartbeats, a jazz-soul fusion that might've been performed for the first time that very evening, or sixty years earlier. We talked and laughed with customers at the bar like we drank there every Tuesday.

Around midnight, we were back on the street when we noticed an odd-looking contrivance rolling toward us. It was a guy named Seamus, a familiar sight most days on the Plaza of the Dirtbags, who was a paraplegic and got around in a special wheelchair, a recumbent, hand-driven bicycle that had been built for him by the UF engineering department.

Seamus was a handsome kid in his early twenties, with a chiseled torso and wavy brown hair, as popular on campus as the varsity football team, though he rarely spoke and never seemed to attend class. As he came gliding up the darkened street, I moved out from the curb to hail him. Seamus wore a bandanna around his head that glowed a bright, surreal green in the dimness, and when he stopped his bicycle-chair, the bandanna started to pulsate under the streetlight.

A dozen of us were spread from the sidewalk into the road, and our visitor eyed us warily. A chubby guy on a mountain bike who was riding with Seamus pulled up a few seconds later and we exchanged nods. I introduced myself to Seamus and told him we were rugby players and wanted to meet him. He shook a few hands, saying hello in a reticent way. He was an athletic-looking guy, built like Dave Farwick, except for his legs, which were bundled together with a little cord and thrust out on the prow of the chair; they looked half the size of what he'd needed to carry around his upper body.

I'm not exactly sure why I stopped him, other to express, somehow, that I—we—were sorry about whatever had happened to him (a motorcycle accident, someone told me later), and that we considered him one of us. As a rugby club, we knew more about each other after that night; intuitively, we just understood things better. And then Seamus had come along, proving that we weren't exclusive—we took people and events for who and what they were. Of course, I didn't say all that, but it was communicated to Seamus through our collective body language that he would've been invited to play rugby with us, if he weren't confined to the chair that student engineers had built for him.

Also, rugby is dangerous; people ended up in wheelchairs playing rugby. In our heightened state, by engaging a guy like Seamus we were, on some level, confronting our fears: *I could end up like that.* So you acknowledged the fear, dismissed it, and kept on going.

Maybe Seamus thought we were just a bunch of "freak-fuckers," as Harry would say. I don't know. He mumbled his good wishes; I shook his hand again, and he rode off followed by the guy on the mountain bike. After they had traveled a block or so, Seamus's buddy turned around and came back to where we were standing.

"Seamus is tired and wants to go home," the chubby fellow said. "But he knows who you are, and thinks you guys are cool."

Chapter 17

Attack of the Clones

After our meeting with Seamus, we slept for a day and a half, and then returned to practice. It was a dynamic week: a lot of running, complex drills under pressure and several full-scale rehearsals of the game plan we'd use in the playoff match. We were a rucking team, compacting one side of the pitch with our forwards, using it to open up space for the speed of our centers and wings. We practiced taking the ball straight at them in the first phase, and going to ground with it; recycling second phase ball off the deck for another stampede through the forwards, then swinging it out to the backs for a third phase, and beyond. It got so we could execute the game plan with our eyes closed.

On the morning of our playoff against Florida State, I took a ride from Surfer to Maria's neighborhood on the edge of the campus. When he stopped to have breakfast with her, I grabbed my kit bag from the backseat of the Egg and began walking toward Norman Hall. I needed $550 to get my car back from a transmission shop over on Fifteenth Street, and had taken to cadging rides from Surfer or using Noel's bicycle to get to class. But on such a fine morning with a current of pregame nervousness running through my veins and my stomach boiling like a kettle, I was happy to take the edge off by hoofing it.

It was already a hot, muggy day, though it was only nine o'clock in the morning. The previous weekend, I'd continued my accelerated education at hooker by playing in four matches at the Gator Invitational tournament. We won our first three games, losing a hard-fought semifinal to the Atlanta Renegades, an experienced Division I men's club. Coming off the field in the oppressive heat, I spoke with Don Morrison, a trim, dark-haired guy from Boston who had the highest rating of any U.S. rugby referee. I told him where I was from, mentioning that I'd be going back to Massachusetts soon. There were several men's teams to pick from in the city, and when I asked Morrison to recommend one, he didn't hesitate: Boston RFC was one of the premier rugby clubs in the U.S., and if I wanted to play with—and against—the best, that's where I should go.

Lugging my bag, I was the first player to arrive at Norman Field, a browned-over, dusty patch of lawn at that time of the year. It was still two hours before kickoff, and the park was deserted. Wearing my sneakers, rugby shorts, and a T-shirt, I set off at a jog, circling the pitch two or three times to reduce my nervous energy. It was a pregame ritual that continues to this day: I can't sit still before matches and have to do a certain amount of running, cool down from that and then go through a rugby-specific warm-up before kickoff.

After jogging a few laps, I returned to the shade and did a little stretching. Before long, Mel Fried's devoted assistant would turn up, a bespectacled, matronly woman known as Irma "Gatorade" Smith. Irma would mix us a few gallons of the local sports elixir in a Styrofoam cooler, and the guys would jibe her about it, asking why it was so watered down. But I was afraid that she wouldn't get there for another half hour or so, and had brought along two quarts of water, a large bottle of Gatorade, and a sleeve of Fig Newtons, my preferred snack an hour or so before a rugby game. I'd always suffered from butterflies prior to competing, but had worked out strategies for overcoming my nerves, and keeping to my rituals was one of them.

Before long, other guys began to show up at Norman Field. Dave

Civil roared into the lot on his motorcycle, his rugby boots fastened to the seat by an elastic cord. He spotted me under the tree and lifted his chin in greeting; as much as we loved to have fun, and appeared as well-organized as an anarchist's convention, we were serious about beating FSU. After the matches are through for the day, rugby players are notoriously social, and just as we'd seen during the brawl at the Sin Sity Saloon, when the Minnesota guys jumped in on my behalf, a rugby player will always side with another rugby player when non-ruggers are involved. But, overall, there was very little affection between our club and the boys from Tallahassee.

Spad rode up on his bicycle without saying a word. Even Carlos was subdued, at least by his standards, talking forty words a minute instead of the usual seventy. This was the first rugby match that I'd ever played in that actually meant something: the winners would be crowned state champions, and go on to the Eastern Rugby Union collegiate championships in New Jersey, and the losers would go home. So I didn't have much to say, either, as game time approached. Conrad was, well, Conrad. He arrived on foot, carrying his rugby boots and a Frisbee. When Greg Taylor and Steve Smith got there, they went onto the field with Conrad and Civil, in their stockinged feet, and began tossing the Frisbee around, their typical Zen warm-up.

One of our new players, Pokey Whelan, an American kid who had grown up in the Panama Canal zone, brought his guitar to the field and sat cross-legged in the grass, tinkering with an original composition he called, "The Ballad of Steve Smith." Stepping out of his car, Van Blokland surveyed this motley scene, laughed, and said, "You can't get much looser than this bloody crew."

While we were lacing up our boots and Van Blokland repeated the starting fifteen and reserves that had been announced at Thursday's practice, a luxury coach eased into the Norman Hall access road, turned alongside the rugby field, and chuffed to a stop. The door opened with a hissing sound, and approximately thirty-five rugby players trooped out with their bags, wending in single file along what Van Blokland referred to as the "car park." Turning at the edge of the grass, the FSU guys continued down the sideline, their faces set like concrete, following their two coaches with military precision.

Despite the rising heat, our opponents wore new sweat suits in garnet and gold, their team colors. A beer company logo appeared on the back, along with the year, and:

FSU Rugby Club
State Champions

It took a moment for this display of hubris to register, while FSU stripped off their new jackets and donned their boots. Kaplan was nearby, fielding kicks from Carlos and our smooth English fullback, Mike May. "What a bunch of assholes," said Kap. Here they were at our field, wearing sweats that declared them state champions, and the game hadn't even been played yet. Before long, one of their reserves said that the sweat suits had been ordered right after our match three weeks earlier in Tallahassee. Whoever placed the order was laboring under the assumption that their 10–9 win that day made them champs. But that was horseshit, and even if it was true, they should've kept the sweats on the bus until after the game.

Guys on our team had fifteen minutes to stew over it before the referee whistled for the captains, going over a few ground rules. Ejections for dirty play, especially fighting, would be swift. The ref also said that if the score was tied after the eighty minutes of regulation, we'd play subsequent periods of fifteen minutes until there was a winner.

Van Blokland whistled with two fingers, calling over all the Frisbee throwers, guitar strummers, and dog walkers to deliver a few last-minute instructions. He urged us to "corner flag like hell," which meant to pursue on defense by retreating toward the opposite corner of the field, cutting off any chance of an overload. His game plan was to starve FSU of tries, forcing them to kick for points, and after he'd gone over that again, we put our hands together and Van Blokland said to "bloody well get after them."

Our New Zealand prop, Martin England, who was captain that year, pushed into the middle of the circle. With his stubby legs, broad chest, and thick, ear-to-ear beard, Martin resembled Taz from *Looney Tunes* and made about as much sense when he was excited. Martin was certainly worked up about this game, because what our

Kiwi prop said after, "C'mon lads," was a bunch of vowels and con-
sonants strung together with compressed air sounds, his face turning red and his fists balled up on his hips. (Surfer used to do a
spot-on impression of him, but not until after the game since Martin
was such a handy player and a jolly good fellow.)

The referee blew his whistle and we ran onto the field and took
our positions. FSU was a good side, and their general hardness, especially in rucking, mauling and tackling among their forwards,
was a persistent aspect of their game. They benefited by playing in
Tallahassee, which, unlike Gainesville, supported a local men's club
as well as the college side, offering a feeder system for the former
and a tough practice opponent for the latter. FSU was anchored by a
set of rugby-playing triplets known as the clones, a fit, skillful trio
who started at loose forward, inside center and fullback, respectively.
Perhaps their mother could tell them apart, but I sure couldn't. Therefore, describing one of them is as good as describing all three: five
ten or five eleven, 180–185 pounds, with narrow hips, a high flank and
a thoroughbred's tapered legs; not a devastating speedster, although
he could run. Dark, almost shoulder-length hair, worn in a North
Florida mullet; sometimes with a thin, porn star mustache, other times
not. Good tackler. Mouthy. Appeared to be everywhere at once: bitch-
ing to the ref, throwing a sneak punch, tackling high. A loud, grating,
feisty nuisance with a disagreeable temperament.

When playing fullback, Clone #1 had this signature move that
always seemed to work, which was infuriating. He was good under
the high ball, and back on defense, he'd often catch a tall, soaring
punt from Carlos or Mike May, and start upfield with it. As the line
of our defense closed on him, he'd hold the ball out in front with
one hand, palm up, then glance down at it and stutter-step, raising
his right leg in a back swing, like he meant to kick the ball over our
heads. Just as the closest defender stiffened up, expecting the kick,
the clone would stab his right foot into the ground, jab-stepping
into the gap between defenders, and continuing upfield. You had to
watch for it, but with three of them out there, it was like playing a
live-action version of the shell game: *Which one of these assholes is the
guy with the fake kick?* After a while, you lost track of the jab-step
clone and fell victim to the fake.

Hitching up my shorts, I made the sign of the cross, spat over the midfield line, and stretched this way and that, loosening up my hamstrings and hips. Wee Wee was ten yards away, closest to their kicker, and looked over and winked at me. Having good, tough props nearby was always a godsend: Wee Wee and Martin played with a nasty streak, and that brought out my own aggressiveness. As a hooker, it was like you were the younger brother where props were concerned.

Carlos had the ball, teeing it up for the kickoff. Despite our unorthodox methods, we had a formidable team. Nonstudents like J.T., Defraites, former UF linebacker Sergio Lopez, Big Harry and Keith Platt were watching from the sidelines. But we had MacFadden, our Scottish scrumhalf; Carlos at fly half; Surfer and Kaplan in the centers; Greg Taylor's raw speed at one wing, and Steve Smith's determined tackling on the other. Mike May was a Brit; Conrad and Civil had been playing since adolescence; Pokey Whelan, who'd been on the team since January, had started playing rugby in Panama at age fourteen. He'd also played at FSU before coming to Gainesville, and for the Tallahassee men's club.

Pokey was the only guy that crossed over midfield before the game, shaking hands with several of the FSU players. An engaging, guitar-picking free spirit, Pokey had serious rugby skills. Curly blond hair, sweet-talking smile, but hard as stone on the field with a creative sense of the game, even under pressure. When Pokey realized that no one else was bantering with the opposition, he put his mouthpiece back in and clammed up.

Carlos sent the ball forty feet in the air but just ten yards downfield, a perfect rugby kickoff. This allowed Wee Wee and Martin and Spad to race underneath it, smashing into one of the clones just as he touched the ball. Conrad and I came piling in, then Pokey and Civil; FSU crashed from their side of the breakdown, and there was a quick whistle; punches flew back and forth over the gain line; then there was a more urgent whistle. About fifteen seconds of the match had been played and I was standing there, chest heaving, blood streaming from my nose, and what felt like molten bands of iron encircling my rib cage, as I struggled to breathe. And I was inclined to think this was the way it was going to be.

Watching sports on television, you grow accustomed to the omniscient view. Looking down from above, you see every player on both teams, and every move they make: the balletic integrity of the game, any game; its thrusts and feints, counterattacks and defensive stands, are revealed in their entirety. But playing in a rugby match can feel like being trapped in a tipped-over phone booth while a gang fight rages all around you. You have a keen sense of tunnel vision, and things come rocketing out of the dark at amazing speeds. Inside the scrums, you hear the quickening of your own breath amid the cacophony of inhale-exhale that surrounds you; the other players bound so tightly it's a wonder you can breathe at all—so close that a knitting needle could not be forced between you and your props, or between your front row and theirs.

The heaving and pushing in the scrum, all with a definite purpose, is like the rolling and pitching of a ship in high seas, making it difficult to maintain your balance; except, at hooker, where I was playing, you were also required to control an overinflated football with either side of your foot, directing it with precision to someone a few yards to the rear that you can't see—and it's ninety degrees and humid (other times it's dark, cold and raining, so conditions vary).

Early in the game, Clone #1 came up through midfield with the ball and just as it looked like he would be tackled, pulled off his fake kick and penetrated into our half, off-loading the ball to one of his brothers. Kaplan caught up from the side and leveled him, but was penalized for a high tackle. Clone #1 smirked at us and made the kick, and FSU led 3–0.

Ten minutes later, Carlos put up three points with a soaring penalty kick from forty yards that tied the score. Thereafter, play settled down, as both teams stiffened on defense, refusing to allow the other side an overload. Occasionally you could hear Van Blokland shouting about a bloody this or bloody that, but the actual soundtrack of the game, recalled in bits and snatches, was a lot of white noise and perhaps Conrad saying "*Quick strike, boofoo,*" or Wee Wee binding onto my jersey, his face two inches away, and his voice like it was inside my head: "*Get under him, buddy.*" At one point, when the scrum dissolved and we broke downfield, chasing after the ball, Civil ran past making noises like he was shifting gears. Carlos, retreating through the line of pursuit to get out with the backs, said, "Beep! Beep!" steering around Civil with his hands out in front like he was driving a car.

Near the end of the first half, the referee whistled for a scrum about thirty-five meters out from our goal line. It was our put-in, and when MacFadden flashed the ball into the tunnel, I was over-eager, striking too hard. By not delivering the ball with the proper English, I missed the channel between our guys' feet, banking it off Wee Wee's shin into their half of the scrum. FSU's number eight, who was twenty pounds heavier than either Spad or Conrad, picked up this tighthead at the back of their scrum and rumbled onto the weak side, traveling seven or eight meters past the gain line before they got him off his feet. It was like indigenous hunters bringing down a wild elephant. But FSU was in easy reach of our goalposts, and again the referee penalized us, this time for killing the ball in the tackle, impeding the other team from playing it off the ground. Clone #1 made the kick, and FSU took a 6–3 lead into halftime.

No one said a word, but it was my fuckup. The way the match was going, with an abundance of hard tackling that had stalled both teams in the middle of the field, tries were going to be at a premium. Our three points had come from a monumental penalty kick; Carlos was probably the only player in the Southern U.S. who routinely made those kicks. But not even the pride of La Plata could slot a penalty from our half of the field, where we were bogged down.

Somebody ran out from the touchline with jugs of water and the Styrofoam cooler filled with Gatorade. While I caught my breath, I tried to disavow myself of the notion that six lousy points would win the game, and the fact that the mistake leading to the penalty kick was on me.

Van Blokland told us to be patient. Push the ball upfield through the forwards, compacting their defense and making space for our backs. I stood outside the circle of players, listening to the coach with my head down. I was getting around the field all right, making use of all the training we'd gone through, but I'd already figured out my primary role was to win possession: in the scrums, lineouts and tight-loose.

The gist of Van Blokland's speech was get the ball to Greg Taylor in space; he was faster than any of the clones, and the FSU winger who was marking him. So far he hadn't touched the ball; FSU had deprived our backline of clean possession to the same degree that we'd starved theirs. When the referee blew the whistle for the second-half kickoff, I was determined to get that one possession back, to balance my own personal account. The rest would take care of itself.

They kicked off to us and things began well, with Martin taking the ball to ground. I dug into the pile for the recycled ball and sent it back through my legs to MacFadden. When I looked up, there was a long pass from Gully that skipped Surfer and went to Kap, who took the ball at a dead run. He broke through their defense and Clone #2, I think it was, corner flagging across the field, drove Kaplan headfirst into the ground like a cowboy wrestling a steer. The referee penalized him for a high tackle, and Carlos put the kick through, tying the score at 6–6.

During the game, I suppose, hundreds of cars zoomed by on SW Thirteenth Street, just behind the end goal we were moving toward. Advice and encouragement from our reserves and ineligible players were shouted from the touchline until voices grew hoarse from overuse. Pretty coeds walked along the sidewalk not five yards from our lineouts, and foreign students passed in and out of Norman Hall, talking in Spanish and Chinese and Arabic. But when I think of the FSU game, all I remember is a patch of ground maybe fifteen yards wide and thirty or forty yards long, running from the left sideline on FSU's end of the field looking toward SW Thirteenth Street. My back to the parking lot, I worked that strip of land, sowing and tilling and hacking for the ball, as diligently as those old sodbusters worked the tenant farms up in Bacon County when Harry was just a stripling.

Except I wasn't looking to produce a crop. I wanted to dig up just one possession that wasn't supposed to be ours, evening things up in that regard, and I was breathing at capacity and spitting blood to do it; Wee Wee at my left shoulder; Conrad floating by, then Civil; the sun bore down on me, and the air was like the inside of a furnace. And when we forced our way inside their twenty-two-meter line, thinking we were about to hit pay dirt, someone spilled the ball and Clone #1 ran it back at us, twenty or thirty yards down the touchline. Greg Taylor had to come all the way across the field to get him, racing fifty yards on a diagonal, collaring FSU's playmaker and slinging him out of bounds. Another penalty, another Clone #1 kick, and we were down 9–6, with less than seven minutes to play.

In rugby, unlike football, when the other team scores, you have to kick it back to them. You can go deep, pinning them in their own end—few kicks get taken all the way back upfield when there're fifteen defenders—or you can go high and short, and try to force the ball loose with a gang tackle. Either way, you must give up possession. Carlos was a very clever player and when he saw that a couple of FSU guys had their backs turned, sucking wind, he quickly put the ball on the ground and topped a little grubber into open space. Conrad and Pokey ran onto it, with Conrad playing it off the ground to Civil, who drove into the opposing forwards. Spad and Wee Wee rucked over the ball, leaving it on the ground; then Martin and I did the same, and Pokey recycled and came over it again. We were drawing in their forwards, trying to create space out on the right side of the field. About thirty meters from their goal line, however, the ball died in the tackle, and over Carlos and MacFadden's multilingual protest—we'd been going forward, and it appeared the opposition had killed the ball on the ground—FSU was awarded a scrum put-in.

Rucking the ball downfield in two or three phases will take the wind out of the most well-conditioned player, at least temporarily. At Acadia, I'd learned that every athlete fatigues at pretty much the same point; whoever recovers the fastest is in the best shape. While the referee picked up the ball, handed it to the FSU scrumhalf and dug his heel into the turf to indicate the mark, I had my hands on top of my head, standing upright, drawing my breath in ragged gasps through my nose, as I'd been taught in college—the idea being that the oxygen has to travel farther by coming in through your nasal passages instead of your mouth. That way, you absorb a little extra and recover a fraction of a second faster than you might have.

I took my bind on Martin and Wee Wee, the scrum readied itself, and the two packs crashed together. There was a slow-motion effect as the scrum compressed; I angled my head to the right, looking for FSU's scrumhalf to tighten his fingers on the ball, and then snaked out my right foot, anticipating his delivery. The ball entered the tunnel mid-strike, and as the opposing hooker made his move, the bone of my ankle blocked his foot sweep, his cleats gashing through my sock. I rolled the ball to the right and backward, and Martin closed off the tunnel and stepped over it; a clean tighthead. Our pack surged; MacFadden darted back to the rear of the scrum to retrieve the ball, and their hooker uttered a soft, though resounding, "*Fuck.*"

Our backs had been up flat, in defense. MacFadden made a quick, blind pass to Carlos, who just touch-passed it to Surfer. He took one step up and off-loaded to Kaplan, who grabbed it out of the air with his right hand, stiff-armed Clone #2 with his left, and got through their line into a sliver of open field. When FSU's defense, scrambling to recover, collapsed in on him, Kaplan put the ball up and over the head of the encroaching winger, right into Greg Taylor's arms.

In that situation, Greg had been the only player besides our full-back, Mike May, who was sitting deep, expecting a kick in the likely event that FSU won the put-in. Running toward that side of the field, I saw Greg veer toward the middle, dekeing one of the clones and then go flat out for the corner. It was a beautiful sight. Once he crossed up the defenders, it was a footrace, and there was no one in Florida rugby who was going to catch Psycho over thirty yards. He sprinted to the end goal and dotted it down, just inside the corner flag. We were ahead for the first time in the match, 10–9.

Not a lot of shouting; just some quick eye contact, and nodding of the head. Our sideline was going berserk, though it sounded like it was ten miles off. From that extreme angle, Carlos missed the conversion, but it didn't faze us. Psycho's breakaway try supercharged the entire team, and when FSU kicked the ball back to us, we ate up the lion's share of the remaining time with a crisp series of rucks and mauls, getting well into their half of the field. Starve them of the ball, Van Blokland had said, and that's exactly what we did. From down on the ground I saw the referee looking at his watch, and then he blew two short and one long blasts on his whistle, and an audible roar went up from our sideline. Wee Wee gave me a heave up from the deck and tousled my hair. "That's the way," he said. We formed two lines and shook hands, and in very short order, the FSU players had their kit bags and championship jackets and were streaming toward the bus.

There's a photograph, taken within seconds of that final whistle, of Kaplan and me walking back toward midfield, his left arm over my left shoulder, and in the half shadow crossing the plane, I can make out a little smile on my face and that Kap is saying something into my ear. I don't remember what it was, and I didn't write it down later when I recorded these events in my journal. But that's all right. We were the state champs, and that was indisputable.

Chapter 18

You Gotta go to Trenton

Maria dropped Surfer, Noel and me off at the Sin Sity Saloon around noon on the day we were heading up to the ERU championships in New Jersey. Two shiny University of Florida vans were parked in front of the bar, and several players were milling around as Mark Carpenter, who was no longer a student and thus ineligible for the trip, scribbled a few parting sentiments on the vans with a stick of white shoe polish. DECADENT BEER SLOBS RULE and FLORIDA RUGBY SLUTS were probably not the kind of signifiers we needed to slip past law enforcement in the eight coastal states between Gainesville and Princeton. But as the guys drank their first beers and laughed, Mark busied himself covering the vans in capital letters three feet high.

Surfer remained in the car for several minutes, canoodling with Maria, while Noel and I stepped into the searing midday heat with our rugby kits and overnight bags. Several cases of Old Milwaukee were already stacked up by the vans, along with enough bags of ice to construct a good-sized igloo. Wee Wee was filling two large Styrofoam coolers with the beer and ice, wearing the kind of little alpine hat my dad preferred when he took us on a Sunday drive into New Hampshire.

"I sure hope my liver holds out," said Noel.

I'd been on many long van trips at Acadia, traveling to compete against far-flung opponents like the University of Maine at Presque Isle, Moncton University, and the University of Prince Edward Island, which also entailed a scenic ferry ride. But those trips were under adult supervision—the coaches always drove. We wore team sweat suits and were given a per diem to cover our meals and a little spending money. Beer drinking was limited, for the most part, to Saturday night or Sunday afternoon, depending on when the competition ended.

Van Blokland wasn't going on this particular trip; we were leaving on Thursday, returning on Monday, and he was busy teaching on those days. That we were even going at all, in the vans and with the athletic department gas card, was a tribute to Wee Wee and his keen understanding of the university realpolitik. Although he was just twenty-three, with his abundant chest hair and sideburns, he looked a lot older, and was treated like a grown-up in negotiations with bar owners, rugby suppliers, and the local constabulary. He was tough on the field and cagey off it, which was great for the team and something that I benefited from personally.

On this occasion, Wee Wee made an appointment with student government, put on a necktie and a decent pair of pants, and convinced them to sanction the trip, lay out the money for gas, and loan us the vans. It was the beginning of legitimacy for Florida Rugby, continuing to this day, with the Gators as established regional and national championship contenders.

One of the conditions was that Wee Wee agreed to drive the lead van and handpick the other driver, vouching for his safety record, et cetera. When Carlos got behind the wheel of the second van, I piled into Wee Wee's van along with Surfer, Boca Scott, Greg Taylor, Mike Siskin, Scholarship, another backup hooker named Freddie Pinot, Noel riding shotgun, and anyone else who had something to live for. The cooler filled with Old Milwaukee was wedged between the bucket seats up front, and the rest of us, along with the rugby gear, travel bags, guitars, et cetera, were strewn over the bench-style seats and in the rear.

As we pulled onto SW Thirteenth Street, Wee Wee announced that he was the pilot and Noel was the head stewardess, and that just like on the major airlines, the pilot's beer should never be empty. When he'd finish a can of Old Mill Water, he'd slam it down on the dash, crushing it, and then throw it against the passenger-side window, which was closed. Noel's first priority was to have a fresh beer in the built-in coaster before the can hit the floor. (A little ways outside of Jacksonville, Wee Wee caught Noel sleeping and rang one off his noggin. Thereafter, he remained alert.)

The plan was to drive all night, visit the U.S. Capitol building in the morning, and then proceed to Princeton in time for the pre-tournament party on Friday night. (Conrad, Civil and Kaplan had exams on Friday morning, and would fly into Newark, New Jersey, later that afternoon.) By the time we were forty minutes out of Gainesville, guys began complaining that they had to piss. Wee Wee further decreed that the vans would not be stopping until we reached South Carolina, handing back an empty Gatorade bottle. When it was nearly three-quarters full, Noel donned a rubber glove from the first-aid kit, picked up the bottle and directed Wee Wee to maneuver alongside and slightly ahead of the other van.

When we were in good position, Noel unrolled his window, leaned out and doused the other van with a golden shower that made Carlos recoil for a moment, then laugh so hard the van nearly swerved into the next lane. Thus began the Piss Bottle Wars, which occupied us a great part of the way and resulted in atrocities on both sides, as will be seen.

We were into Georgia at dusk, speeding northward on I-95. The floor of the van, especially around the door wells, was sticky and cluttered with empty beer cans. I laughed just thinking what Dan Palov, my wrestling coach at Acadia, would've thought of it. He was a hell-raiser in his youth, a former University of New Brunswick running back who was also an assistant football coach. Coach Palov enjoyed Saturday nights on the road as much as we did; after dinner, he'd send a case of Schooner to our room at the motel. I usually bunked with the other Americans: Barnesy, and Jay Buckler from Massapequa, Long Island, and redheaded Joe Fleming from Weymouth, Massachusetts, and our 178-pounder, Marty DeMarzo from East Orange, New Jersey. We'd sit around drinking beer and telling stories, including how Buckler used to play street hockey in Carlo

Gambino's driveway. Gambino was a New York mob boss and when he'd roll up in his Caddy, one of his goons would climb out and give the kids each five bucks to get lost.

Approaching midnight, the Florida rugby caravan pulled into a truck stop near Florence, South Carolina. Stiff-legged and woozy, twenty-four rugby players got down from the vans and went into the restaurant. Inside was a tiny gift shop peddling fake Native American headdresses and rubber-tipped lances, corny-looking postcards, foam-billed South Carolina Gamecocks' hats and other useless junk. Across the wide, rectangular space was a lunch counter, adorned with a small pasteboard sign announcing that the four or five chrome stools were RESERVED FOR TRUCKERS.

This tickled Mike Siskin, one of our fleet-footed wingers. He was a sturdily built, long-legged fellow, a one-time college hurdler, with an animated golly-gee-whiz manner of speaking that at first seemed like a put-on. Mike and I'd gotten off on the wrong foot the previous semester, because he'd gone out with Darcy before I did, and for a while there was that natural enmity between two guys who'd dated the same woman. But Darcy and I'd long since broken up, and I used to hang out with Siskin after games to hear his whimsical pronouncements on life.

There was another sign over by the bathrooms, which were doing a brisk business, stating that children under the age of five should not enter—here Siskin interpolated, "unless accompanied by trucker." Behind the restaurant/gift shop was a run-down string of tiny cabins, and a steep-sided, concrete swimming pool filled halfway with an evil-looking greenish-blue goop. As players walked past on the way to the bathroom, glancing at the pool, Siskin admonished them to refrain from swimming "unless accompanied by trucker."

Two heavyset fellows in CAT Diesel Power ball caps were eating chicken-fried steaks at the counter and eyeballing us. Several guys ordered cheeseburgers or heating-lamp pizza, and stood around in groups pounding fountain drinks and talking in a din. The truckers' eyes narrowed even further when Pokey came in (his real first name was Bernard, but everyone called him Pokey, because he moved so slowly, at least off the field). He was shirtless, wearing a sleeveless winter vest, blue necktie, red sweatpants, rubber boots, and carrying an open umbrella that looked like it had been through a typhoon, with an acoustic guitar slung over his back.

Pokey went through the chow line with the umbrella riding over his head like a parasol, grinning at the truckers while he bought a couple slices of the oily pizza. Seeing that he had a captive audience, Pokey bolted his meal and swung his guitar around, putting down the umbrella for the moment.

"Ladies and gentlemen, good evening, and welcome to the Florence, South Carolina, I-95 Luncheonette and Gift Emporium," he said, tuning his guitar. A few of the guys clapped; Noel whistled; Wee Wee looked on with his arms folded, like he was watching his child perform at a school pageant.

"I've prepared a little number that I like to call 'The Ballad of Steve Smith,'" said Pokey, strumming his guitar.

More applause ensued, and Steve Smith was pushed forward in the crowd of rugby players. He looked back at us, his white guy's Afro bobbing to the music, and forked a "V" with his fingers and stuck his industrial-length tongue through it.

The best thing about the impromptu concert, which stymied the truckers a little bit, was that Pokey is a decent guitar player and has a nice singing voice. He began playing louder, and sang:

> Well thinking of man's accomplishments can make
> your mind spin 'round
> How Einstein found relativity from Newton's ups and downs
> The Wright brothers gave us wings to fly, then
> Yeager boomed through sound
> Ah but all these things seem trivial when Steve Smith
> comes around.

The song had a good beat, and one of the truckers was patting his hand in time on the counter, until his friend gave him a dirty look and he quit it. As soon as Pokey launched into the first chorus, however, the redneck truckers put their hands together like they were at a barn dance.

Because he's had three hundred girls or more, who knows
how many more is in store?
For every hair upon his head, he'll have a woman in his bed.
And the thing that's hardest to believe is that he's not
dead yet from some disease
So take your hats off if you please when Steve Smith
comes around.

You'd be wondering how he does it after hearing his approach
"Do you go down on strangers?" just don't work for normal blokes
He'll say "I want to lick your asshole" and
"Your body is so intense"
And they're lining up to take him home, it really makes no sense.

Wearing a smirk and his gold medallion, Smitty struck a theatrical posture, stage right. The truck stop probably hadn't seen that much excitement since Pretty Boy Floyd drove past in '32, with the highway patrol in close pursuit.

Well it's easy from this song to see the man's a living legend
He's had notches on his bedpost since the age of seven.
He's done threesomes, he's done foursomes,
he's engineered some lengthy trains.
All his friends think he's a hero but his mom
thinks he's deranged.

Conrad, blow off school today, let's play some liar's dice.
Wild Bill and Spad are here now, we got drugs and beer on ice
Frank, you don't need an education, look where it's got me
Not one in three hundred asked about my degree.

By the time Pokey came around to the fourth chorus, it was a regular hootenanny in there. When he concluded with a rousing, "So take your hats off if you please, when Steve Smith comes around," Wee Wee doffed his little alpine chapeau, mopped his brow with a handkerchief, and bellowed, "Let's go, Gators. We're leaving."

A little woozy from getting a buzz on and sobering up on the same ride, I staggered out to the tarmac. Carlos was in his van with the window rolled up and I went over and stuck my tongue out at him, running it up and down the glass while moaning like an idiot. Wee Wee yelled at me to stop fucking around and get in the van; soon after, we were back on I-95.

A couple of hundred miles down the road, both vans exited the highway when Carlos and Wee Wee decided to consult on the best route into D.C. It was approaching 3 A.M. when the caravan lurched into a little turnoff beneath a grove of sassafras trees. Most of the occupants of our van were trying to catch some shut-eye, with generally poor results. Other than Scholarship, who was irritating Surfer by nudging him and talking in a loud voice, guys had quieted down over the past hour and were in pretty foul moods.

But it was a night for musical performances, even here beneath the glittering stars of North Cack-a-lacky, as Noel referred to his home state. Suddenly the door on the side of our van was drawn back with a grating sound, and an a cappella group of six or seven nitwits asked where I was. Scholarship pointed to me like Judas's idiot kid brother, and the visiting troubadours serenaded us with an original composition, sung to the tune of Hall & Oates' "Kiss on My List":

> Our piss, our piss, is on your lips
> Because our piss you can't resist
> Our piss is on your lips when you turn out the lights

Someone growled at them to shut the fucking door. No one in our van knew what I'd done at the truck stop, though it would soon become a defining moment in team lore—one that I would never live down. But just about every guy on the team eventually had his moment, either heroic or ignominious, and there was no real shame in it.

For the time being, I was happy to be anonymous and nudged Psycho to move over. Before Wee Wee had the van back in gear, I shuddered off to sleep, if you could call it that.

I awoke to the stench of the van, with a taste in my mouth like I'd been chewing on a muddy rugby boot. Outside the window was the

U.S. Capitol building, its golden dome shining in the early light, and Wee Wee got us onto the sidewalk like a bunch of parolees. He marched us down to a fast-food joint for breakfast, and then up the long, wide stairs to the Capitol, still wearing that little hat that made him look like a junior high school principal.

The entrance to the Capitol building was wide open in those days: no pat-downs, metal detectors or zigzag waiting lines, just a sleepy-looking Capitol policeman who nodded to Wee Wee and directed us inside. No sooner had we gotten under the dome, in the vast stone chamber of the U.S. Congress, than Pokey Whelan took a rugby ball from his backpack and started tossing it around. On the very spot where such notable wags as Alexander Hamilton, Ulysses S. Grant, and Millard Fillmore had smoked cigars, scratched themselves and told bawdy stories, we did U.S. history no further injustice by playing a game of skip-pass beneath the Rotunda. After all, ours was a government by the people, for the people, et cetera, even people like Gully MacFadden, Mike May, and Conrad, who weren't even U.S. citizens.

Before we departed from Washington, Carlos and Wee Wee looked over the map, and a spirited disagreement arose over the best route to Princeton. With the vans idling on the Mall, Carlos, wearing his wraparound sunglasses, gestured in the direction of the mighty Potomac, and said, "To get to Preeenz-ton, you gotta go to Treeen-ton. You gotta go to Treeen-ton to get to Preeenz-ton." Wee Wee insisted that he was Able One Leader, and that Carlos would fly in formation behind him, then we mounted up and zoomed off.

The Piss Bottle Wars had continued through the night. Each of the vans had a patina of crystallized urine, and my decision to lick Carlos's window had become common knowledge over breakfast (with guys saying things like, "Hey, Pissy Lips, pass the ketchup"). Just the way Carlos had acquiesced to Wee Wee's authority in D.C. made me suspicious, and I kept glancing over at those guys as we drove along. Peering into the recesses of the other van, which was alongside on the right, I caught a glimpse of some commotion behind the rearmost seat.

Someone handed an object I couldn't make out all the way back there. Robby DeReuil, who could play loose forward and prop, took whatever it was and disappeared from view, the guys in the middle seats laughing and congratulating each other. Robby was a quiet, friendly guy who wore a pair of wire-rimmed specs off the field and had a dry sense of humor. We called each other "Mister Sir" for some reason, and always embraced upon meeting.

A couple minutes later, I saw the object—a Big Mac container—return to the front seat, and Carlos stomped on the accelerator, shooting past us. He sure could drive, that kid, and with horror-struck tourists from Virginia and Delaware flying along on both sides, Carlos shot a van length ahead of us, edging closer, until only six inches of pavement separated the two vehicles. Sensing danger, Wee Wee tried to escape, but he was boxed in by an eighteen-wheeler on the other side. He started to decelerate, and as we lost power, Carlos leaned out from his window with a devilish smirk on his face and tossed out the Big Mac container.

It flipped up and over, coming toward us in slow motion. The faces of the players in the other van, contorted as though in a fun house, careered past in a silent procession—then all the sound came rushing back, as the container upended on our windshield and a large brown smear obliterated Wee Wee's view. Men screamed. Children in passing station wagons cried, seeking comfort from their mothers. Before I could shout *Don't turn on the wipers!* it was too late, and Wee Wee had spread the essence of Robby DeReuil all over the windshield.

We were stunned. Then we started laughing, until the noise was so loud it was like the bedlam express, the guys in the other van howling and pointing at us and us pointing back and howling at them. It was a far cry from the Acadia U team trips I used to take across the frozen barrens of New Brunswick and Nova Scotia, spitting into a cup to make weight. We were loose on the American highway, *Preeenz-ton or Bust,* and mothers were duly advised to lock up their daughters, and post Steve Smith's picture on every telephone pole from the Virginia line to Jersey City.

Late that afternoon, Wee Wee strolled into the office of the Sleepy Hollow Motel in Princeton, New Jersey, and booked us a room, chatting with the sallow-faced clerk about the local weather and other inanities. We kept out of sight, the vans parked in a far corner of the lot, beneath some trees. The motel was about as attractive as the desk clerk's complexion, a single row of dinky, slope-floored rooms, leaky faucets, coin-operated televisions, et cetera; definitely our kind of place. Surfer noted that it was a good spot for a murder, as we dumped our bags on the floor and headed out to find the rugby fields.

By the time we'd stopped for something to eat and driven over to the campus, the pretournament party was well under way. It had begun raining, and most of the revelers had gathered under the beer tent, a great, circuslike structure that some Ivy League genius had decided to erect at the foot of a small, grassy hill. With four dozen rugby teams in town, playing for the East Coast championships across three men's and a women's division, a throng of people had amassed on that hillside. It was like Woodstock with muscles.

Fueled by a row of kegs, a large, naked group of ruggers (it was 95 percent UF guys) had lined up to slide down the muddy hill on their backsides, piling into the legs of the people standing inside the tent. It was a naked luge run, minus the actual luge.

As soon as they saw this, Civil and Conrad took off all their clothes and ran to the top of the hill. It was a little disconcerting to be talking to the scrumhalf from the U.S. Naval Academy and have a muddy, naked Dave Civil go rocketing past you on the beer-slickened grass. I found Wee Wee in the crowd and told him that something had to be done about this; he agreed, and we went to the far end of the tent and bought a couple of beers. While we were drinking them, trying to somehow appear not from Florida, a blood-curdling shriek went up from the hillside. Noel whistled in a sharp blast, calling us over.

Apparently, Scholarship was running the naked luge with the rest of them and flayed his skinny ass wide open on a beer can top. He went trotting by on his way to seek first aid, the blood running down the streaks of mud on his legs. Wee Wee touched his beer against mine. "Out of the lineup," he said.

Around 11 P.M., after Greg Taylor had done a naked pole dive from about halfway up the big top, and Pokey had led the assembly through a rendition of that rugby classic, "Father Abraham," followed by a muddy elephant walk through the tent, Wee Wee rounded up a dozen guys who wanted to go back to Sleepy Hollow. As we exited the tent, I stopped for a word with Noel, who was checking IDs and charging a two-dollar cover charge to unsuspecting Jack-o's, funneling the proceeds to guys who didn't have any money.

"Rob from the overprivileged, and give it to Conrad," said Noel, after fleecing some dude from Brown University.

We got back to our crummy motel just after midnight. Some of the guys were amusing themselves by watching Steve Smith have sex with a cute little blonde, parked in a car in front of our room. How he had met the girl, and then convinced her to park there, in the three or four hours we'd been in town was anybody's guess. Wee Wee yawned, scratching himself as he walked past where Mac-Fadden and the stitched-up Scholarship were peeking through the blinds. He was like the circus ringmaster going by the monkey cages; didn't matter how spectacular the trick, he'd seen it before.

I stretched out on the floor between the two beds, a wadded up mattress cover for a pillow. The television opposite played a war movie, *The Big Red One,* with the sound turned low. A few of the guys were sleeping, or at least trying to, but I knew that wasn't going to happen for a while yet. Ever since I'd cracked the A-side, I never had more than a couple of beers the night before a game, and it perturbed me when some of my most valuable teammates insisted on getting shitfaced, like they were sailors on leave and wouldn't have another opportunity to get drunk for six months. It was one of the things that was starting to bug me about the Gators: sometimes we would throw away wins in exchange for a premature good time.

We were one of the best college sides on the East Coast, and that meant, among other things, that there were no pushovers in our bracket. Conrad and Civil and Carlos and Pokey had all played in cup finals and league championship matches before, so perhaps it was no big deal to them. But as I lay in the narrow trench between the beds all I could think about was how much I wanted to win. There would be plenty of time to drink afterward.

Presumably, I got some sleep, though I don't remember any of it, just the *chok-chok-chok* of the war in France coming from the television, along with Lee Marvin's hard-bitten observations. At quarter to seven, Wee Wee turned on the lights and went to fire up the vans, since we were playing in the first match, which was a little over an hour from kicking off. Wee Wee discovered that a few guys had wandered in so late they just crashed in the vehicles, not wanting to miss their rides to the pitch. And one or two guys hadn't turned up at all, including Pokey Whelan. Inside the room, groans and cavity noises and trips to the bathroom occupied the next ten minutes. I could taste that moldy old rugby boot again, and made sure to brush my teeth.

Our first-round opponent was none other than Princeton University, the hosts of the tournament. Staggering up to the field just ten minutes before kickoff, we were treated to the sight of the Ivy Leaguers, resplendent in their striped jerseys and crisp white shorts, running through a series of precise-looking drills at their end of the field. A few of our guys were still trickling in, either on foot or in strangers' cars, when we set off on a couple of warm-up laps. Circling the goalposts, we saw Pokey rise up from the weeds beyond the rugby fields, weaving toward us with his umbrella.

Conrad and Civil and two or three others had been out all night, and were still loaded. Even in the open air, they stank of booze and cigarettes, eyes glazed over, their tongues inert. Noel was in his rugby kit but wearing a pair of aviator sunglasses to stave off his headache. On the far sideline, he began humming the theme to *Chariots of Fire* as we ran along.

A couple of guys laughed, but within a few seconds everyone had joined in. Soon Noel was in front of the group while jogging backward and waving his arms like a symphony conductor: "da-da-DA-DA-DUM. Da-da-da-DUM." Life Chiropractic College of Atlanta, a formidable side that we'd hosted at the Gator Invitational, was warming up on the adjacent field. When they heard us, they began smiling, and put together a "Hail, Florida" cheer when we ran past them.

On the way to New Jersey, Wee Wee had told me that since Freddie Pinot and Scholarship were making the trip, the selection committee decided that each of them would play a half, and I'd play the rest of the time (each team was guaranteed at least two matches; more if you were winning). We were especially light in the pack: Martin had to skip the tournament to complete some research toward his Ph.D.; Big Harry King and Keith Platt were ineligible; and Eau Gallie was injured. Spad was moved to tighthead prop, and with Scholarship out, Wee Wee decided to put Freddie in for the first half of the Princeton match, allowing me to play the rest of the tournament.

Eight or nine reserves populated our sideline when Carlos kicked off, and I was probably the only one who wasn't hungover. We were frustrating to watch: dropped passes, missed tackles, penalties and no sense of connection between our forwards and backs. In one of the early scrums, Freddie Pinot didn't get himself set in time and the two packs crashed together without him. He was left standing up in the midst of the engagement, the other forwards bound together and shoving back and forth. Freddie had a puzzled expression on his face, gazing off at the horizon as their scrumhalf grinned and put the ball in unopposed, since Freddie had no view of the tunnel.

It was bush league, embodying the futility of our opening half of championship rugby. Princeton scored two unconverted tries and a penalty, and were leading 15–0 at half time.

Guys sobered up. The sun had risen over the campus, and the temperature was climbing into the seventies. Teams were allowed four substitutions in this format, and I came into the match with Pokey, Boca Scott and Mike May, which gave us a lift. About ten minutes in, Pokey and Carlos manufactured a break culminating in a long try off the wing by Mike Siskin, with Carlos making the conversion. Later, Carlos put a magnificent penalty kick through the posts from near midfield, and at an extreme angle.

With the score 15–9, and approximately five minutes left, we had taken over the match, driving the ball forward in second and third phases. Getting well into their half, we were awarded two scrums in succession, then ran a series of quick rucks off that, bending our possession right, right again, nearing their twenty-two-meter line with Conrad and Civil doing the bulk of the work. Princeton buried the ball in a tackle; the referee whistled another scrum put-in for us, and we got the ball out to Kaplan, who scissored back to the forwards, crushing their scrumhalf as he went to ground. Wee Wee picked the ball up about ten meters from their goal line and crashed again, as the rest of the forwards formed a controlled maul.

A converted try would tie the match, giving us a shot at overtime. Rolling off the maul to rejoin at the back, I saw the referee look at his watch and then blow the whistle. A round of cursing ensued. The game was over, with the ball in our hands less than ten meters from Princeton's goal line.

Coming off the field after shaking hands with the Princeton guys, who were more than a little smug about their victory, I was limping along beside Wee Wee; tired, hot, dehydrated and pissed off. Staying out all night had delayed our true entry into the match, and time had simply run out on us. Also, we never had the chance to stock up on water and Gatorade before the game, and Princeton, as tournament hosts, had failed to provide any, which normally would've been the case. Instead, they directed us toward a concession booth over by the entrance to the park. After stopping to retrieve our wallets, Wee Wee and I circled the rugby fields, arriving at the stand pestered by a ferocious thirst.

A smarmy dude told us there was no water or Gatorade; all they were selling was Coca-Cola at two dollars a can.

"This is one of the wealthiest schools in the country, and you're selling tonic for two bucks a can?" I asked.

The kid shrugged. "How do you think we got that way?" he asked, delivering a civics lesson along with my Coke.

Nursing our sodas, we walked over to the master board to look at the other scores, and to find out our next opponent. Our second match was at 1 P.M., against the University of Maryland. We needed to win that game, or we were out. Back at the field, most of our players were resting in the shade. I lay down, pulled the brim of my Houston Astros cap over my eyes, and tried to catch a nap.

U Maryland had a large pack of forwards and they gave us trouble in the first half, shoving us around and scoring a try off a back row play. Standing on our goal line while their fullback teed up and missed the conversion, Wee Wee spat into the grass, eyeballing Spad and me.

"That ain't happenin' again," he said.

We scored a try on a fluke play about ten minutes later. Boca Scott charged down a kick deep in Maryland's end, which deflected off his hands at a weird angle. Greg Taylor snagged it on the fly and ran six or seven yards to the corner for an easy try. Carlos missed the conversion, and Maryland's fullback made a twenty-five yard penalty kick before the half, to give the Terrapins a 7–4 lead.

Playing against men's clubs and our extended winter schedule were a boon in matches like this. No one panicked. Even with C.J., our tall, skinny, extra winger, filling in at second row, our scrummaging improved over what we'd done against Princeton. I was striking as soon as our shoulders touched the opposition, and our nimble back row—Civil, Conrad and Pokey—was taking the ball straight from the back of the scrum, standing up in the tackle, and then getting it to MacFadden, preventing Maryland from using their big, ugly tight five to push us around, and from releasing their own loose forwards early to harass our backline.

Conrad and Pokey said that recycling the ball through two quick phases, instead of a straight pass from the back of the scrum, would work against these guys, and it did.

In the second half, our pack began to move them a little bit. For a forward, particularly in the front row, this is one of the most satisfying things that can happen in a rugby game; for the team getting pushed backward, it's one of the more psychologically damaging. They're going in reverse, and can't seem to do anything about it. And when the pack doing the pushing is smaller and lighter—we were giving away an average of fifteen pounds a man, at least—it robs the other forwards of their momentum, and confidence.

With fifteen minutes left, we were still down by three points when the referee awarded us a scrum put-in about thirty meters from the Terrapins' goal line. In the first half, when Maryland was using their combined weight to distinct advantage, I was striking on contact and our loose forwards were taking off with the ball in hand. Now, Wee Wee put on a call for a normal strike and then a controlled shove, using all eight forwards, trying to catch them leaving the back of the scrum too early.

The ball was put in, and I went for channel two, hooking it back to Pokey's feet at number eight. He called out a cadence and we advanced in short, synchronized shoves, pushing them back incrementally. Their back row started to peel off, realized we weren't going to run the ball off the back, and hastily rejoined the scrum. The referee signaled a penalty but let play continue, since we maintained the advantage. They were disorganized, and we pushed them back two yards, then three, marching in unison, Pokey dragging the ball along with his foot, keeping it within the confines of the scrum. Our reserves were going nuts on the sideline.

Big, powerful guys in Maryland's scrum were giving way, pushing and scrambling as individuals, instead of eight men working together. It was probably the highlight of the tournament and our season, thus far—at least from the narrow perspective of the front row.

When we crossed their twenty-two-meter line, with all the Maryland forwards committed, heads down, pushing frantically, Conrad and Pokey took the ball to the weak side, went to ground with it, and MacFadden recycled; in the next phase, Carlos set up Noel with a neat little pop pass, and he barreled over their fullback, stumbling toward the goal line.

Wee Wee and I were just emerging from the ruck when Carlos got the ball in his hands. We ran to the right in support, but Noel regained his balance, stiff-armed the off winger coming late, and got into the try zone right between the posts.

"Fuck, yeah!" said Wee Wee, looking straight into my face. He shook my hand while we were still running that way. "There's your two-dollar fucking Coke," he said. Carlos made the straight-on conversion, and a few minutes later, we'd won the match 10–7.

That evening, we went to a local steakhouse for dinner, and then wandered the Princeton campus. We were scheduled to play West Point in the quarterfinal at ten o'clock the next morning. Then, as now, a collegiate rugby powerhouse, Army had solid professional coaching, a top-notch rugby complex, five day a week practice schedule and seventy or eighty super-fit, competitive athletes with nowhere else to go because of the strict rules at West Point.

On campus, we gravitated to Prospect Avenue, known as "the Street," one of the main thoroughfares at Princeton. Instead of fraternity houses, Princeton operates an array of eating clubs, a string of mansions that appeared in F. Scott Fitzgerald's novel *This Side of Paradise*. The street was busy at nine o'clock on a Saturday night, with sporty young swells arriving at the curb with their shiny females in tow, piling in the clubs amid stiff-jawed greetings from Biff, Phineas, and perhaps even Nick Carraway himself.

Conrad had fun mocking the pretensions of this scene, puffing on a cigarette and laughing when some Jack-o told us we weren't dressed appropriately.

"Why not? You're dressed like an absolute fool," said Conrad. "Didn't mummy tell you never to wear a dinner jacket with shorts?"

At the next club, we tried sending Noel and Pokey up to the door, our most convincing wheeler-dealers, but again no dice. Finally we lifted a case of beer from one of the porches and sat on a wall overlooking the Ivy Club, drinking and harassing passersby. We were a bunch of singing fools, and sometime around eleven o'clock, Noel arranged us in choir formation and we serenaded the arriving and departing guests with our team song, which Surfer had composed in the van on the way up—a variation on the official University of Florida fight song.

We are the Boys from Old Florida
F-L-O-R-I-D-A
We'll drink all your beer
And offer a cheer
Then drag all your wenches away

Hey
We are the Boys from Old Florida
We came to Princeton to play
With hearts full of lust
Your women we'll thrust
They'll cry when we all go away

Hey
We are the Boys from Old Florida
Land where the old gators play

We all come together
With whips, sticks and feathers
Play rugby the Florida way
THE FLORIDA WAY

The next morning, Army arrived on their bus at precisely 8:30 A.M., according to several witnesses. When we rolled up, almost an hour later, they were about halfway through a rigorous pregame workout, following which they assembled their first fifteen, marched onto the pitch, and began dismantling us. In the opening minutes, when their biggest guy, playing number eight, ran down Greg Taylor from behind and rag-dolled him to the turf, Pokey Whelan looked at me, and said "Oh-oh."

West Point was big, fast, fit and well drilled, going up by three converted tries just fifteen minutes into the game. Regret lingered over the result versus Princeton, a team we should've beaten, but we could've played Army nine times with the guys we had on this trip, and lost all nine matches. There was nothing to be done about it. Army had superior numbers and fitness, which didn't really surprise us in the end, since Surfer had played there and told us what to expect. But we went down swinging.

Late in the match, trailing 24–4, Army backed us up to our end goal for a series of hotly contested scrums. They were trying to push us over from five meters out, scoring a last, emasculating try in the waning moments of a game they'd already won—the ultimate indignity in rugby. Even with our makeshift pack, and very little to gain from resisting so fiercely, we were staving them off: wheeling the scrum, collapsing it, even incurring a referee's warning (and several punches from the opposing front row) when Dave Civil dived into the tunnel from his spot at wing forward, disrupting their foot rush.

On their sixth attempt, Army succeeded, all that pressure directed inward and downward, to where I came unbound from Wee Wee and Spad, ending up facedown in the muddy end goal with some buzz-cutted oaf stepping on the small of my back.

Wee Wee and Spad leaned over, hoisting me to my feet.

"That sucked," Wee Wee said.

"Tell me about it," I said.

The Naval Academy defeated West Point in the semifinal and was, in turn, beaten by Life Chiropractic College in the championship match. Almost immediately, various protests were lodged against the format, especially the inclusion of a professional school like Life. By offering the equivalent of rugby scholarships to what was a team made up only of graduate students, Life had dominated collegiate competition in the East. This resulted in a significant rule change: grad students were no longer eligible to compete for collegiate sides in NCAA-sanctioned matches. So I'd come along at precisely the right time to take my shot at it.

Wee Wee and Carlos drove the vans through the gates of the rugby venue, across campus and out toward the highway by midafternoon. Our vehicle seemed especially full, and Greg Taylor and I climbed all the way into the back, stretching out on the piled up kit bags. We had stopped for gas over near the interstate, when commotion erupted from the middle seats, nearly invisible to Psycho and me because of the stacked luggage. It had something to do with Freddie Pinot, my freshman backup.

We hadn't seen much of Freddie since the disastrous first half of the Princeton game. So it was pretty surprising for Psycho and me to hear that, not only had Freddie met a girl in town somewhere and brought her into the van for the ride back to Florida, but she was only fifteen years old.

"Even I'm offended," said Steve Smith.

Wee Wee got out of the van. A light drizzle was falling, and the gray New Jersey woods loomed all around. Through the window, Psycho and I watched our loosehead prop explain to Freddie that what he was attempting to do—transport a minor across state lines for the purpose of carnal relations—violated the Mann Act. (While Conrad was mature and worldly at eighteen, Freddie was nineteen but looked and acted like a muscle-bound fifth grader.)

The girl stood a little ways off, a fresh-faced kid wearing a ski coat. She was carrying a plastic grocery bag with a few things in it, and someone remarked that she probably had a teddy bear in there.

When Wee Wee finished his lecture, Freddie started to walk away from him toward the girl. "What're you doing, Fred?" asked Wee Wee. "Get in the van."

Freddie gripped his kit bag tightly, staring back at Wee Wee. "I love her," he said, which were the first words I'd heard him utter all weekend.

"Hell, so do I," said Steve Smith. "But I don't want to go to federal prison."

Freddie came over to the van and slid the door shut with a resounding boom, walking off in the rain with the girl. "You don't see that every day," said Boca Scott.

Riding through downtown Philadelphia on the raised expressway, Psycho and I entertained each other with stories of losing teams we'd played on as kids. For me, it was a Pop Warner football team, the Methuen Bengals, who went 1–13.

"You know that feeling," I said. "You run onto the field, and you just *know* you're going to lose."

Most of the other guys were asleep by now, and Wee Wee was listening to Warren Zevon sing "Lawyers, Guns and Money" over the radio. Greg related a story about his junior high wrestling team, and how they lost every dual meet all year (though by his senior year, he was one of the team captains and went undefeated).

Then we drank our beers, and gazed out the window at the rain falling on the Philly skyline. I realized that I loved these guys and loved playing with them. But I also wanted to see how far I could go in rugby, and that meant my time in Florida was coming to an end.

Chapter 19

Salad Days

At the last FADC meeting of the year, a dozen rugby players convened at our place to watch televangelist Ernest Angley perpetrate his fund-raising con on the rural South. A few of the boys got off the sofa or the floor to "lay [their] hands on the set," in a futile attempt to rid themselves of their "alcohol demons." During the broadcast, I related the tale of their ancestor Scooter Riddell's indignation over this same program while attending an FADC in Wolfville, prompting his announcement that the old bunko artist "wasn't cool."

Within a couple of weeks, the Bunker was up for sale ("includes free cable" was in the advertisement). Noel and Surfer had enlisted in the Marine Corps and were heading up to Quantico, Virginia, for Officer Candidates School. In the meantime, I'd arranged to sublet Maria's house over by campus, where I'd bunk with teammate Barry Fisher and an old high school buddy of mine for the summer. Gainesville was quiet when the spring term ended, and I'd have plenty of time to finish my degree.

At Maria's place, a well-kept ranch with a carport and private, fenced in yard, I took the master bedroom, complete with a walk-in closet, private bath and Maria's ample collection of albums and cassette tapes. Loretta spent most weekends there, and I occupied myself through June and into July refining my thesis and retyping the stories. My roommates weren't around very often, and I usually had the place to myself: Loretta and I grilled steaks or chicken beneath the carport, drank a few beers and stayed up late watching *Letterman* or old movies on the bedside TV.

In mid-July, when Loretta was pulling double shifts at the hospital, I became ill with the worst case of the summer flu I've ever had. Hardly anyone I knew was in town, and for two days I lay in bed with a high fever, the cupboard empty and not even a bottle of aspirin in the medicine cabinet. My back ached, my stomach muscles were sore, even my knees were stiff; it felt like I'd played two rugby games back to back, got drunk, laid, and beat up, while aging forty years in the span of forty-eight hours. Finally, on the third day, I heard Barry Fisher banging around in the kitchen and began calling to him in a weak voice; I felt like an invalid in a William Faulkner story, laid up in bed and complaining about the misery.

Fisher was a tall, cadaverous fellow, with a scouring pad of dense, curly hair, high cheekbones and an abraded, sanguine complexion. Equipped with a powder-dry wit and an air of perpetual conspiracy, Barry reminded me of Franz Kafka—if Kafka had played high school basketball in Polk County; or more likely, rode the bench, since Barry, like old Franz, really wasn't much of an athlete, and was possessed by a wry, sarcastic, almost melancholy self-awareness.

Barry was also habitually agreeable, and when he came into my sickroom, he promised to rush out to purchase ibuprofen, nighttime cold medicine and a quart of ginger ale for my aching throat. I handed over a twenty-dollar bill, which was all the cash I had, and Barry stuck it in his billfold.

Vowing to return within the hour, Barry left the house, and I listened to his departing footfalls anxiously, my temperature spiking and my throat reddened and raw, like I'd been gargling with kerosene. It was the last time I'd see Barry in the month of July. It wasn't malicious; it's just that Barry was mostly concerned about Barry, and finding that extra twenty in his pocket a few hours later was probably a nice surprise.

After a while, I staggered out to the living room and went through a list of phone numbers that Maria kept by the front door. I knew that Conrad was around for the summer and though he didn't have a telephone, his girlfriend April's number was in there, and I called her, left a message on the answering machine and stumbled back to my room.

Less than an hour later, Conrad and April were standing by the bed, looking on with mild concern. "Get up, boofoo," Conrad said. "You look like shit."

April was a wholesome, apple-cheeked blonde who was endowed with, among other things, a tremendous amount of patience—a requirement for dealing with Conrad and his bonehead pals. She drove a little foreign car, puttering the dozen or so blocks to the campus infirmary, where they dropped me off before proceeding to Albertson's to buy the ibuprofen, et cetera. Inside, I produced my student ID and took a seat in the waiting room, plagued by light-headedness and nausea. Finally, a pudgy, bespectacled man in his early thirties wearing medical scrubs directed me into an examination room. A physician's assistant, he took my temperature and asked a perfunctory question or two.

Almost immediately, this fellow decided to inspect one of my key glands. As an English major, I'd never had occasion to take an anatomy and physiology course, so when the PA mentioned the gland by name, I began probing my neck, squeezing my windpipe and contemplating my ravaged throat. "Yeah, maybe . . . ," I said.

Before I could say Jack Robinson, the guy had snapped on a rubber glove, lubed his index finger and was checking my tailpipe: it was then that I discovered where my prostate was located.

Pronouncing it healthy, the guy suggested I take a couple of ibuprofen, drink several glasses of water and return home to bed. In a matter of seconds, I was standing in front of the infirmary in the broiling midday sun, wondering what'd just happened. April honked from down the block, zooming into the loading zone to pick me up. When I described the limitations of this weird exam, Conrad thought it was the funniest thing he'd ever heard.

"That guy examines your prostate no matter what," he said, laughing at me.

The following day, I submitted three copies of my thesis to my committee, with the oral defense scheduled for that Friday. My thesis consisted of four stories: "A Small Penance," "Taxi-Dancing," "Overnight," and "Flyers"; and when I came out of the department with two spiral-bound copies under my arm, I felt like Hemingway rushing through Montparnasse with the printer's galley of *Three Stories and Ten Poems*. Over time, I was hopeful that I'd do better work than what I'd written thus far, but I'd gotten started—I was on my way.

In early August, I went back to Massachusetts to see the family. That week, we were also treated to a visit from Uncle Jack, who had driven down from his home in St. Stephen, New Brunswick, to acquire a New Hampshire driver's license. We all crowded into the living room to hear his stories including my mother and father, my grandmother Dorothy (Maynard) Atkinson and my sisters, Jodie and Jill. Uncle Jack had a cup of black coffee in his hand, and kept a glass of my father's whiskey at his elbow, from which he took an occasional sip.

Jack Maynard was an enterprising guy. Already taking a small pension from the British navy, as well as a decent-sized one from Canada Power, where he'd worked for years, he was also a member of the boilermaker's union that was headquartered in Boston. Uncle Jack kept his union card active by driving down on weekends, vacations and holidays to work in the area, often staying with my grandmother on Newport Street, or with Uncle Johnny and his family in Litchfield, New Hampshire.

There he sat on our couch: a black-eyed, ruddy-faced man, with square shoulders, thick forearms and dressed in a blue Local 29 T-shirt and dingy work pants. Uncle Jack was born in 1927, and shipped out with the British navy in 1942, when he was just sixteen. He'd been born to my great-grandmother Gertrude five years after my grandmother left for America, one of the eventual seven Maynard children scrapping for food and attention at 74 Edgerton Street in Middlesbrough, Yorkshire, England, in the 1920s.

Uncle Jack always insisted he lied about his age to join the navy so he could get enough to eat—with adequate nutrition, he grew a foot that first year of his enlistment—but there was also a war going on, and he wanted his shot at the Nazis. His transport ship was torpedoed and sank, and he ended up in the chilly waters of the north

Atlantic. After the war, he worked on commercial lines and jumped ship in San Francisco after having his appendix removed. He hitch-hiked across the country to visit my grandmother, selling pints of his blood to buy candy bars. When he arrived at my grandmother's, she thought he was some ne'er-do-well friend of my dad's and told him to come back later. He had to explain that he was young John, the brother she'd heard about in letters but never met, and that he'd come to stay with her.

During the Korean War, Uncle Jack served in the Royal Canadian Navy as a gunnery officer, again returning to Methuen when the war was over. I sat beside him on the couch listening to these stories with rapt attention. Maynard, as he was called, could not sit still for long: typically, he wouldn't come to your house unless there was a bathroom that needed remodeling, or a garage door to be replaced. But there was time for one last story.

When my uncle Johnny was five or six years old, and Jack was living with them after the Second World War, he would carry Johnny on his shoulders from the house on Newport Street to the Wonder Bar in Lawrence, two and a half miles each way. Uncle Jack was lean and muscular in those days, with a deep chest, a laborer's knotted arms and lank, blue-black hair that fell over his eyes. A handsome sight, my mother called him.

The Wonder Bar was a small, dark-paneled establishment with a wooden bar on the left-hand wall and a couple of pool tables. Uncle Jack would seat his young nephew on one of the stools, buy him a Coke and hustle pool or arm wrestle with strangers for pocket money; either that, or he'd execute a favorite trick of his, as part of a wager. Jack would bet skeptical newcomers that he could stand with his belt buckle touching the edge of the bar; then, with a full glass of beer in his hand, he'd perform a standing vertical leap, landing on the bar top without spilling a drop.

This feat of agility and strength drew the attention of the proprietor's wife, a platinum blonde who drove a '51 Cadillac and favored diamond earrings and necklaces. She had a pretty daughter, too, just eighteen years old. The owner of the bar had underworld connections, and Uncle Jack was taking a gambler's chance, pitching woo to the man's wife and his daughter at the same time. But Maynard was so gregarious and likeable that the proprietor invited him to dinner, in their rooms above the bar.

The four of them sat at the table, glasses of beer all around, with the proprietor standing up from his chair to carve the roast beef. As he did, the edge of his jacket fell open and Uncle Jack spied a large revolver nestled in the holster under his arm.

"I stopped going around with the wife after that," said Uncle Jack with a wink, and we all laughed.

I flew back to Gainesville at the end of August, and Surfer and I moved in with Gully MacFadden at Landmine. My high school hockey pal Rick Angus was only supposed to visit for three weeks the previous spring, but Surfer and Noel, driving him to the Jacksonville airport, convinced Rick to stay and just showed back up with him when we were living at the Bunker. At Landmine, Rick and I shared a room, while Surfer, who stayed at Maria's several nights a week, bunked with MacFadden.

Right before classes started, Surfer's birthday was the object of a major bash held out by the pool: three kegs; team chorus on a naked "Singin' in the Rain," leading to an elephant walk and nude belly-flop contest; all furniture broken; cops there twice; a command performance by Surfer and Noel in the cheerleader outfits, made even more disturbing by their high-and-tight haircuts—a typical beginning of the season bash. Van Blokland had organized our first live scrimmage that morning: Noel, Wee Wee, Sergio, Defraites, Platt, Civil, Conrad, Pokey, Psycho, J.T., Smitty, Martin, et al, the entire gang plus a few capable recruits. The team looked even better than it had the previous spring.

Loretta and I had broken up at the end of the summer, and Surfer's party offered an opportunity to meet the attractive coeds who lived next door. Gully MacFadden was in love with one of our neighbors, a shapely, blue-eyed girl named Tara, who was from a well-known family in West Palm Beach. Tara had zero romantic interest in MacFadden (his nickname was "the Dull Man"), but she was friendly and used to drop next door to watch TV with us sometimes. I thought of her as a high-society girl, very smart and good-looking, dynamite figure, but just slumming a little bit on her way to Florida's upper crust.

Tara's best friend and roommate was Missy Fitzgibbons, a spec-
tacularly endowed brunette with a definite wild streak, although
she made Silent Cal Coolidge sound like an auctioneer, she was so
quiet. Missy was a rugger hugger extraordinaire, the poster girl for
the job. Steve Defraites had dallied with her during a time when he
and Suzy were broken up, and a few months later there were rumors that Missy and Boca Scott had some weird nocturnal adventures. (One time, we were heading next door for Sunday dinner
with the girls and Boca reached us in the nick of time with a cryptic
phone message: *Don't eat anything green.* The girls made spaghetti
and meatballs, and Surfer, Rick and I spent the first half of the meal
passing the salad around like a bowl of hand grenades, eyeing the
cucumbers and zucchini warily.)

The notion of a rugger hugger is grossly misunderstood. In fact,
it's a term of affection, not derision, among the rugby community.
Just last spring, years after I'd left Florida and in the midst of my
recovery from ankle surgery, I was summoned to play for the Vandals RFC in Stamford, Connecticut. This was a scene I'd replayed
hundreds of times in my career: showing up tired and yawning in
some desolate urban green space, on Randall's Island in New York
or Worcester, Massachusetts, lugging my rugby kit and a lawn
chair, ready as I'd ever be for the rigorous pleasures of a daylong
rugby tournament.

Only this time my blood brothers and I weren't going to play
rugby: we were scheduled to portray ruggers in a scripted television series airing on Showtime, *The Big C*, starring Laura Linney
and Oliver Platt. On the show, Ms. Linney plays a put-upon high
school guidance counselor, wife and mother who discovers she has
cancer while living in Minnesota, two sobering prospects. Her husband, the tall, chunky and affable Platt, is an immature corporate
type who's been kicked out of the house, and in a fit of adolescent
pique has decided to start playing rugby again.

An army of technicians, production assistants, extras and actors
had set up the day's shoot at a park across the street from Showtime's
headquarters where, ostensibly, Oliver Platt was going to play in a
rugby match. While they were preparing for the first shot, one of my
longtime Vandals teammates, Super Dave Laflamme, a thick-legged

hooker and prop from Providence, Rhode Island, and I were lounging against a fence. Forty rugby players were all jostling each other, trying to get the director to notice them, but Super Dave and I remained aloof.

"Let him come to us," I said. I raised my arms overhead, palms pressed together, gazing at the sky. "One mustn't *try* to be selected. One is merely selected. There is no effort required."

Just then a guy wearing a headset motioned to us. "You two guys," he said. "Get your bags and a rugby ball and come with me."

I winked at Super Dave. "Zen rugby," I said. Super Dave stifled a giggle, and we went over to our marks.

Oliver Platt was sitting in a make-believe Volvo with no rear window and Minnesota plates, wearing a loose-fitting rugby jersey. In this scene, his character was approached by a slinky, forty-year-old brunette in tight jeans and a push-up bra. On about the third take—Super Dave and I were supposed to walk past the Volvo pantomiming a conversation—the guy in the headset left the shooting script on the hood of a car. I looked over the dialogue that Oliver Platt and the actress were running through, and when the assistant director returned, I called his attention to a detail of the script.

"It says here that the girl Oliver is talking to is a 'rugby slut,'" I said. "That should be amended. The proper term is 'rugger hugger.'"

At that moment, the director called out, "Background. Action," and Super Dave and I went in motion. "I'm going to slap her on the ass when we go by," whispered Super Dave. "I mean, if she's the rugby slut, I was with her last night, right?"

Later, we were waiting for the camera to be repositioned when the director, a fortyish, curly-haired guy, asked why rugby shorts have pockets. "So you can play with yourself," Super Dave said. "I'm doing it right now."

Back in my Florida days, I went home with Missy Fitzgibbons once or twice after last call at Big Daddy's, encouraged by an abundance of the amber-hued social emollient. After that, I couldn't get rid of her. Missy would show up at Harmonica Joe's or Dub's, and follow me around without saying a word. One time I was on a date with the curvy blonde from *The Gainesville Observer*, and when we arrived at Landmine around 1 A.M., Missy was waiting on the sidewalk. She didn't say anything, just walked along beside us like Buster Keaton, with that same melancholy expression. The blonde got spooked and went back to her little red sports car and drove away, saying that she'd catch up with me later. I had to sit on the curb with Missy and explain to her that she couldn't sneak up on me like that, making it clear that I wasn't her boyfriend. She just looked at me with a sad face and plodded away in those little white tennis shoes she always wore.

MacFadden had a split personality. He was like a terrier on the rugby field, a tough, skillful halfback who always made the right decisions, and whipped the pack of forwards into a ball-producing frenzy. Off the field he was an old woman: nervous, fussy, always poking his Edinburgh nose in everyone else's business. At nineteen, he was a narrow-faced Ichabod, wiry haired, long necked, with an adolescent's blotchy complexion and a high-pitched voice to match. Right before the rugby season, he shattered his elbow playing table tennis, of all things, and was out for the year, which made him even more jumpy and meddlesome at home. He was a penny-pincher, too; one blazing hot day when Surfer and I climbed up to the Dutch oven of the attic and hot-wired our TV into the junction box, providing us with free cable, the Dull Man clasped his hands together and started jumping around like we'd won the Irish sweepstakes.

When Noel and Surfer patched into the underground cable at the Bunker, their handiwork remained out of sight, and they took the further precaution of sending me around to the neighbors to make sure there was continuous service. But it was stifling in the attic that day and after cutting and refastening the line, Surfer left our new black cable tangled in a nest of bright yellow wires hanging there. We jumped straight into the pool to cool off, and then drove to Mama Lo's restaurant for some soul food.

After we returned from practice a few nights later, the Dull Man was pacing up and down the sidewalk like he was awaiting the gas chamber. While we were gone, the Gainesville police had stopped by with a citation for theft of services, and would be returning around 8 P.M. to serve us each with a court summons.

"We have to get our stories straight," said MacFadden, following us into the house.

Exhausted, overheated and hungry, Surfer and I began assembling the pots, pans and foodstuffs necessary for Surfer John's Nuclear Nachos and Tacos, along with a pitcher of sweet tea to wash them down. (We used so much chili sauce, we used to eat dinner bare-chested, with our T-shirts knotted around our heads like turbans.) But the Dull Man persisted, hounding us while we slathered the taco chips with refried beans, garnishing each of them with a jalapeño pepper and dusting the sheet with handfuls of Monterey Jack.

"But guys, what are we gonna *do*?" asked MacFadden, his voice cracking.

Surfer and I had begun chopping up the tomatoes, onions and lettuce for the tacos. "We're gonna plead guilty, and throw ourselves on the mercy of the court," I said.

At the hearing, Surfer, Rick Angus and I wore clean shirts and endured a brief lecture from the judge, who rightly insisted that an aerospace engineer, x-ray technician and graduate student should know better than to steal cable. MacFadden sat apart from us, the only one of the accused who'd hired a lawyer. MacFadden shook in the dock like he'd been accused of murder, and when the judge fined us each fifty dollars and dismissed the case, the Dull Man raced down the steps of the courthouse like he'd been acquitted of the Lindbergh kidnapping.

About midway through the fall season, I was home alone on a Tuesday night, wearing a pair of gym shorts and watching TV from a beanbag chair, which was our only piece of living room furniture. During a rerun of *M*A*S*H,* the front door opened and MacFadden came in with Tara. He'd taken her to dinner at the Brown Derby, and they were both a little tipsy. Tara looked magnificent in a tight-fitting cocktail dress made from some kind of stretchy, iridescent material, her perfect breasts spilling out of the top and her auburn hair falling about her shoulders.

While MacFadden rummaged around in the fridge for a couple of beers, I walked past the kitchenette and said good night, figuring he'd want to be alone with her, though he had no shot. At the top of the stairs was a full bath and I closed the door behind me, washed my face, and was brushing my teeth with my eyes closed, humming the theme song from M*A*S*H, when I heard a tiny unlatching noise.

I was astounded to find Tara in the bathroom with me, the door closed again behind her, giggling with her index finger to her lips in the "ssshh" position. A gob of toothpaste fell onto my bare chest, and I caught a glimpse of myself in the side mirror. I looked like a kid who had asked for a ten-speed bike for Christmas, and then found a Maserati beneath the tree.

The bathroom had a second door, behind which was a tiny anteroom containing the bathtub and toilet. Tara put her hand on my chest and guided me in there, to the edge of the tub where I sat down abruptly to keep myself from falling in. Downstairs, MacFadden was calling for Tara in a puzzled tone, coming through the living room, and then back to the kitchenette and out the front door into the parking lot. Tara had made it clear to the Dull Man, and the rest of us, that she considered him a friend, that's all, and when they were out together, other people were usually around and she paid her own way. But I never had a clue that Tara had her eye on me, and had been stunned into my own Buster Keaton impression by this turn of events. It was an early Zen moment.

Sometimes, when I was home from Acadia, my mother and I would sit up watching the late show on TV, romantic comedies starring Cary Grant and Irene Dunne, or some unlikely tale of Bing Crosby and Rosemary Clooney falling in love and opening up an inn in Vermont. My mother didn't care for most contemporary love stories, with their graphic depictions of lust and sex, preferring the suggested trysts of those old classics, with their hint of physical sparks.

"I think it's much sexier when they just go into a room, and the door closes behind them," my mother said. "It leaves it to your imagination."

And I had to agree when Tara groped backward with her foot and shut the anteroom door.

Chapter 20

Chesapeake Bay

My old pal Glenn Gallant, a Methuen firefighter, had been flying down to Gainesville on occasion to ride his motorcycle, which he stored in the garage at Sigma Nu, and to hang out with the guys on the rugby team. Glenn was a frequent visitor to my home in Methuen, even when I was away, and on very good terms with my dad, whom he called the Big Guy, often stopping in for a beer upon completing his shift at the firehouse. After Glenn bought his tickets to come down for Halloween, he convinced my dad to go along, which I was thrilled about when I received the phone call. We were playing a home match against Tallahassee that weekend, and Glenn, my father, and Mike Ewing, another former classmate who was a cop in Methuen, would all be staying at Landmine with us.

On the road against the St. Pete Pelicans the week before, our undefeated start to the season was in jeopardy right away. We were losing 10–4 when the second half kickoff tumbled straight into Wee Wee's arms at midfield. Usually a prop forward will rumble five or ten yards with the ball, choose a defender, and punish him by dropping a shoulder and taking the man on; it's called setting up in the tackle, an effective way to secure possession, recycling the ball for a second phase of the attack. But Wee Wee had pretty good speed to go with his size, and after catching the ball on the run, he let out a war cry, freezing the initial defenders. Burning past them, Wee Wee split the opposition in half, coming straight up the field. The full-back and winger on that side flung themselves at him, but Wee Wee had the momentum, staving them off with his hip and then a stiff arm, chugging into the try zone to dot it down, unassisted. A straight-up kick return for a try almost never happens.

(The only other time I recall seeing it was years later, when Joe Dudek, a one-time dark horse candidate for the Heisman Trophy— *Sports Illustrated* published his photo on the cover with the headline WHAT THE HECK, WHY NOT DUDEK?—appeared in a match with Amo-skeag RFC. Playing tailback for Division III Plymouth State College in New Hampshire, Dudek had broken Walter Payton's collegiate record for touchdowns in a four-year career, 76–66, and later played a couple of games for the Denver Broncos, rushing for 154 yards and two touchdowns. In that one rugby game, I was running along be-hind Dudek when he caught a booming kick at our twenty-two-meter line and weaved back and forth, eluding at least ten defenders on his route to the try zone.)

Running downfield against the Pelicans, I caught up with Wee Wee beneath the goalposts. I laughed and mussed his hair, drop-ping to one knee. "My liege," I said, bowing my head. Carlos made the conversion, and we ended up getting away with a tie, 10–10.

Noel drove up to Jacksonville to get Glenn and Mike on Wednes-day, and I went the next morning to pick up my dad. Old school and a self-made man, Jim Atkinson always traveled by air dressed in what he called the uniform—dark blue blazer, oxford shirt, gray slacks, knee-high black socks, and a pair of black loafers; the only variation being that he omitted the necktie he always wore to the office, preferring an open collar for such occasions. Then fifty-two years old, my father was a burly, Sebastian Cabot kind of guy, with enormous shoulders, a large, well-set head, black hair, which he kept short and parted to one side, and a full but neatly trimmed beard, marked by two small streaks of gray at the corners of his mouth. He wore a thin gold chain around his neck, hung with a small medallion figured in his birth sign, Virgo, or the Virgin.

My dad was a large, gregarious man, popular in the little town square where he kept his business, and beloved by his friends, co-workers, fellow Rotarians and, most of all, by us, his family, consisting of his five children (I'm the oldest), and his smart, pretty wife, the former Lois Mae Bower, of Camden Street. Both my parents had grown up during the Depression, in the section of town known as the Arlington District; a collection of dingy, narrow streets and rickety tenements along a segment of the Spicket River that ran behind a row of old mill buildings. Nobody who ever lived on Camden Street ever had a trust fund, that's for sure.

If my father had a weakness, it was that he was a lifelong salary man, never going in for the main chance by starting his own business. My mother would point out that his customers remained loyal because of my dad's loyalty to them—as well as his professionalism, diligence and personal charisma—and that they didn't know or care who owned the agency. But the Big Guy had watched his own father struggle through lean times with Atkinson's Bakery, and always preferred a steady paycheck to the all-consuming worries of the sole proprietor. Consequently, my dad had a keen appreciation for the value of a dollar, along with an abiding respect for higher education; and since I was the first of his children to earn a college degree and venture out from home, he smiled warmly as he came down the Jetway.

"Hello, son," he said, embracing me.

Back at Landmine, the Big Guy occupied my room with the rest of us sprawled out on the living room floor. That first night, my dad took us to dinner at the Yearling restaurant, fourteen miles away in Cross Creek, where we dined on alligator tail, "cooter," or turtle, and frog legs, all of which pretty much tasted like chicken. The next morning, my father sat on our tiny concrete patio reading *The Gainesville Sun* and drinking a cup of coffee. I heard the slider open next door, and Missy Fitzgibbons walked by in a tiny pair of shorts and a bikini top, heading for the pool.

My dad tracked Missy until she lay down in the grass, and when he came back into the house he winked at us. "You need a couple of pickets to Tittsburgh to ride that train," he said, prompting guffaws.

Our match that afternoon was a battle of undefeated teams: we were 4-0-1 on the season thus far, and Tallahassee was 5–0. My dad had never seen a rugby game in his life, and stood on the touchline with the guys from Methuen. Glenn and Rick had participated in a scrimmage or two, and explained what little they knew about the sport while Mike Ewing also listened in. We had our club side on the field: with a solid pack including Martin, me and Wee Wee up front; Sergio Lopez, the former Gator linebacker, and Harry King in the second row; Keith Platt at eight man, and Civil and Conrad at loose forwards. MacFadden was out with his Ping-Pong injury, so Pokey Whelan was at scrumhalf, his natural position.

It was a warm day, and the pitch was hard, dry and dusty. Talla-hassee had an experienced pack of forwards, and we played them even in the scrums; Sergio jumped at number two in the lineouts, a wide body with a great pair of hands, and I threw quick little darts to him all afternoon, sometimes just on eye contact without any ca-dence or signal. The muscled giant would leap up and over his op-posite number, rising to the spot where the ball would suddenly appear, snagging it out of the air.

Rolling mauls ensued, with Harry King and Platt coming out with the ball and leveling people on the second phase. At one point in the tight-loose, I picked up a ball that Martin had taken to ground, hopped over his prone body, and dodging two or three guys, who each had fifty pounds on me, brought the ball to the deck for Pokey. He served it off the ground to Sergio, who ran over the opposing fullback and one of their loose forwards for the try.

When I turned back upfield, my father was there on the sideline. "Way to go, Jay," he said.

We won the match by a try and a penalty kick, to remain unde-feated. Sin Sity Saloon had kicked us out after yet another dustup, and the party was held at a small, open-air bar on East University Avenue near City Hall. At the drink-up, my father, wearing a pair of navy-blue chino shorts, an Acadia wrestling T-shirt, and a straw cowboy hat, occupied a table with Mel Fried and Van Blokland, the three of them drinking beer and eating chicken wings. At the bar with Surfer and Civil and a few other guys, I made plans for the an-nual Halloween bash, which fell on a Sunday that year. Looking

over at my dad, who was listening to the coach tell a story punctuated by hand gestures and a table's worth of laughter, I caught his
eye and he winked at me. These were his people, too.

Late the next morning, a big gang of us went to Mama Lo's for a
soul food breakfast of chitlins, collard greens, scrambled eggs and
grits. Upon our return, the town house began to fill up with rugby
guys preparing for the Halloween party, traditionally held outdoors
at the band shell. The group costume that year was Native American; we filled our bathtub with warm water and several bottles of
red food coloring, each of the players immersing himself for a few
minutes, until his entire body took on a copper hue. Downstairs,
Noel and Surfer had arranged bunches of feathers, chamois loincloths, strings of beads and amulets, and other junk from the novelty
store, with each of the guys accessorizing as he saw fit. I was taking
my dad to the Jacksonville airport for the five o'clock flight back to
Boston, and had to refrain from wallowing in the dye. At length, my
dad said good-bye to the fellows, shaking hands with a procession
of red Indians in beaded loincloths and headdresses. It looked like
some kind of peace treaty ceremony, with General Grant turning
them out to the reservation, every last one of the erstwhile warriors
carrying a quart of Budweiser.

At the airport, I was divided between staying with my father,
who I hadn't seen much of in the past two years, and racing back to
Gainesville for the big Halloween party. I shook my dad's hand on
the concourse overlooking the gates and then hustled down the stairs,
heading for the parking lot. Crossing the lobby, I had the sudden
urge to look up at the second-floor gallery. There amid the passing
throngs was my father, his hands resting on the steel rail. I waved,
and with a strange gesture that induced a pang in my chest, my dad
raised his big mitt in the air, his gaze steady despite the crowd, and
bestowed a solemn benediction on me. Then I turned and went out
through the electric doors into the glare of the parking lot.

As the semester wound down, I had to admit to the English department chairman, a sour-faced little man who clashed often with
Harry, that I had no intention of taking the Ph.D. qualifying exam.
Thus, it became official—another month, a handful of rugby games,
and I was through at Florida.

Late one night, Rick and I were awakened by whispering from the crawlspace between our town house and the next. We could make out someone groping along the cobwebbed passageway, accompanied by the sound of feminine giggling. Half-sized emergency doors separated the two units, and we heard ours creaking, followed by more whispering and strangled laughter. The door to our bedroom was ajar and before long it swung open—in the reflected light I could make out two curvy silhouettes, Missy Fitzgibbons and Tara, who closed the door behind them and padded into the room. Dressed in tiny panties and baby doll T-shirts, they slipped into my bed without saying a word, one on either side, their warm flesh pressing against me and hands reaching for my hair, my neck and my hips.

Tara kissed me, long and deep. "Hi," she said.

Across the room, Rick peeped out from beneath the covers, speechless. While I lay there like a cigar store Indian, wooden all over, I contemplated my options. I knew that my old buddy had dated Missy a few times when we were away on rugby trips. Silent as usual, Missy was doing all her talking in sign language at the moment, her hands describing an encyclopedia's worth of sensuous pleasures while her tongue explored the crevices of my ear. A line from a Clash song echoed in my head: *"Should I stay or should I go now?"*

Tara whispered that she and Missy knew I'd be leaving soon and wanted to express some fairly complex and rigorous farewell sentiments, if I was willing.

Part of me was. But with my best friend from high school just fifteen feet away, I felt self-conscious, and more than a little guilty. In a strained voice I noted that Rick was in the other bed, and probably getting a bit lonely by now. Missy climbed out from beneath the sheet and went over and got in Rick's bed. The Dull Man was sleeping down the hall, and amid all the fuss and smothered laughter, Tara whispered that she and Missy would go back home through the attic, and in a few minutes I was invited to follow them over to their room, thereby solving the problem.

It was a tempting offer. Excusing myself for a moment, I lifted the sheet and went into the hallway, ostensibly to visit the bathroom. Instead, I crept downstairs to the telephone and called a number that was written on the wall. Conrad answered on the first ring and I provided a brief description of the situation and asked if I could drop by, perhaps even stay the night.

"Sure, boofoo," said Conrad, a little bewildered. "Come on over."

I took a pair of rugby shorts from the laundry basket at the foot of the stairs, lifted my car keys from a hook on the wall, and tiptoed over to the front door. I cast a wistful glance up the darkened stairwell, and slipped out to the parking lot. Surfer had developed a set of koans that we called Surfer John's Rules for Life ("Never shit in a bar"; "Never trust a man in a kayak"; "Piss when you can, not when you have to"), and as I started up the Monte, one of them popped into my head: "It's not where you go to sleep that counts, it's where you wake up."

Conrad and Civil were in the living room at #9 when I arrived, listening to music with a basketball game on the television, the sound turned down. Quickly I explained what was going on, and how I didn't feel comfortable staying there with the girls for a couple of reasons, which I enumerated. Dave went out and got me a beer from the fridge. When I had finished my story, he tried to reason with me: loyalty was commendable, but when a man had the sort of opportunity that had been handed to me, well, he had a duty—no, an obligation—to see it through. Besides, what would Steve Smith think? Furthermore, if I turned down the girls' offer, it would create some kind of X-rated butterfly effect, whereby some poor bloke in Christchurch or Madagascar would be denied a chance at a ménage à trois he never even knew he had.

Civil threw up his hands, finally. "You talk to him, Conrad," he said. "I'm going to bed."

The two of us sat drinking beer and watching Duke versus UCLA. "Guess it's the way I was brought up," I said, admitting that I was little old-fashioned.

Conrad squatted by the turntable, changing the record in the greenish light from the dials. Shirtless and disheveled as usual, he looked like a wild-haired shaman. "It's who you are, boofoo," he said.

University of Florida provided a wealth of free concerts, and in just a few months we'd seen the Grateful Dead, Talking Heads, Peter Tosh and the old R&B group The Spinners. Near the end of the year, the rugby team congregated in front of the band shell to hear Southside Johnny & the Asbury Jukes, a band from New Jersey that, like Bruce Springsteen, got its start at the Stone Pony in Asbury Park. They were kitted out in their trademark dark glasses and pegged pants, accompanied by the famous roving brass section, the Miami Horns. With a blare of trumpets, they cranked out that raucous Northern sound I'd grown up with, parked on some dead-end street with my pals after a hockey game. We'd drink beer and eat Squirrel peanuts, arms extended as we sang along to the Jukes' version of "The Fever," or Springsteen's "4th of July, Asbury Park."

Southside Johnny was the front man, a suave, soulful punk right off the boardwalk: tight black suit with his shirttails out and a loosely fastened skinny tie, his voice halfway between a growl and a lament. When Southside hushed the crowd with a raised fist, the band struck up their unofficial theme song, "I Don't Want to Go Home," and I was possessed by an urge to quit the field right then and there, rev up the old Monte, and just head for the highway with my rugby kit in the backseat. Civil was bopping back and forth, and he caught my attention, lifting his chin toward me in that what's-up? gesture. I leaned over, shouting to be heard above the chorus that I was ready to go somewhere.

Civil yelled over that it would be good for me. There at the concert we decided that it would be au revoir and not adios when I finally left. Civil kissed me on the cheek, saying, "I'll miss you, brother," and I knew that it wouldn't be easy to leave these guys.

My last rugby competition as a Gator was the Florida Cup, a tournament held in Orlando early that December. A formidable lineup of clubs was participating, and once again, we drew a tough bracket. Our first round opponent was the Atlanta Renegades, Southern U.S. club champions for three years running. We had stayed with them at the Gator Invitational the previous spring, losing by a converted try. Although we'd added players and improved since then, so had the Renegades; Stormin' Norman Litwack was on their sideline, wearing the unfamiliar jersey, red with a yellow stripe and black outline. He looked over at Surfer and me during warm-ups and gave us a grim-faced little wave.

We'd put up a good fight against them in the spring, but the

Renegades wore us down in the second half with their larger, more experienced pack, a tactic they expected to repeat in the Florida Cup. As a result, they thought it would be funny to play Norm at fullback against us, instead of tighthead prop (where he would be an A-side stalwart for the next decade, and a Georgia Select Side player). We were competing as a club side, and had added several good players; my own rugby had continued to develop, and I was named pack captain for the final two matches of the fall season, as well as the Florida Cup.

In the early going, our tight scrummaging and quick strikes, along with the clever halfback combination of Pokey and Carlos, kept the Renegades pinned in their end. Mike Siskin got loose on the outside, bringing the ball back in to Mike May, and we scored a try about fifteen minutes into the match. Carlos made the conversion and we were up, 6–0. Sergio was jumping at the front of our lineout, and I was hitting him with a hard, flat pass; even in his late thirties, he was so big and agile, Sergio was able to break away from their forwards, and I'd already be running downfield after I threw the ball in, close on his heels. When they gang tackled him, and the 240-pound jarhead started to go down, I'd burrow in and take the ball, placing it on the ground for Pokey, just as Wee Wee and Civil and the rest of the support crashed the pile. With Sergio taking them on like that, we were rucking the ball with the efficiency of a rototiller, which flummoxed the Renegades.

Their fullback made a long penalty early in the second half, and Carlos responded with a nifty drop goal a few minutes later, making the score 9–3 in our favor. There were only thirteen minutes left in the game, according to the referee, and it appeared that we were on the verge of an enormous upset; the Renegades had only lost a handful of games in three years, not one of them to a Florida club.

In the next sequence, we took a questionable penalty for killing the ball right at midfield, to which the referee tacked on ten and then fifteen more yards of advantage when guys started talking back. While we were arguing, the Renegades ran a quick tap from the referee's mark and their eight-man broke through for a try. The conversion was good, and in a matter of seconds, it was 9–9.

The Renegades put together four successful phases of play on the ensuing kickoff, leading to another try, which went unconverted. They closed out the scoring with a midrange penalty a couple of minutes later, winning the match 16–9.

These were the type of games I wanted to get serious about and win—no more fucking around. After the final whistle, I embraced Stormin' Norman and then sat by myself in the shade for a while. I got so worked up during games, back then and over my entire career, that I'd avoid even my best friends for at least fifteen minutes afterward. It's a sport that has to be played with your blood at a rolling boil, and I needed to lower the heat before I could be myself again.

In our second match, we defeated Montgomery of Maryland 8–0, with unconverted tries by Greg Taylor and Kaplan. After the match, I glanced around at Kap, Surfer, Civil and Conrad; Noel, Pokey and Platt; Big Harry and Defraites and Carlos and Psycho, all talking and laughing, and I realized that our final match that afternoon, against Brevard County, would be the last time we'd be on the same rugby field together.

I played with my heart in my throat. Things went our way early, which is always a godsend in rugby, a sport that depends on momentum like no other. Brevard was awarded a scrum about ten meters out from their own goal line, and I was so attuned to the rhythm of play that I could distinguish the individual breathing of everyone in the scrum. Their halfback lowered the ball and I flashed out my right foot at the peak moment and brought a tighthead back before their hooker even flexed the tendons in his ankle. Platt grabbed the ball at number eight, went to the weak side and laid it off to Psycho just as he was tackled, and Greg Taylor plunged over for the try.

Stealing Brevard's first put-in messed with their heads, and the hooker and scrumhalf bollixed their timing so much that I seemed to have a better chance than my opposite number when they put the ball in the scrums. We worked long lineouts to the back, and Platt was catching them over his shoulder on the fly and just running through people. We won the match 12–4 and as I was leaving the field Van Blokland showed me the statistics he kept on a little card: Brevard had won only seven scrums in the entire match. I took ten balls against the head, all of my own, and all of our lineouts ended in clean possession but for two.

"That's the stuff," said Van Blokland, shaking my hand.

Soon thereafter I stopped by Harry's office for the last time. Our meeting was brief and unsentimental. He went into a drawer and brought out a small hardcover book with a simple title, *Dispatches*, by Michael Herr, *Esquire* magazine's correspondent in Vietnam.

"Everything you need to know is in there," said Harry. I stood up and he reached over and shook my hand. "See you in ten years," he said, and I left his office puzzling over what he'd meant.

Rick was going back to Methuen for Christmas vacation, and on the morning of our departure, I had returned to Landmine from the auto parts store when the Dull Man accosted me on the sidewalk, his arm still encased in a grimy sling.

"There's a *girl* here," he said. "She came by twice, looking for you."

"Who is it?" I asked.

"I don't know. She's really cute, though. She said she'd just wait up in your room until you got back."

I went inside, washed my hands in the downstairs bathroom and then pounded up the stairs. The shades were drawn, the room hung with gray shadows despite the early hour. Sitting on the edge of Rick's bed (I'd given mine to Defraites, telling him it was magical) was Loretta, in a white cotton skirt to the knee, a red leather belt, red pumps and a red and white striped jersey; her nails were painted fire engine red, and she was tanned so dark that her green eyes burned like pilot lights in the dimness.

We hadn't spoken to each other for two or three months. I had entered the room quickly, leaving the door open, and Loretta got up, crossing behind me to shut the door with a gentle click. When she turned, her face wore a shifting look of remonstrance, sadness and pique: her lips quivered for a moment, and we sat on the edge of the bed, holding hands while Loretta fixed her gaze on the opposite wall. For several moments nothing was said, until she glanced at me, her face very close and the bedroom adrift with her scent.

"I just wanted to come and say good-bye," she said.

Afterward, we got dressed, handing each other items of clothing and moving around the bed in a ritual still familiar from the previous summer. She kissed me on the cheek, patted my neck with a kind of half smile and descended the stairs with her little red handbag, going past MacFadden, who had been hovering around downstairs like an enraptured schoolboy.

"Wow," he said, as Loretta got into her car. "Who was *that*?"

In the afternoon, Rick and I changed the spark plugs on the Monte; replaced the air filter, and changed the oil; flushed and filled the radiator, and went out to check the tire pressure and fill the gas tank. Upon our return, Karen Koffler was sitting out front, talking to Surfer and Maria, who came by to see us off. (Surfer would leave for Quantico and the Marines a few days after Christmas.) Rick went to Joe's Deli for lunch with Surfer, Maria and the Dull Man, while Koffler and I leaned against the Monte in the low winter sunshine, talking quietly. We laughed over missed opportunities, like the night I troweled off her roommate's lipstick at the Winnjammer.

As soon as Rick got back, I threw the last few things into the trunk, embraced Koffler again ("Bye-ee," she said, in my ear) and shook hands all around. Koffler was headed for medical school at the University of Miami, and I was bound for somewhere, though not even I knew which direction I was going in.

Surfer came over to shut my door. "Later," he said.

By the time we were on I-75 north, it was late afternoon. The plan was to go straight through to Virginia Beach, where we'd stay at my cousin Larry Crane's house. It was raining like the devil all the way through Georgia, but I was rocking out to the Boss and The Clash and Elvis Costello, playing a cassette tape that Conrad had made for us.

We arrived in Virginia Beach the next day. When we were growing up, Larry Crane was my consigliere of cool, the guy I modeled myself after, the walk and the look and the way he talked, in smart-ass little asides; he and his brother Steve were like the older brothers I never had.

Come nightfall, Larry, Rick and I were parked in the bitter cold at the foot of the Chesapeake Bay Bridge-Tunnel, drinking Canadian beer and talking about the summer vacations that Larry and I had spent together as kids. Navy ships moored in the bay were festooned with Christmas lights; the bridge portions were also illuminated, stopping at a few points in the darkness where the tunnel intervened, and then starting up again. I remarked to the others that it was a great place to woo a girl, if there was one to be wooed.

The next morning I was driving again, and I stumped the lady at the bay bridge tollbooth when I paid her the nine dollars and asked, "Will they be showing a movie on this flight?"

Rick dozed in the passenger seat and I gunned the Monte down that long, eerie stretch of pavement, the seas turned cobalt blue and lapping against the trestle on both sides. We were leaving the South. It was like I had been carrying a helium balloon for two and a half years, and there on Chesapeake Bay, I just let it go, feeling not so much unburdened, since the whole thing had been lighter than air, but unencumbered.

Chapter 21

O Canada

During those early years, I always made it home for Christmas, even if that was the only time that I did. In the months I'd been away, my parents moved the family down the street to a new house; even though I'd been living in Nova Scotia, Colorado and Florida for the previous seven years, I was awarded my own room, much to the consternation of my four younger siblings, who had to double up. Built in 1880, the house was a small, neat, clapboard-sided colonial, with a central hearth, a small plot of land and a terraced garden that I could see from my second-floor bedroom in the rear of the house.

My father had given me an old manual Olympia typewriter, and after paying twenty-five dollars to have it reconditioned, I hauled it up to the second floor of the house. It must have weighed fifty pounds. Struggling up the narrow staircase, I put the antiquated machine on a little table in my room that overlooked the garden, a mass of broken stalks poking up through the snow.

I planned to start looking for a job and a rugby club right after the holidays, and spent the waning days of a very good year doing things outdoors and working on my first novel, *Local Talent*. The book had grown to more than eighty pages of manuscript, the longest thing I'd written to date, and it was a marvelous experience to sit at the typewriter in the early morning, a cup of tea at my elbow, snapping at the keys and watching my old friends and the antics we'd pulled in Canada take shape on the page.

On Christmas Eve, my father got nostalgic, which was rare for him, and called an old army buddy he hadn't spoken to in thirty years, Phil Saccone of Jackson Heights, New York. Mr. Saccone was so surprised to hear from the Big Guy that he kept repeating my father's name, and then began to cry.

My dad stood in the kitchen with the phone cord wrapped around his forearm, the disks of his eyeglasses clouding over from the emotion, as well as the heat of the turkey baking in the oven. After they hung up, the Big Guy said that Mr. Saccone had cancer and they planned to get together in March, before they both died.

We had a quiet Christmas at home, and the next day I got up early to work on my novel, finishing chapter four. In the afternoon, my dad and I went cross-country skiing in the town forest, a heavily-wooded twenty-four-acre parcel on the western shore of Forest Lake. The park was closed to traffic in the winter, and we left the family car outside the gate, pulled our skinny skis out of the back and trod through knee-deep snow to the old fire road.

About a hundred yards in, the road forked and my dad took the lower half, skirting the lake, an immense white space, barely visible through the trees. Choosing to herringbone up the slope, I bypassed the road altogether and went off alone in the woods. The sun was going down in the hills and the trees, mostly seventy- and eighty-foot pines with a few oaks sprinkled in, were set close together; a single crooked fir illustrated how vertical the others were, its trunk crossing some of its neighbors at a forty-five degree angle.

Along the road, the snowpack had been worn thin by all-terrain vehicles and snowmobiles, but it was heavy among the fir trees, so deep in places it was more like snowshoeing than skiing: one foot lifted up, shaken free of the snow, and placed in front of the other.

It was a study in black and white. The woods were empty, and when I deigned to look up, the clouds loomed with an impending storm and I couldn't hear a thing except my own breathing. Occasionally, a pine tree would move, creaking amid the stillness, though there seemed to be no wind, and it was like someone getting up and leaving the room during a lecture.

This was a different world than the one I'd been living in, but it was a world that I knew; pausing at the top of the hill to catch my breath, I spotted my father making his way along the edge of the lake. I took the road going down, picking up speed through one long wide turn, which I tempered by thrusting out my heels. Meeting my dad by an empty lifeguard chair, we stood on a low wall overlooking the flat white disk of the lake. In summer, this was the public beach, thronging with kids and their families. Now the concession stand and bathrooms were shuttered, and the pavilion was drifted over with snow. As a boy, I'd camped here in winter with the Boy Scouts. My cousins Steve and Larry Crane were in charge of the Flaming Arrow patrol, and we bivouacked in old army tents, huddled against the stone wall to keep out of the wind. We built up our campfire in the morning and kept it burning all day, feeding it with deadfall; then we foraged over the hill and back along the old fire road, identifying local animals by their tracks. In the afternoons, we shoveled off a rink-sized area and went skating on the lake.

Now it was deserted, silent and white, the half-dozen or so picnic tables piled high with snow. They resembled a row of giant wedding cakes.

My dad reached into his anorak for a tooled silver flask. He unscrewed the top and took a drink, handing it to me. The whiskey burned my throat, and I gave it back and he took another shot. We didn't speak. After a while the two of us chopped sideways in our skis, describing a half arc until we were facing the way we came. My father pushed off toward the low road, gliding along in a steady motion, and I climbed back up the hill, planning to go telemarking down the long slope on the other side.

I scanned the want ads, but finding a good job proved impossible. After vacation ended, I put in a couple of applications for substitute teaching and called a temp agency. One of my high school friends, Jeff Ness, was working at a local golf course removing brush and cutting down trees, and hired me occasionally as a day laborer. Tall, dark haired and gap toothed, Jeff was a hard worker but an easy companion, especially in the woods, where we both felt at home. Chain saw roaring, Jeff would drop the trees that were marked with a blaze of orange paint; huge, gnarled oaks with dead limbs that were crowding the fairway, and skeletal pines clustered around one of the water hazards. I'd follow after him, splitting and stacking the two and a half foot lengths.

That winter, Jeff was living on the beach in Salisbury, Massachusetts, with Glenn Gallant; at their insistence, I packed some clothes in an old hockey bag, and stayed on their couch during the week. It was a seasonal place, a two-story cottage that rented for $900 a week in the summer, but could be had from October 1 to May 1 for $750 a month. Their apartment was a second-floor walk-up with a huge stone fireplace, the wood piled in neat lengths on the back porch; and a table and chair by the front window with a view of the surf, which was gray, tangled and wild. The first time I stayed there, the other guys left for work before 6 A.M., and I put on long johns and sweats and went for a run on the beach, a forty-minute slog through the sand at low tide.

When I returned to the house, I banked up the fire, which had been smoldering all night, took a shower, and brewed a pot of tea. I'd purchased two new typewriter ribbons and a ream of bond paper, and laid out *The Sun Also Rises, Dispatches,* and my notebooks on the table overlooking the beach. It was my first day as a writer, and I was eager to get started.

In the afternoon mail, I received letters from Dave Civil ("rugby team is kickin' ass, I'm getting laid, sun's a shinin', life is good"), and from Surfer. The Marines were already trying to boot him out. Apparently, they hadn't investigated his dismissal from West Point until after he was commissioned as a second lieutenant, and had decided that they didn't want him, in spite of the fact that he'd finished his advanced training ranked second overall in the platoon. Surfer wrote that it would take a few months to sort out, and then he'd probably be assigned to the Marine Corps' Individual Ready Reserves and get sent home.

Included in the mail was a card from Jeff the Ghetto, my old Hollywood rip-off pal from Acadia. It said he'd call me on the following Sunday, and that he had a job for me. I reread the card and put on an album by Lightnin' Hopkins, staring out the window at the ocean. The afternoons were growing longer by a minute each day; the sun fading at 4:35, 4:36, 4:37, and it was strange, but I was somehow conscious of it, could tell without looking at the clock. Glancing back through the mail, I noticed a postscript on Civil's letter: "Play rugby and write, write and play rugby . . ."

A week later, I was on a plane to Toronto. After leaving Acadia to play football at San Diego State, the Ghetto dropped out of college altogether and moved back home to Burlington, Ontario. He took a job as a personal trainer at the local health club, and when the owners filed for bankruptcy, the Ghetto, always a hustler, borrowed money from the government and took over the club. Busy trying to manage its day-to-day operation, the Ghetto needed someone he could trust to lend him a hand. The economy was bad and getting worse, and I said yes to the offer before he'd even articulated the terms.

The arrangements were quite agreeable, especially in light of my current situation. I was to be paid $400 a week, under the table (the Ghetto had dual citizenship, and I was hired as a consultant to a business he'd incorporated in Michigan, where his mother was born). Also included was the use of a brand new Pontiac Firebird; and a free place to stay, once Jeff had closed on a property in nearby Waterdown, atop the glacial escarpment overlooking Lake Ontario. But the sweetener was the proximity of a good rugby club, the Burlington Centaurs RFC. They fielded three teams in the Niagara Rugby Football Union, and had recently made the jump to the first division.

Burlington Wellness and Strength was a two-story, yellow brick structure with four thousand members, tons of free weights, Universal and Nautilus equipment, an indoor track, squash courts, swimming pool, the whole deal. Ghetto introduced me as the new general manager, making it clear to the chubby housewives, coronary shoo-ins, and shifty salespeople that I was his eyes and ears in the club. (He employed a former used car salesman named Dave who was fond of making cash deals for so-called lifetime memberships, charging $2,000 and then writing $1,500 on the application. I put a stop to that right away, earning my first sworn enemy in the real world.)

Burlington is located on the Golden Horseshoe, a string of attractive communities on the western shore of Lake Ontario. I fell right back into the swing of living in Canada, buying "pain" and "lait" by the kilogram and liter, drinking Molson, and chatting with total strangers at the grocery store, a rare occurrence back in Boston. I could turn on the only real TV channel, CBC, and watch a show starring Ronnie James, an actor and comedian who'd been in my modern drama class at Acadia. Despite its geographical immensity, Canada had that small town feel I always enjoyed.

One benefit of the fifty-five-hour workweeks was that I got to train a lot, early in the morning, at lunch, and on my breaks; out on the gym floor I made the acquaintance of Ray Williams and his brother Adrian, two middle-aged, transplanted Welshmen who played for the Burlington Centaurs' third side. When I moved to Ontario in February, three weeks before the Centaurs began practicing, the Williams brothers, without seeing me play, vowed that I'd make the A-side. That year, the Centaurs had aspirations for a championship season; a lot of young Welsh expats filled out the first side, including tighthead prop Tony Spencer, who had played for the national team, along with several other regional and provincial select side players. This was shaping up to be a good team and even though they had a Welshman, an Englishman, and a local kid who had come up through their youth program vying for the A-side hooker's job, the Williams brothers started promoting my candidacy among the club elders well before the season began.

Jeff was known as the Ghetto because of how he dressed, and for a proclivity toward beating the system, just on principal. His sartorial style was what my mother called "unmade bed." For two years at Acadia, he wore the same thing every day: milkman's overalls, a cutoff Acadia football T-shirt, and a tattered down jacket that leaked feathers everywhere. Before he split for California, the Ghetto, Drew Cooper and I were always together; coming and going from the gym and dining hall, at our regular table at the Swingin' Axe or downtown at the Anvil, and sitting up late in the Ghetto's room at Eaton House, drinking beer and listening to Al Stewart's *Year of the Cat,* which was Jeff's favorite album.

The Ghetto was the starting middle linebacker for the Axemen, and Coop was an All-Conference tight end; when football season ended they'd be out six nights a week, at the Axe and the Anvil, or sneaking into all-night bonspiels at the curling rink, where you could drink after hours. It's not an exaggeration to say that I was a more serious student, dependent on my academic scholarship to ease the burden on my parents. During the winter, I had to cut weight, too, going down from 170 pounds during soccer to my wrestling weight of 142, and spent most nights in my dorm, reading Heraclitus and Plato and Aristotle in my search for what the Greeks called *arete*, or virtue. Sometime after 11 P.M., when I'd be nodding at my desk, a heavy tread came along the hallway, accompanied by boisterous voices. In a flash, I'd close my book, switch off the lamp, and jump into bed.

Pounding on my door, Ghetto and Coop would shout, "At-kin-son!", startling my neighbors, who would peek into the corridor, spot this pair of behemoths, and retreat without protest. Coop might give up after a few minutes, but Ghetto would persist, saying, "I know you're in there, Blade." He'd shove ten-dollar bills under my door until I'd open up, promising to go out for a beer. Because I wasn't allowed to work in Canada on a student visa, I had to survive on $100 American per month (about $121 Canadian at the time), which limited my social opportunities.

Ghetto had the same take-no-prisoners attitude in the real world. At the health club, I'd be giving a tour to prospective members, a husband and wife, for instance, explaining how thirty minutes a day on the LifeCycle or a refreshing game of squash would jump-start their metabolisms (and their libidos), when Jeff would appear, coming from the opposite direction. Dressed in the same dark blue suit, white shirt, and red tie he wore every day, he would walk by, nodding professionally, greeting me as an esteemed colleague.

When the couple looked away, Ghetto would throw a quick fore-arm, shoving me against the wall of the squash court; or he'd turn quickly and mimic the husband's facial expression while making lewd thrusts in his wife's direction. I'd struggle to keep from laughing, push Jeff away, and usher the couple toward the swimming pool.

The free lodging that came with the job turned out to be a run-down, two-story brick farmhouse on a two hundred-acre strip miles out in the boonies. Situated on a rise and surrounded by browned-over fields, it resembled the setting for a Hitchcock movie: no central heat, a big hole in the trap beneath the kitchen sink, and an abundance of bare lightbulbs, cracked plaster and nocturnal sounds. I'd arrive there after a twelve-hour workday and two-hour rugby practice, the landscape stubbled and black for miles around, a piece of the new moon riding above the house. Clutching an ax handle I kept by the door, I'd take the key from under the mat, let myself in, and creep upstairs. Then I'd lock myself in the front bedroom, where I had a foam pad and comforter, portable radio and my clothes and rugby stuff. I'd scribble in my journal for a while, then shudder off for a brief, nightmare-filled sleep.

By March, I was playing rugby three times a week, and at practice the Centaurs' coach, a voluble, ruddy-faced Welshman named Cye Beechey, had me working with the A-side front row: at tighthead prop, Tony Spencer, a solid, thick-legged Welshman in his early thirties, and an enormous Englishman at loosehead prop named Alf Glazebrook, a philosophical gent with a gunfighter's droopy mustache. The Burlington Centaurs, established in 1973, had a first-class sporting complex at Sherwood Forest Park, one of the finest rugby facilities in Canada. It featured an international-sized pitch, with what's known as a compound cambor, a slight peak in the middle, allowing for proper drainage. Permanent regulation goalposts, a pop-up sprinkler system, beautifully groomed practice fields—a far cry from the hard, dusty pan of Norman Field.

The park also contained a clubhouse, locker rooms and a cozy pub. Blotchy-faced old Welshmen greeted me there after training sessions, in their vests and soft wool hats, insisting they buy the evening's first pint. Rumors of a competitive tour to England and Wales echoed through the clubhouse, along with talk of the club's first serious run at the Niagara RFU championship. It was rugby heaven for a guy in the prime of his fitness, with no other serious obligations and an ever-growing keenness for the sport.

The trial match was held on the first weekend in April, the annual intrasquad game among the Centaurs' best players, from which the selection committee would choose the first, second and third men's sides. It was a dark, rainy afternoon, favoring the Welshmen on the roster, as this was the weather they'd grown up with. Of the fifty players taking part in the trial, roughly half were from the British Isles, having played rugby since the age of seven or eight. In the locker room, I was given an old team jersey—dark blue with the small orange figure of a Centaur—and then I went outside into the gloom, jogging around the park to get my head straight for the match.

It was a fast, physical and muddy affair: more competitive, and a lot dirtier, in every respect, than the club scrimmages we'd had on the two Saturdays leading up to it. I played the entire match between Tony and Alf; the Englishman and the local kid split the game on the other side, with the Welsh hooker begging off with an ankle sprain. (This was not the last time a teammate would duck head-to-head competition by claiming an injury. Sometimes I lost my spot, but I always showed up.) After the game, I was filthy, exhausted, and soaked to the skin by the needles of cold rain that had fallen throughout. A huge red welt appeared on my thigh, where an opposing player had stomped me in a ruck. But I'd played pretty well, capitalizing on my fitness in getting around the pitch, often keeping up with the loose forwards. And I had a quick strike in the scrums— taking one against the head from each of the other two contenders for A-side hooker, and giving up none.

The players all shook hands, and I went off beneath one of the oak trees bordering the field. Putting on my sweatshirt, I was in the midst of cooling down when the first-side scrumhalf, an easygoing Welshman named Phil, called over that Cye was about to name the first side. By the time I changed into my sneakers and ran over to the clubhouse, one of the committee members was announcing the third side for a match the following Saturday, versus Brampton RFC.

I was standing by the bar in my wet shorts and IT'S NOT A GAME, IT'S A BLOODY RELIGION Florida rugby T-shirt, when Cye Beechey approached, dressed in a striped club tie and dark blue sweater, with a serious look on his face.

"Young man, I truly hope . . . ," Beechey said, laying a hand on my shoulder, "that you'll dress better than that when we go over to Wales. I was born there, you know."

The coach revealed a crisp, new Centaurs jersey that he was hiding behind his back. It was printed with a large white "2" on the reverse, the hooker's number. "Here's a first-side jersey for you," he said. "Wear it proudly, lad."

Over at one of the tables, Ray Williams was sitting with his brother, Adrian, a local policeman. They beckoned to me, and I couldn't help grinning as I went over. "First of the day, son," said Ray, handing me a pint of stout.

We won our first three matches, over Brampton, London Ontario RFC, and the Toronto Nomads, during which I solidified my place on the first side. Playing with Tony Spencer made that a lot easier. Just three years removed from his international playing days, with a broad back that gave him the heft of a jukebox, Spencer would tuck me under his arm like a little bird and pile drive into the enemy front row. We were up against some formidable packs, but he was an immovable object. With Glazebrook's length effectively holding off the opposing tighthead, I had plenty of room to swing out from my right hip and sweep the tunnel with that foot, my calf practically touching the grass I was so low. We feasted on other teams' balls. I even made the front page of the local newspaper, churning my way through a melee of Nomad players with the ball in my hands.

The Centaurs played the same forward-driven style we'd used at Florida, though their approach to game preparation couldn't have been more different. Beneath heavy gray skies, we warmed up as a team, usually on an adjacent field out of the opposition's line of sight. When the referee blew his whistle to summon the captains, we ran onto the pitch: a tight, silent mass of dark blue jerseys and emotionless faces, spreading out to our positions without a word, all business. I'd finish up with a little stretching and a silent prayer, then I'd push down my socks, spit into the grass, and insert my mouthpiece.

Things were going well at the health club, so smoothly in fact, that I'd spoken to Surfer on the phone about flying up to Ontario. His reserve appointment had come up sooner than expected, and he was looking for a job and a rugby club. I'd already told Cye Beechey and the Ghetto about him, and now I'd have someone to hold the ax handle when I unlocked the door to the spooky old farmhouse, which I'd dubbed the Estate.

One morning at work I was showing a middle-aged couple and their two bored teenagers around the club, trying to interest the husband in becoming a member. After completing the tour, the man surprised me when we entered the little sales cube overlooking the gym. He asked how much a lifetime family membership would be and when I said $2,500, he wrote a check for the full amount, shaking my hand vigorously after signing the agreement.

Within seconds, the Ghetto had heard about the sale, bounding down the stairs from his office and herding me back into the nearly soundproof cube. "Blade, this is key," he said, using my old nickname. He bombarded me with forearms, throwing me against the wall, a move that startled a group of weight lifters out on the floor. "Bonus! You just made the quota for the weekend. Good ol' Blade. We'll go out tonight and celebrate."

Jeff gave me a fifty-dollar bill. "Start without me, if I don't make it in time," he said.

After lunch, I was at the front desk, talking to the receptionist, Janet, a buxom young brunette, when Dave, the so-called head of sales, buzzed to say that someone wanted to speak to me. I asked what it was regarding, and Dave said, "His name is Mr. Mustakas. He says it's a personal matter."

I didn't know anyone by that name. But I was on a roll, and ready to sell Lake Ontario to Mr. Mustakas, if he was even slightly interested in water. Intrigued, I zoomed out to the sales area.

Dave was in his cube, talking on the phone. I didn't trust that beady-eyed son of a bitch as far as I could throw him. In the next office was a couple in their mid-thirties; the man, wearing a dark suit, trim and mustachioed, looked like a squash player. The woman, plain and unsmiling, was dressed in a conservative skirt and fake pearls, looking out at the gym.

I bounced into the room and shook the man's hand. Confirming who I was, he said, "I'm Officer Mustakas, and this is Officer Russell, of Immigration Canada."

He showed me a badge. "Did you realize, Mr. Atkinson, that after working one day in Canada without the proper papers, that you

violated the immigration laws, and you may be subject to deportation, or two years in prison, and a fine of two thousand dollars?"

Officer Russell nodded in agreement, and Mustakas continued:
"You're under arrest, Mr. Atkinson. We'd like you to accompany us
to our office downtown."

Chapter 22

Operation: Frog Hop

Ghetto smelled a rat. Whether it was the boxy sedan that Officers Mustakas and Russell had arrived in, or the cheap, government cut of their clothes, something propelled my old buddy from his second-floor office and down the stairs before I'd even received the bad news. Just as Mustakas was preparing to escort me out, the Ghetto appeared in the doorway with a shit-eating grin on his face, welcoming these first-time visitors to Burlington Wellness and Strength and pumping Officer Mustakas's hand like he was the lord mayor himself.

All a misunderstanding, the Ghetto insisted, just a matter of dotting the i's and crossing the t's on the right piece of paper; confounding government red tape, made it difficult for a legitimate businessman to stay afloat when he had to remain abreast of a thousand federal regulations that seemed to change every week. But he was all about compliance, Jeff said. As my employer, he felt compelled to accompany me to the employment center, but apologized for not shaving that morning, asking Officer Mustakas if they could postpone the initial hearing to the following day, which would allow time for proper grooming, et cetera.

Jeff talked to people in such a bullshit way, I was amazed when

Mustakas didn't even flinch (*shaving!*) during this ridiculous monologue. Instead, he agreed to the postponement, after taking my Massachusett's driver's license and Social Security card. Upon mentioning they'd be contacting the FBI about my case, Officer Mustakas and his partner bid us a good afternoon, and left the club.

Jeff waved cheerfully, and then we raced upstairs to his office, locking the door behind us. Immediately the Ghetto telephoned half a dozen barristers, starting with Jason, his personal attorney, but all of them were either in court, meeting with clients, or on the golf course. In between these calls, I phoned my mother, telling her to plead ignorance if the FBI called. Always calm and levelheaded, my mom said that she'd let my father know right away, and that I should be honest and do the right thing.

Taking the phone back, the Ghetto answered a page from the receptionist: Jason was on the line. The slippery Toronto barrister instructed Jeff to play up the Acadia connection, his ignorance of the finer points of the law, and the fact that he and I were great pals. Jason also said that we needed to draft a letter to Mr. Daniel Allantosh at the Canadian Employment Centre in Hamilton, stressing my unique qualifications for the job and that, by hiring me, the Ghetto had expanded his business, creating jobs that hadn't existed prior to my employment (he'd hired a kid to clean the pool).

Consequently, I went over to the typewriter and began writing to the honorable Mr. Allantosh, calling this most pressing matter to his attention; that I, Jeff the Ghetto, had encountered many obstacles in administering to my business, and after careful analysis had arrived at the fact that I needed a well-qualified general manager, who I could trust implicitly; the letter being typed on good paper—best cream-laid—and sealed with the Burlington Wellness and Strength crest—an Olympic barbell next to a winged foot—concluding with a plea to the foreign labor office to allow me to continue employing twenty-two full- and part-time staff, and assisting the health and well-being of local residents by retaining Jay Atkinson's unique services, yours most sincerely, the Ghetto, et cetera.

The next morning was rainy and cold. I was feeling as glum as the weather when Jeff met me in the club parking lot at eight thirty, opening the door to his Caddy for the ride over to the employment center. It was a drab collection of particleboard cubicles reminiscent of 1950s Soviet décor. Inside a windowless room, I signed a document with my name, place and date of birth, permanent address and Social Security number, admitting that I had worked in Canada illegally. A Cold War vibe permeated the entire ordeal, with a handful of bureaucrats in ill-fitting suits looking on. It appeared that I'd really stepped in the shit this time.

Officer Mustakas turned out to be all right. He said I could request a hearing and thereby risk certain deportation, or leave the country of my own accord within seven days. Once I was processed through at the border, said Mustakas, I could cross back an hour later, so long as Canadian Customs allowed me to return as a tourist. I simply was not permitted to work, unless I was able to obtain the appropriate visa.

The Ghetto shook hands with Mustakas and a couple of other functionaries who were standing around, then led us back through the maze of cubicles, into the threadbare lobby and onto the street. Walking to his car, the Ghetto began to pummel me, and said, "Fuck 'em. The government's just a bunch of flunkies, anyhow. We'll rally 'em at their own game." He threw me against the Caddy. "We'll have the last laugh, Blade. It's a good scam." Ghetto pounded me with a left to the body, and a slap to the head. "Good man! Good man, the ol' Blade."

Two days later, Jeff and I drove to the U.S. border, stopped on the bridge over to Niagara Falls, and handed the exit document to a U.S. Customs agent, who smiled and waved us through: I hadn't broken any American laws. Then we looped around Niagara Falls, New York, barely noticing the phenomenon that attracts thousands of daily visitors. Trying to find another route back to Canada, the Ghetto passed through a grimy industrial area that contained a huge Shredded Wheat plant, belching gray smoke that smelled like they were making cereal by recycling old tires.

Eventually Jeff stumbled upon a narrow, two-lane bridge with signs pointing to Canada. At a tiny booth, a young woman in a blazer stopped the car, asked two or three questions, and leaned down for a moment to scrutinize the two of us. The Ghetto smiled broadly. And there was such a fine, frank, openhearted manner about him—coupled with his Rudy Valentino eyelashes, rosy cheeks and sporty attire (the Burlington Wellness and Strength polo, wide-wale corduroys and spotless tennis shoes), with Gordon Lightfoot crooning "The Wreck of the Edmund Fitzgerald" from the car stereo—that the pretty young customs officer just laughed, allowing us passage.

In a little more than two hours, I'd departed Canada, had a letter authorized that I'd indeed left, and then returned, semi-triumphant; officially, I had a clean slate for an additional three months, provided that I didn't continue working without proper authorization.

The Ghetto turned up the stereo, roaring along the Queen Elizabeth Way. "Operation: Frog Hop a success," he said. "Fuck 'em. I ought to send Makookas [his version of the immigration officer's name] the bill for gas. Just another useless government expense." He cuffed me on the side of the head. "Beat 'em at their own game. Fuckin' good ol' Makookas. Way to go, Blade. Good man, good man."

That weekend the Centaurs played a match against the Harlequins in Brantford, Ontario, notable for being hockey star Wayne Gretzky's hometown. The Harlequins facility included three regulation-sized rugby pitches, a clubhouse, concession stands, and a pub. We were playing every weekend now, and I was amazed at the well-maintained rugby facilities scattered across the Golden Horseshoe. Leaving the Harlequins clubhouse following another first-side victory, I couldn't help wondering what sort of a rugby player I'd be if I'd grown up in the sport. Still, with another win under my belt, I was happy that rugby had found me, and glad to be part of it.

After picking up my car at Sherwood Forest Park, I headed into downtown Burlington to a pub called the Duke of Buckingham. The Duke was located on the old village square, a rustic, low-ceilinged place with mahogany furnishings and an upholstered bench in red leatherette running along the walls. According to a newspaper article, the Duke of Buckingham pub had been there for a hundred years.

Before long, the Williams brothers had entered the pub, followed by Cye Beechey; our scrumhalf, Phil, and his wife, Denise; John Kennedy, the winger; our star fullback, Collin Calloway, who'd played professional soccer, and his obnoxious second wife, Rachel; and the only other American on the team, Duff Santamaccia, who was from Pennsylvania and had played college football at Pitt. Santamaccia had a good job with an American company doing business in Toronto; sometimes he'd pick me up from the health club in his Porsche for the drive over to rugby practice. When he passed the oddly named local grocery store, Duff would shout, "Food Master—discipline me!"

After a few pints and some laughs, the jukebox blasting, I'd just begun to loosen up, asking the fellows where we were heading next, when Phil and his wife got up to leave, then Cye, and Adrian Williams, who had to work a shift that night and was drinking club soda. Even Santamaccia, a rakish fellow with dark hair and a slick black mustache, cut out early: he had a date with a waitress over in Oakville.

Sitting there with Ray Williams, I lamented over the dearth of hell-raising among the Centaurs: no singing, nudity, or late-night party crashing. Ray had a family to get home to, and standing up awkwardly from the little table, his back sore from the third-side game, the Welshman reached over to pick up the check.

"It's never going to be like Florida," he said. "But you're playing for a good club. That's what it's going to be about now, son: the rugby."

Surfer bought his airline ticket with the promise of a job; a free, if run-down and decrepit, place to stay; and a first division rugby club to play for. By the time my old pal arrived, neither one of us had gainful employment, though Jeff maintained that he wouldn't quit until he'd secured our working papers. As a result, he paid his attorney to draw up some official-looking documents, listing Surfer and me as company officers. Meanwhile, we worked out at the club, spent our afternoons painting the interior of the house, and went to practice in the evenings.

It was cold for late April, going down below freezing at night, and it rained nearly every day. After rugby and a quick beer at the Poacher, we retreated to the Estate with a space heater one of the guys had loaned us. Two big pieces of foam covered with old sleeping bags nearly filled the room; a bottle of orange juice, gallons of springwater, aspirin and a six-pack of Brador were kept in the unheated, walk-in closet; writing paper and envelopes and books: *Walden, Sometimes a Great Notion, The Hotel New Hampshire* and *Madame Bovary*; the walls painted a monastic white, and the gabled roof and gothic window giving way to peeking stars, the full moon and the vast ominous shadow of the lake. It was the ideal rugby house, and sometimes at night I dreamed of inviting Dave Civil,

Psycho, Noel, Wee Wee, Conrad, Carlos and Pokey Whelan to come up and play for the Centaurs: what a team that would've been.

After two weeks of running around, and all the time Surfer and I spent creating incorporation papers, signing trumped up documents and filling out forms, Immigration Canada denied our visa applications. Disgusted with all this bureaucracy—first the Marine Corps, then the Canadian government—and nearly broke, Surfer decided to pack it in. One cold gray afternoon, I drove him to Buffalo to catch a flight home. The final indignity occurred at the border when U.S. Customs searched the car with a drug-sniffing dog. Buffalo is a dismal place, especially in the rain, and I had to drop Surfer off in a hurry. I was supposed to be in Niagara Falls within the hour for a last-ditch meeting at the provincial employment center.

Neither Surfer nor I said very much on the ride from the border to the airport. I felt bad for dragging him up to Burlington for a job that never materialized, spending the last of his military pay to get there and then going back with nothing. The rain fell in pattering drops and at the terminal, Surfer ran around to the hatchback, grabbed his bag, and we shook hands quickly.

"See you whenever," I said, and we both looked away. Then I jumped back in the Firebird and gunned it out of the airport.

I'd given him a slew of nicknames—Surf, Beamer, Bean, Tab Hunter—the smiler, the optimist, the workout partner, the eternal pragmatist; once called by me a new kind of Neal Cassady, one not beaten down a single iota by melancholia. The beach bum, the laugh track, the horniest white boy in any man's land, the golden boy with the gutter mouth, the lad of the short hangover, had finally hit the road and gone his own way. Ray Williams was right: Florida was over.

An hour later, I was waiting on Jeff at the labor center in Niagara Falls. He sure was a persistent son of a gun. At Acadia, we'd pretty much exhausted the ways to sneak into a beer garden—fake tickets, fake hand stamps, leaving windows unlocked and taping down the latch on one of the rear doors. In a memorable ploy, the Ghetto once took the extraordinary step of hiding in a cabinet in the weight room. It was the size and shape of a large coffin, used for storing Olympic plates, and after spending the afternoon working out, the

Ghetto pretended to exit the building, doubling back and climbing into the cabinet like a pumped-up Dracula. Exhausted from three hours of heavy squats and dead lifts, he fell asleep, awakened at 8 P.M. by the thump of disco music.

At the appointed time, he opened one of the rear doors to the field house, and Coop and I scurried inside. "Bonus," said the Ghetto.

At the labor center, Mr. Allantosh handed me a piece of paper known as a 1097, a thirty-day temporary work visa, recorded as "Discretionary entry" and stipulating "must work in a managerial capacity *only* at Burlington Wellness and Strength Institute. No change of status or extension to be considered without approval from Canada Employment Centre. Must verify departure from Canada on or before 4 June." The document also stated "Foss neg," which meant that I'd passed a thorough background check by the FBI.

After we'd driven through customs again, Jeff in his Caddy and I at the wheel of the Firebird, we pulled up beside each other on the bridge. The sun was breaking up the clouds, and there was a hint of spring in the air. Ghetto leaned out and said, "Carpe diem. We fucked 'em all, buddy." I laughed and said, "Right on," and we roared off.

With Surfer gone, I spent Thursday evenings after practice at the Duke of Buckingham or the Poacher, having dinner and talking with the rugby players who stopped in. Duff Santamaccia had just purchased a twenty-seven-foot cabin cruiser for tooling around Lake Ontario, and after a couple of pints, he invited a few of us to go barhopping down the coast.

It was just after eight thirty at night. Phil and Denise, John Kennedy, Collin and Rachel, and Duff and I clambered down an alley to the local marina, and Captain Hindgrinder, as Duff referred to himself aboard ship, fired up the engine and sailed out of the harbor.

Drew Cooper's younger brother Todd was also on board, a native Montrealer who Ghetto had hired at the club and who also played for the Centaurs. Our cruise to the Riverside, a waterfront bar in Oakville, was smooth and uneventful. Captain Hindgrinder moored at their dock, entering the Riverside like a rock star in his white dinner jacket and dark glasses. We drank and mingled, and when the bar closed Todd and I shanghaied two attractive girls onto the boat, a pair of sisters who had gone out dancing.

My date was named Isabel, a pert-nosed redhead in a gold lamé top, white yoga pants, and high heels. Duff had a fully stocked liquor cabinet down below, and Isabel and I helped ourselves to the vodka and orange juice, retiring to the aft cabin. We were an hour out of port when the engine suddenly went dead. The boat rocked back and forth on the swell, and the ignition revved weakly as Duff tried to restart the engine. Nothing doing.

I left Isabel in the cabin and went topside. Waves almost three feet high pushed the boat this way and that. Duff was at the wheel, cursing his rotten luck: out of gas. No reserve tank. No radio. No food. We were a mile offshore, far enough out to prevent us from being seen. A complete novice on the water, Duff had a lot of money and self-confidence, though he sometimes lacked a thimble's worth of common sense.

Rachel discovered a flare gun beneath one of the seats and began firing it at the low, black sky. I whispered to Collin that we'd probably need those in the morning, when more boats were likely to be about, and he tried to get Rachel to listen but she was on the verge of hysterics. Four times, a thin line of red quivered into the night sky, popped open in a circle of light, and then fizzled out. Finally, Collin disarmed her. He handed me the gun and I checked under the seat: there were two flares left.

I went below, ducking into the tiny cabin where I'd left Isabel. She was curled up against the back wall in the dark, and the news stunned her. Phil and his wife crawled down into the cabin, not knowing we were there, and Denise began crying and, in her lovely Welsh accent, said, "We're going to sink. Oh, Phillip. The children!"

Feeling a rush of claustrophobia, I took Isabel by the hand and got out of there. On deck, I huddled with Santamaccia, Todd and Kennedy. My advice: Save the last two flares, drop anchor, and get some sleep. In the morning, another boat was bound to come along and we could flag them down.

The next day, things only got worse. I dozed for maybe an hour, waking up to several of the crew puking over the side. The water was still rough, and though it wasn't yet raining, a storm was brewing on the horizon, and there wasn't another craft in sight. We hung around at anchor until 7:30 A.M., the water turning glassy and dead—the calm before the storm.

Calloway and I started paddling for the town of Grimsby, which appeared to be close by. Up front, Todd and Duff also took turns, feet locked into the chrome hitches, heads hanging down over the bow, trunks perpendicular to the water. It was excruciating, but at least they could get an actual stroke going. Collin and I and John Kennedy worked the stern, armed with the other paddle and a pair of water skis, our ribs pinched against the side of the hull.

We rowed while the others slept, or puked, and the morning and then the afternoon dragged along. In the end, Captain Hindgrinder and his crew were rescued, when a trio of salmon fishermen spotted our last flare and towed us to shore. We didn't know until we got back to town that our friends and teammates thought it was much worse than it was, or appeared to us. Phil's babysitter had called one of the other Centaurs after 2 A.M., who, in turn, phoned the Burlington police. A report had already been filed of a boat matching the description of Santamaccia's that had gone down not far from Oakville.

Some began to think the worst. They called the harbor police, the Ontario Provincial Police, and the RCMP. They almost called Phil's mother over in Britain. By late Friday afternoon, the Poacher was hosting a deathwatch while the police broke into some of our cars looking for suicide notes.

No chance of that with a bunch of rugby players. When we finally turned up at the Poacher after dark on Friday, several people were ticked off—especially at Santamaccia—although a festive mood prevailed. The bar was filled to capacity, and Cye Beechey stood on a chair, shouting to get everyone's attention.

"Ladies and gentlemen, concerned citizens and well-wishers: I just want to say that, from now on, I don't want Jay and Phil and Collin to go anywhere together, ever again," he said, provoking widespread laughter. "The first team can't afford it."

But I could see the writing on the wall. We finished the spring season 3–0 in league play, and 6–1 overall. My visa ran out in June, and the Ghetto had failed to make any headway on an extension.

He wanted to keep trying, but in a phone conversation my dad said I should come home: getting deported would prevent me from attending reunions at Acadia, and visiting my Canadian buddies in the future. Besides that, I'd been invited to tour England and Wales with the Centaurs and wanted to come back to Burlington in September to practice with the team.

I packed my bag, said good-bye to the fellows at the Duke of Buckingham, and flew home for my sister Jodie's wedding. She was marrying her college sweetheart, John Berry, who'd been a high school quarterback and cocaptain of the football and track teams. On the morning of the wedding I came down to the kitchen in just my striped ascot and underwear, cracking everyone up.

A few days later, I overheard my dad talking to my sisters. "Down at the office, you can tell the difference between the educated and the uneducated salesmen, like me," he said. "[Educated salesmen] can deal with—talk to—other educated people, our best clients. Sometimes, in meetings, I can't follow a lot of what's being said. Half my age, and I work for two-thirds the money—successful, working my tail off, but for the nickel and dime."

Fourth of July weekend I drove to the Cape with Glenn Gallant and an old soccer pal, Brian Raymond. We banged around the nightclubs, went swimming, and Brian and I took a long run on Seagull Beach. Coming home on Route 1, the day was hot and sticky. I took up the map and explained to Brian that Nahant Beach, a thin jetty of land over near Lynn, Massachusetts, was actually an isthmus.

"I bet it gets busy around isthmus time," he said.

I was still laughing when they dropped me off at home. My sister Jill was right inside the door, crying on the phone. She hung up, looked at me, and said, "Dad had a heart attack."

Chapter 23

Visiting Hours

There he is, dead. Lying with his eyes closed, my father's heels are pressed together and the great barrel of his chest is still. His eyeglasses are on the table beside the bed, and the air smells of disinfectant.

My mother cries without making any sound, hugging herself, and my sisters grasp her by the elbows, slowing moving forward. It's late, and the hospital is quiet. My father's room is a tiny glass enclosure on the cardiac ward, the curtains drawn, just as they had been that afternoon in the cubicle next door. Inside was a thirty-year-old woman with a bad case of ventricular fibrillation and while we stood around my father's bedside, making small talk, nurses began rushing into the woman's room and one of them closed the curtains. Dread overcame my father and he took off his glasses. He didn't want to see what was happening, but we could all hear the beeping heart monitor, the squeak of rubber-soled shoes, and the whispering. His glasses missed the table and there was an etching sound as they struck the floor. I picked them up and rested them on the table just as a voice over the PA said that visiting hours had ended. My father shook my hand, and his grip was cool and dry like iron. Neither one of us spoke.

Next to the broken eyeglasses is a wrinkled peach pit, representing my father's last meal. We had watched as he savored it, joking that the peach would help get his blood pressure down. An intern came by for my father's chart and the man extended his hand, offering to take the slimy peach pit. But my father ignored him, dropping the stone onto the table.

Now the intern is sitting in the corner. Apparently my father was up late and fretful, and asked if the attendant would stay and keep him company. But my father didn't say much, and just kept watching the clock. The doctor had revealed that if there was going to be a second attack, it would occur within forty-eight hours. Shortly after midnight my father sat up in bed, clutched his chest, and died. The intern has told us this with a strange note in his voice, like he has proven something.

The black tubes of a stethoscope around his neck, the cardiologist enters the room, saying that my father's heart blew out like a tire. An autopsy won't tell us much, and he suggests we call a funeral director. The doctor touches my arm, saying he's very upset about all this, but mostly he looks bored. I hope my mother doesn't notice, and then thankfully, the doctor leaves.

There are a hundred things to do. Relatives who've been waiting for some news, like my grandmother, have to be told right away. My sisters must clean the house and begin making food for all the people who will be coming.

Now my mother leans over the bed, toward my father's corpse. His lips are brown and sunken into his beard. This kiss is different from the one this afternoon, when we were leaving and my father pulled my mother toward him. That went on for several seconds, embarrassing my sisters and brothers and me. Get a room, someone said. This is my room, said my father.

My mother brushes the narrow, papery lips. Her shoulders are shaking. Oh, Jim, she says. Finally the intern gets up from his chair and goes out. It's just family now. We stand on all sides of the bed, looking down at my father. He'll never eat a peach, or make small talk again.

My sisters usher my mother from the room. Against the crisp, white sheets, my father is a big man. His shoulders are broad like a weight lifter's and his legs are thick and hairy. His hands fall neatly to his sides and I can see his wedding ring, squeezing the girth of his finger. I pick up my father's eyeglasses and put them in my pocket and take up the peach pit. It flies directly from my hand into the empty wastebasket where it lands with a ringing sound. For an instant I can see the line the peach stone described through the air, and then it disappears.

My mother is waiting in the car, her knees drawn up and elbows pressed against her sides. Stuck above the visor is an envelope that contains my father's life insurance payment. We have to stop at the post office and mail it or they won't pay on the policy. For someone in the business, my father is poorly insured and unlucky to have skipped his premium this month. But if we get it postmarked right away, at least they'll honor the policy.

The town square is deserted. I leave the engine running at the curb and emerge with the premium envelope in my hand. The Fourth of July celebration is over and burnt metal sparklers and the gray casings of firecrackers litter the roadway. Next to the post office, my father's office is dark, his parking space empty. The name is printed on the awning and there's a sign that reads SORRY WE'RE CLOSED. *I drop the envelope into the slot and hear it falling down the chute. My mother turns her head and looks at me through the window. It's a brand-new sedan, a company car with leather seats and a nice radio. Soon we'll have to give it back.*

My grandmother lives a mile outside of town. When we were young, my sister Jodie and I would stay at Grandma's on weekends during the summer. The house includes a long farmer's porch with rattan curtains on three sides, where we'd lie on the planks, the shade penetrated by spindles of light and the air sweet with mown grass and honeysuckle. Inside, Grandma would rummage around the kitchen, making rhubarb jam and Yorkshire pudding.

Tonight the house looks abandoned. My mother waits on the porch while I go around and climb in the window. It's always unlocked; my father used to get in this way when he was home from the army. I creep through my grandmother's rhubarb patch, shove the window upward and hear the weights rattling in the wall. Pulling myself up, I dive through the narrow opening, the toes of my sneakers pawing against the shingles. My hands grip the edges of the sink and I thrust myself over, into the kitchen. My father's eyeglasses slide out of my pocket and the cracked lens bursts in the sink. I brush the particles into the drain and pick up what's left.

On the sideboard is a strawberry-rhubarb pie covered by an old tea towel. I hear the clock ticking and pass through the living room and unlock the front door. Grandma is asleep upstairs, and my mother and I go into the kitchen and wait.

It's 3:30 A.M. Grandma is an early riser but not this early. For a long while we just sit listening to the clock and an occasional nightingale. My mother glances over at the teakettle but nothing is said. Finally we hear the complaint of bedsprings and my grandmother laboring to her feet. On the kitchen table, my mother's hand closes into a fist. But there's only the sound of coughing and then the bed settles and it's quiet again.

When Grandma stirs the next time, there's light seeping through the windows. Now I can make out a few details: the table scratched and scored by fifty years of eating and drinking; a photograph of my father in his army tunic, smiling with his hand around Grandma's shoulder; a magnet stuck to the refrigerator that proclaims IT'S GREAT TO BE BRITISH. My grandmother came over on the boat in 1922. She was sick the whole way and vowed she'd never go back.

Grandma descends the staircase, and my mother's face is as white as the tablecloth. At the bottom of the steps Grandma enters the bathroom without noticing us. Each day she lets the waste build up in the toilet and then flushes and cleans it in the morning, an old habit to conserve water. This takes a couple of minutes. Then we hear the tap running in the sink as my grandmother washes her hands.

The light grows stronger throughout the house. Dressed in a shabby old nightgown, Grandma tips open the bathroom door and stands in the hall blinking at us, her hair matted to one side and markings on her cheek from the pillow. After a moment, she realizes why we're here and staggers toward the table. From deep in her chest comes a sound like woo-hoo *that makes gooseflesh on the back of my neck. I rise from my seat, and the eyeglasses slip from my pocket again and the other lens shatters on the floor. Grandma wails a second time and my mother gets up to fill the teakettle. Rugby is a million miles away, and I'm pretty sure I'll never play again.*

Chapter 24

The Night Shift

A New York lawyer who was an old friend of the family said that my dad's wake equaled that of a U.S. senator's; and he knew what he was talking about, having recently attended one. Grown men did, indeed, cry, attending in droves to pay their respects, none more emblematic and pitiful than the little fellow in the rumpled suit, no tie, going bald, who did a brief herky-jerky dance in front of us, and said, "I didn't know him so good . . . I think we had lunch once. He seemed like such a good man."

Later, when the crowd had boiled down, I went to the rear of the chapel to stretch my legs. Uncle Jack was sitting in a metal folding chair, wearing an old sport coat, dark slacks and a pair of zippered dress boots with white socks. The stench of flowers was overwhelming. I sat beside him for a while, staring at the opposite wall. The replay of my dad's last hours had filled me with a retroactive dread, as he lay there waiting for what he must've known was coming: the second, fatal heart attack.

I started to talk about it and Uncle Jack put his arm across my chest to stop me. "Your father's troubles are over," he said. "Yours are just beginning."

Returning to the house afterward, I came across a floral arrangement that had been delivered when we were out. It was a large horseshoe composed of navy-blue roses and other dried flowers, girdled by a sash imprinted with: DEEPEST SYMPATHIES. BURLINGTON CENTAURS RFC.

For the next few weeks, I didn't get out of bed earlier than noon, and hardly accomplished a thing when I did. I soon found out that I couldn't read for too long at a stretch, or do any real writing, and had zero interest in watching television, listening to music or going out with my friends. A two-mile jog around the neighborhood left me exhausted.

One of the temp agencies I had visited before I left for Canada phoned to say they had a few openings. I was broke, and took a second shift job at a gigantic warehouse twenty minutes away in Woburn, Massachusetts. They stocked thousands of computer parts, from the size of a bread box to chips so small you couldn't see them inside the little plastic bags, each coded with a serial number. Orders came in for diverse parts in different combinations; we gathered these components, and shipped them express to various locations around the world.

Though it was a humid summer, the warehouse was cool, quiet and dimly lit. Early on, my boss figured out that I had a pretty good memory and an eye for detail, and he began giving me the most sophisticated orders. At the beginning of the shift, I'd receive a printout with a list of numbers, and then drive around in this little electric cart, piecing together the order. The shelving rose thirty or forty feet toward the ceiling—the cart had a lift mechanism that boosted me to the upper levels—and cruising around in that half darkness was like exploring the canyons of the moon.

Each order was like a puzzle that took about an hour to solve, and time passed quickly. Sometimes my boss and I would talk for five or ten minutes at the start of the shift, going over the things he wanted me to do. It was the perfect job under the circumstances: I had to think, but not too much, and people mostly left me alone.

Around the first week of August, I received a phone call from Cye Beechey. It had been nearly a month since my father had died: a hard, dreamlike four weeks. I'd be lying if I said that things had returned to normal, but Jamie and Patrick had gone back to hanging around the house and throwing their clothes on the floor. Jill was starting to pack for college, and Jodie and her husband were leaving for Dallas soon, where John had taken an engineering job. My mother was selling real estate again, and meeting for coffee with her radical friends: a group of middle-aged women determined to save the town's historic buildings from demolition and redevelopment.

Cye asked how I was doing, and inquired about my mother and the rest of the family. Presently the conversation turned to rugby matters, including the Centaurs tour to England and Wales, now just a month away. The team was practicing in earnest, Beechey said, and had acquired commitments from several good clubs over-seas to provide the Centaurs with matches. An extensive fund-raising campaign had proven successful, and those players who participated in the eighteen-day tour would only need to pay for their airfare. The club would supply accommodations, meals and travel within England and Wales. In addition, each player would receive a blazer with the Centaurs insignia, a club sweater, tie, golf shirt, two T-shirts and a kit bag. A send-off dinner was planned for the night before the trip, and the local newspaper, *The Burlington Post*, had assigned a reporter to keep track of our fortunes by telephone, from which he'd contribute articles to the sports section.

I was in lousy shape, returning from work pretty tired just from riding around in a golf cart. When I informed Cye that I hadn't been training, he said, "Look, son, the lads on the first team would really like to have you on tour. So would I. You're a very useful player."

I began to clear my throat, but Cye went on. "Above that, you're a popular *person* on the club. Get running again, and be in Burlington by the twentieth. That's plenty of time to sort things out."

I told Cye that I wasn't sure if I was up to it.

"Not only will you enjoy this tour, but you'll treasure it for years to come," he said.

A week later, I'd completed my fifth consecutive training day—a fifteen-minute jog to the high school track, a hard mile, eight fifties, sit-ups and push-ups and star jumps, then a jog back home—and handed in my notice at work. The local Rotary Club had decided to honor my dad, a recent past president, by sponsoring part of a new exercise trail in his name. That evening, I ran a mile up to the woods surrounding Bon Secours Hospital, where the trail was located. The current Rotary president had asked me to choose which segment of the course our family would like to see dedicated to my father's memory.

Running the loop at dusk, I chose a nice uphill grade that curved off through a stand of white birch. At the top of the hill, chest heaving, I stopped to unzip my sweat jacket, producing a tooled silver flask.

"Here's to you, Big Guy," I said, taking a drink. The whiskey burned my sinuses; I spit, laughed, recapped the little vacuum bottle and headed down the backside of the hill.

By early September, I found myself in Aberavon, a gritty seaside borough along the road between Cardiff and Swansea in South Wales. The touring party sat in the grandstand for a first-class match between the Aberavon Wizards and Llanelli; afterward, in the members-only bar, a few of their club men treated us to a good look around, a Wizards' centenary program, and a few pints of Toby.

The barmaid, Angela Morgan, was a lovely, young, raven-haired girl, with luminous blue eyes, a creamy complexion, and a pleasing figure: long legged, buxom and coltish in her movements. Standing nearby, a Wizards supporter, an old gent in a waterproof coat and striped club tie, was refreshing his inner man and eyeing us kindly. He saw Angela wink at me through the crowd, pushing a slip of paper that contained her phone number over the bar to me.

The Wizards supporter grinned, and said, "All right, son?" a greeting favored by all the Welshmen I'd met. He bought Jeff Coles, Alf Glazebrook and me a round of whiskies, and after they were passed around, I had the heavy little tumbler in my hand when the old gent sighted over his glass of rye, his face crinkling up as he smiled.

"To be your age, in Wales, playing rugby? It's magic," he said. "It's the best time of your life."

We won our first match, against Harrow RFC near London, 6–3, but I was a reserve, since I'd be going back home after the tour, and the club was auditioning a couple of replacements at hooker. Before the game, several of the boys visited Trafalgar Square, thousands of pigeons wheeling overhead in great flocks, possessed of an eerie group mind. While we were loitering near the statue of Admiral Nelson, a pigeon lit on a young girl's hand. It took the crust of bread she was offering, and defecated on her wrist and forearm.

Attempting to soothe the girl, Cye Beechey went over. "Oh, don't worry, that's lucky," he said.

Puzzled, the little girl said, "How's that?"

"Lucky it didn't shit on your head," Beechey said, and the girl laughed so hard she had tears in her eyes.

On the outside, Beechey appeared as a lovable old sot, unguarded in his comments and intemperate in his habits, an opinionated, garrulous, beet-faced old thruster, most at home within an arm's length of the clubhouse bar. Then in his mid-forties, Cye was a successful salesman and shrewd rugby strategist, however; despite coming across like a blustery gent straight out of *Fawlty Towers,* he'd put together a team that got the club, after only ten years of existence, where the club committee wanted to go: the Niagara Rugby Union first division championship.

On the bus ride over to Chepstow on the Welsh border, Beechey, our self-appointed historian, pointed out a medieval castle on the banks of the River Wye. "Two Welshmen held that castle for months against fifteen thousand Englishmen," he said. "Eventually, the English found out it was a trick. There were three Welshmen."

Wales was much as I'd imagined: with darkened skies and lush green valleys, the water rolling right up to the edge of seaside farms. In the small towns, the cottages were neat and immaculate, set close together on narrow cobblestone streets, a sprinkling of pubs and shops tucked between them.

In Chepstow, I was billeted with the Centaurs first-side captain, Steve Carter, a gruff, grizzled, bowlegged flanker, originally from Gloucester, England. Carter, at age thirty-seven, was white-haired with a little Vandyke beard and dark blue eyes. A man of few words on the pitch and off, Steve could silence a group of chattering rookies merely by glancing at them, and some of the boys discreetly offered their condolences when they found out he and I were rooming together.

Welsh hospitality was superb: civic receptions in the villages where we played, during which we'd be greeted by the lord mayor in his powdered wig and vestments; we were given club souvenirs, and a hot meal when we stumbled home to our billets at two or three o'clock in the morning; opposing players with names like Basher and Slasher and Cyclops making sure everything was just the way we liked it.

Chepstow had just been elevated to the Welsh premier division, and when Steve Carter and I were wandering through town, we struck up a conversation with a few of their players, including the first-side hooker, who was out with a leg injury. When he heard what position I played, this fellow emitted a low, sinister laugh.

"You're going to earn your wings tomorrow," he said, as he shook my hand.

Steve Carter just shrugged, offering no explanation for this remark. He'd cut his teeth on the sort of rugby played in Gloucestershire, and if I didn't know what to expect or how to handle it, that was my problem.

The match was played on a well-maintained pitch flanked by two boxed wooden grandstands. After dressing in silence, the starting fifteen gathered in a little anteroom in the clubhouse, our cleats knocking against the stone floor. There we sang a surprisingly emotional version of "O Canada," and ran onto the field. A smattering of applause floated down from the crowd. The home team was already out there, going through pregame drills. They had two kickers, a lefty and a righty, who were booming punts worthy of the NFL, and putting balls through the goalposts from unworldly angles and distances. Although that sort of finesse was quite different from the grinding of the forwards, the kickers' performance sent my heart rate soaring: I hadn't felt this much anxiety since my first match, back in Nova Scotia, against the coal miners from Stellarton.

I didn't have to wait very long for their hooker's prophecy to come true. Chepstow's lefty kicked off, the ball on a rising parabolic flight that barely cleared the required ten yards. No sooner had Alf Glazebrook taken down the kick when several opposing forwards piled into him, and the ball was buried in the tackle. The referee awarded the ensuing scrum to our side, digging in his heel to show us the mark.

The Centaurs regular tighthead prop, Tony Spencer, the former international, hadn't made the trip. Glazebrook had moved back to second row because of our shortage there, and up front I was playing with two guys I hadn't scrummaged with very much, except in training sessions. Jeff Coles, or Colesy, was a closemouthed Gloucester man like Steve Carter; a no-nonsense thirty-year-old who's motto was "retaliation first." Of all the players on tour, I knew Jeff Coles and Steve Carter the least, though I'd played with them back in Ontario. Being Englishmen, Colesy and Carter favored their young countryman for the A-side hooker's position, at least that was my guess; and both players knew I was going back to Massachusetts after the tour and wouldn't be playing with the Centaurs. So there was a measure of coolness in their attitude toward me.

With his bulky torso, black eyes and large rounded brow, Colesy looked like a gun-toting thug in a Jimmy Cagney movie, though with a sly sense of humor and an intelligent glint in his eye. I wasn't too worried about Colesy. To my left, our loosehead prop was a former wrestler and middle linebacker who had been playing rugby since high school. But when we solidified our eight-man pack, took our binds and prepared to engage with Chepstow, their front row, just a yard away, resembled a trio of bridge abutments. With mangled ears, sloping shoulders and wide necks, the Chepstow props and hooker stared across at us, chests rising and falling in unison, the veins standing out in their foreheads.

Just as the referee said, "Engage," I could make out the evil glimmer of a smile pass across their tight head's face.

Immediately the scrum compressed in a manner I had never experienced before: our shove, coming mainly from the second row, was somehow harnessed—*managed* is a better way to describe it—by the momentum of their tight five shooting across the gap; the result being that I was initially pushed downward, so low that my chin was between my knees, and with tons of force simultaneously coming from behind and in front of me, I was robbed of my breath.

Next, as Chepstow's pack surged, all eight churning in lockstep, the downward pressure rolled upward—the line of their shoulders was beneath ours now, lifting me up, higher and higher, until my feet were off the ground, pawing at thin air.

My neck was at an ungodly angle; for half a second, I flashed on the image of Seamus in his wheelchair. My head was pushed downward; my chin denting my upper chest, and my legs flailing as I tried to get my feet down. Still, Chepstow moved forward; using my peripheral vision, I saw Colesy, all 225 pounds of him, lifted into the air. Our front row was completely off the ground, our scrum coming apart—it was terrifying.

I resisted the temptation to cry out. I'm not sure I could've opened my mouth anyway, and it would've been a sign of weakness a minute into my first match on tour. I could hear the cervical vertebrae grinding in my neck, the tendons stretched to their limit. But I kept my cool, relaxing as much as possible given the position I was in. I was hoping that the ball would exit the scrum—at either end, I didn't care which—or the referee would blow the whistle for dangerous play. (A few years later, lifting the front row would become illegal, since a number of players at various levels of competition were catastrophically injured that way.)

Besides, I was pissed off—at my helplessness; over being dominated from the get-go in front of so many people; at the tighthead prop's little smirk; and at the notion that I was "earning my wings."

Finally, the whistle blew; the pressure relented, and Colesy and I thudded to the turf. Colesy got up first, stuck out his hand, and yanked me to my feet. "All right, mate?" he asked.

"I'm all right."

Immediately, we faced the trial of another scrum, only this time it was Chepstow's ball. For the first time in as many matches as I could recall, I kept both feet in a pushing position, never attempting to strike at a tighthead. That was part of the reason for Chepstow's tactics—intimidation being the other part—and I needed a minute or two to regain my senses; to swallow the fear that had welled up in my throat, and start playing rugby.

Twice more in the first half, Chepstow lifted our front row despite our resolve to win the ball. It was frightening and demoralizing each time. There was nothing to be done about superior technique, and I lost three or four tightheads that way, which had never occurred in North America. I struggled in those set pieces to keep my nerve, and afterward had to calm myself, steadying my feet and my throwing arm when the referee called for a lineout. Every scrum arrived with a sense of dread, though I received little sympathy from the referee and none from the opposing forwards. It was the closest I'd ever come to life and death in a sporting event, and the seconds crawled by like hours in the brief span before the ball came in the tunnel.

In the second half, fatigue among the players on both sides reduced the danger in the scrums, and the pace of the game, to some extent, began to come back to my level. It was a lesson that I'd carry with me in the hundreds of matches that I'd eventually play: hang on for the first few engagements, maintain your nerve, and let your fitness take over. I didn't come anywhere near stealing a tighthead, but I was getting most of my own ball, at least. Trying my best to contribute in other aspects of the game, I made a couple of tackles, cleaned up a few loose or bounding balls, and threw a clean lineout in Chepstow's end that led to a penalty against them, and three points on the kick. But lose the scrummaging and you lose the match, which we did, by eighteen points, and I walked off with my head down when the ref blew his whistle for full time, going straight off the pitch and alongside the painted wooden façade of the grandstand.

In the changing room, I hated every one of those Chepstow sons of bitches, especially their front row. To my mind, they had deliberately tried to injure my teammates and me, and I was furious about that. When I finally got up in my shorts and flip-flops, carrying a towel, an attendant said there weren't any showers, just something called a Welsh bath.

It was a square, featureless room, with two facing doors, no windows and a row of wooden pegs along each of the blank concrete walls. The doors opened into the home team's and visitor's changing rooms, and sunk into the floor was an immense tub, three feet deep, which took up nearly all the available space. Filled to the brim with scalding hot water, the bath, obscured by thick piles of steam, had a concrete bench all the way around that permitted you to sit in the water up to your neck. As I entered the warm, vapor-infused chamber, hanging my towel on a peg, players from both teams were easing themselves into the bath, talking and joking now, mostly in Welsh.

There was just room enough for all thirty players, arranged cheek by jowl. Since the field had been muddy and there was no place to rinse off, as more fellows climbed into the bath, the water turned a dingy gray color. There wasn't any seating arrangement and when I lowered myself into the water, so hot as to be nearly intolerable, I found myself jammed between Chepstow's loosehead prop and number eight. Their other prop was wedged in next to Colesy across the way, and the Chepstow player gestured toward me with his chin, saying something in Welsh to the guy beside me, and their loosehead slung his arm over my shoulder and replied in his native tongue, winking at me.

The changing room attendant was a thin, porcupine-headed fellow, past the age of fifty and dressed in black trousers, white shirt, and an apron that hung to his knees. He had a long, dour-looking face, a nose like a shattered red pear, and pendulous earlobes that fluttered when he came around with a tray and handed each of us a cup of hot tea. It seemed odd to have tea immediately after a match, when the usual impulse was to guzzle cold water or Gatorade, but the tea, brewed strong with a dash of milk, was just the right thing after playing eighty minutes of rugby.

After the cups had been given out, fragile bits of eggshell china imprinted with the Chepstow RFC insignia, the same long-faced, porcupine-headed attendant came back around and handed each of us a biscuit—a small, hard, shortbread-flavored cookie that you dunked in the milky tea while soaking in the bath.

We lounged in the tub for half an hour, until the water turned black and tepid, and our voices rose in a din as we kidded each other and talked about the match. No one was allowed in the bath except the players and the lone attendant, and he only when he had business there; when we finally climbed out, possessed by a keen sense of fellowship, we adjourned to the changing rooms to get dressed. We entered the clubhouse bar in our tour blazers and ties, where I leaned up by the taps with Chepstow's props and Colesy, who smacked me on the head and placed a pint in front of me.

The bar was snug and cozy, paneled in dark wood that rose head high, then a few feet of white plaster wall. Hung in this space and ringing the bar were a series of portraits, varying from old-fashioned oil paintings near the entrance, to black-and-white and then color photographs. These portraits depicted the first-side captains that had graced the Chepstow pitch since the club's inaugural season, in 1878. (The Welsh Rugby Union was formed three years later, in 1881.)

Armed with my pint, I took a tour around the small, crowded pub, studying each of these ruddy-faced lads, seated on a stool and wearing the club jersey and crest, which hadn't changed much in a hundred years. Rugby was compulsory in the Welsh schools, part of the national identity, and the country itself, with a population roughly equal to the state of Connecticut, had been an international powerhouse since the origin of the sport. Every little village had a rugby pitch and a clubhouse, and most had a ring of portraits like the one I was looking at. Traditionally, when the men came up from "the pit," the coal mine, grimy from head to foot, they blew off steam in a vigorous game of rugby and then climbed into the bath for a "cup of char," or tea.

Once all the players were in the bar, Chepstow's president, a tall, white-haired gent, welcomed the visiting tourists and remarked on the hardness of the match. Cye spoke next, his face squeezed crimson by his tight collar and tie; he thanked Chepstow for being such gracious hosts, and got choked up when he said how pleased he was to be home again, in Wales, after the passage of quite a few years.

Next, a dozen or so Chepstow players, all wearing club blazers and neckties, were formed into a choir against the wall. Accustomed as I was to bawdy songs, I was surprised when the Chepstow boys launched into a medley of traditional Welsh hymns. Blending their voices perfectly, the choir, including their loosehead prop and scrum-half, who I'd been looking at all afternoon, sang "Pantyfedwen," "Men of Harlech," and "Speed Your Journey," with a great deal of skill and feeling. Some of the fellows had long, drooping mustaches, like lancers or dragoons, and while they sang, I compared their bruised and abraded faces to the portraits from the club's early days, noting that little had changed in that part of the country.

The Welsh singing was a far cry from "I Used to Work in Chicago" and "I Don't Want to Join the Army." When the choir finished, one of our wingers, John Griffiths, who was from Cardiff originally and had played rugby there, set aside his pint and went over in front of the choir. With the others providing background harmony, Grif matched his beautiful tenor voice with the old Welsh standard, "Myfanwy." A lament of missed chances and lost love, in Welsh it begins:

> Pa ham mae dicter, O Myfanwy
> Yn llenwi'th lygaid duon ddi?

His hands clasped in front of him, Grif sang in a sweet, mellow tone, his eyes turned upward like an angel in a painting by Raphael. Though I couldn't understand the words, by the final chorus the emotion of the song was clear to me, as well as the hard guys ranged all around, their faces thoughtful, their aspect more childlike than they ever appeared on a rugby field.

> Forget now all words of promise
> You made to one who loved you well
> Give me your hand, my sweet Myfanwy
> But one last time, to say farewell

All I could think of was how much my dad would've enjoyed being there, standing with Cye and the vice chairman, dressed in his blazer and wingtip shoes, holding a pint glass.

The next day, we were off to Swansea in our well-upholstered coach. Rolling along through the green vales of the countryside, most of the boys hungover and lulled by the hum of the tires, Beechey interrupted our reverie by announcing, "If you look to the right, lads, you'll see the house where I was born." Then, from the back of the coach, Adrian Williams said, "And if you look to the left, you'll see the pond where he learned to walk on water!"

In every town, guys had the opportunity to change roommates and when someone asked Steve Carter if he wanted to swap, the old Gloucester man said no. "Jay's not so bad," Carter said, "for a Yank."

Houses in Wales are quite small by North American standards, and in Swansea, a coastal town of some 150,000 souls, Steve Carter

and I billeted with a young married couple and their infant daughter. Steve and I were to sleep in the couple's bed, while they bunked
in a glorified closet with the baby. Before I left Boston, I'd purchased
a cache of sports paraphernalia in a shop near Fenway Park, which
I'd been told would please our hosts when given as gifts. But in the
tiny kitchen the next day, I learned that the young couple had quar-
reled when the husband refused to take off the Red Sox cap I'd
given him—even after they'd gotten into bed.

From there we traveled to Llandeilo, losing a heartbreaker 4–3,
and two days later, the Centaurs had a match against the Vultures,
an alumni side from Cambridge University. Beechey sat me out against
Llandeilo, though my name was in the official game program (my
opposite number was a fellow aptly named Stuart Quick), and then
I got the starting job against the Vultures. When I ran onto the pitch
with Steve Carter, Jeff Coles and the rest of the Centaurs, I spotted
Angela Morgan, the sexy young barmaid I'd met after the Aberavon-
Llanelli match a few days earlier. Apparently, she'd seen a notice of
our match in the local papers and took the train over from Port Talbot, with her "brolly" (umbrella) and stylish, double-breasted raincoat,
to watch the game.

When the captains went out for their instructions, Steve Carter
returned to say that the referee was none other than Clive Norling,
the most well-known and highly rated official in Wales. Before he
retired, Norling, an imposing fellow who didn't take any guff, had
refereed thirty-five international test matches, including a quarterfinal in the World Cup. That he was refereeing what was, essentially,
a social match between two non-Welsh sides on a public ground
was unusual, to say the least. But Clive Norling is a bona fide rugby
man, prone to show up anywhere, anytime, for love of the sport.

At the kickoff, rain was falling in earnest. Though the Vultures had
a few reserves on the sideline, they were short a hooker, creating the
opportunity to play a half against each of the other two Centaurs,
the Englishman and the bowlegged Welshman. That was fine with
me, because after the Chepstow match these two were overheard
griping about not playing, and how I hadn't been any use in the
front row. (There was no mention of Jeff Coles, a formidable player,

being lifted off *his* feet.) So my Irish was up, and I looked forward to playing against these guys in front of the selection committee, since there were two matches remaining after the Vultures.

Norling was an efficient, authoritative presence, only inserting himself when necessary, allowing us to play on when there was an advantage even if the other side had committed a penalty. My fitness had caught up after the long layoff, and despite the cold steady rain, which pelted our backs in the scrums, I was getting around the park without difficulty. We scored an early try through the forwards, with Colsey bowling over their number eight after an efficient series of rucks.

In the waning minutes of the first half, the Vultures' inside center, a dashing, rangy fellow, kicked a little zigzag grubber through our defense that wobbled and bounced all the way past our twenty-two meter line. I was corner flagging across the pitch, and with the ball topping along in dangerous, open ground, I set off full bore in that direction. Their inside center was right on my heels, and a Vultures' flanker just a few meters behind him; racing for the ball, I could see that the nearest friendly jersey, worn by Steve Carter, was half the width of the pitch away.

The temptation with a rolling ball is to grab it on an easy, charitable bounce, jab-stepping to reverse course, and taking it back upfield. I'd seen gifted players do just that, feinting and spinning in one smooth motion, and then kicking the ball away, thirty or forty yards on the fly. If you mistimed that sort of thing, however, the first opposing player at the breakdown would keep one hand down low, out of the referee's sight, and give you a clever shove right over the ball. You'd both go sprawling, which would leave the ball free on the ground for the next Vulture to pick it up and scoot in for an easy try.

My best option was more in keeping with my skill level, and personality. I could hear the Vultures player right behind me, panting at my ear. When I reached the bouncing football, a scant fifteen meters from our in goal, I slid down on my right hip in the mud, gathered the ball in the crook of my right arm, securing it with my left hand as well, and popped to my feet; immediately the opposing center smashed into my right hip, driving us both into the mud.

In rugby, once on the ground, you must release the ball and make an attempt to get back on your feet. Crabbing away from the first tackler, who slid a couple of feet on the greasy turf, I jumped up, bringing the loose ball with me, as well as the certain knowledge that the opposing flanker, a stout fellow who was coming full tilt, would drive his shoulder into my kidneys a half second later.

After being drilled to the ground again, I released the ball and gathered it a second time. When I regained my footing, Steve Carter had arrived, coming around to take my little pop pass. He took a couple of strides and punted the ball out of bounds, relieving the pressure on our line.

Those two tackles had exhausted me, though I'd protected the ball just long enough for Steve's clearing kick. While I was bent over, hands on my hips and gasping for breath, Carter mussed my hair and said, "They can send a third man next time, if you like."

Cold rainy days like that, familiar to me from Acadia, made it easy to catch my second wind. Later in the match, I was chasing down a kick that ran over the touchline and when I got to the mark, John Griffiths and I were the only ones there. I motioned for him to chuck the ball in to me, before the other team arrived at the mark—this sort of quick throw-in is allowed, provided the ball travels at least five meters and is thrown in straight.

Behind me, I could hear the Vultures protest as the play was occurring, but as I grabbed the throw-in, Clive Norling bellowed, "Play on."

I dashed along the right touchline, ten, twenty, thirty meters flashing by, with a good portion of the Vultures defense angled toward me and running like devils. Glancing ahead, I realized that I wasn't going to beat the first tackler to the goal line, and determined not to be pushed out of bounds (which would mean a turnover in possession), I halted abruptly and veered inside, the nearest opposing player skidding past.

Squaring up, I ran at the next tackler, quite aware it was their number eight, one of the largest players on the field. At the last second, I made slight contact and went to the ground at his feet, causing the Vulture to go flying over me, and leaving the ball for Grif to pick up on the run. He took it forward into a tackle; the mob of Centaurs in pursuit secured the ball, recycled it, and Alf Glazebrook thundered in for a try.

I stole a handful of the Vultures' scrum put-ins, didn't surrender any, and we won the match, 17–4. Leaving the field covered in mud, I reached over to shake Clive Norling's hand, thanking him for the match.

"That was good ball you were throwing," he said, imitating the American football motion I used in the lineouts.

On the way to the changing room I was encircled by kids, who pressed in with tour programs and pens, clamoring for my autograph. I signed them all, wondering how any athlete can say no to children.

After I'd cleaned up, I found Angela Morgan waiting by the grandstand. She was a lovely girl, just turned nineteen; tall, poised and curvaceous, with dark hair, startling blue eyes fringed with long lashes, well-shaped hands and that musical accent that cut me to the quick. Huddled beneath her umbrella, we loped along Swansea's narrow streets, gazing at each other instead of the shopwindows, splashing through the puddles and kissing beneath every streetlight, which had come on early, the sky had grown so dark. In a quiet pub, after I'd asked the barman if he'd have one himself, and he'd said that he didn't mind if he would, I brought a shandy—half lager and half lemonade—and a pint of bitter over to the table, and Angela and I sat with our hands entwined, watching the rain against the window.

Angela met me in Cardiff on our off day, and when the team moved on to play Birchgrove, we spoke frequently by telephone, laughing when we couldn't understand each other's expressions or instructions. Against Birchgrove, another side not to be trifled with, I got my third start of the tour. We lost a hotly contested match, 12–6, again playing in the rain, and afterward, in the members-only bar, I asked Cye if I could address the team, since it was my last match on tour, and in the Centaurs jersey. We'd just exchanged team pennants and other gifts with Birchgrove's club president, and Cye motioned me over.

"That's a poxy knot you've done there, Atkinson," Beechey said, straightening and tightening my club tie. With his head next to mine, he said, "That's a good lad. Played well."

Holding my pint, I turned to face my teammates, who'd gathered in a loose ring. "Hey, I just wanted to say, thanks for having me on tour," I said. "It was a rough summer . . ." Whenever I thought about my father, or tried to summarize my feelings about what had happened, it was like gazing into an enormous hole in the ground, a pit more than a grave, just a vast, empty space. "Anyway, it's been a privilege to play with you guys."

Steve Carter got a big laugh by saying, "I get to sleep with him," before leading the barroom in a few choruses of "For He's a Jolly Good Fellow."

The Centaurs played the final match of the tour against Abercarn a couple of days later. Chosen as a reserve, I was surprised when our English hooker went down with an injury just minutes into the game and Beechey pointed at me. When I ran onto the field, Steve Carter shook my hand.

"Gave your speech a bit early," he said.

It was the last night of the tour, and after the game, I walked down the hill to the station and met Angela's train, which was up from Cardiff. We went along the dripping streets to the Abercarn social hall; I was dressed in my blazer and tie with the club insignia, and Angela wore a cocktail dress she'd purchased for a hundred quid on a trip to London.

Seated at a table after dinner, Angela and I held hands and danced to the Motown hits being spun by a local deejay. Every time I returned from the men's room, I was treated to the amusing sight of Angela fending off the locals; she smiled, shook her head, and pantomimed, "No, thank you," over the strains of "You Can't Hurry Love" and "This Old Heart of Mine".

After several drinks, Steve Carter ambled over to our table, insisting that I introduce him to Angela, while intoning, in a loud stage whisper, that she was "a cracking piece."

Carter bowed, kissing her hand. "I'd crawl across a rugby field of broken glass to get to you, if I wasn't a married man," he said.

Then he straightened up, throwing his arm over my shoulder. "This is the best Yank you'll ever meet," he said. "I'll have a beard down to my feet before I know a better chap than what's this fellow."

Later we went back to our billets and Carter was so loaded he curled up in the dog bed next to the stove, turning away the actual dog, which looked upon him with morose eyes.

With the rain dashing against the windows, Angela and I had the bedroom to ourselves and slid beneath the heavy comforter, tickling and poking each other. In the morning, when our hosts drove us back to where the team bus was waiting, Angela hugged me, smiling a little through the tears. The boys cried *"Come on, Atkinson!"* and *"Let's go, Jay!"* and I left her in the car and ran to the bus, shaking hands with the Abercarn players as I hurried past, with them wishing me all the best, and never once looking back.

Chapter 25

My Dinner with Andre

My old teammate Tim Moser, a fearsome, shaggy-haired second row who played for the U.S. Eagles, once remarked that when someone mentioned Boston, he never thought of the city itself, or its familiar historic landmarks, including Faneuil Hall, Fenway Park and the Freedom Trail.

"I think of the Boston Rugby Club," said Moser, who was a stalwart there, along with his late brother Tom, an orthopedic surgeon.

Founded in 1960, Boston RFC is one of the most storied clubs in the U.S., instantly recognizable in their black socks, black shorts, black jerseys and the buckled pilgrim hat with an arrow through it on the left breast. For decades, Boston's enduring rivalry with Old Blue RFC of New York City has provided some of the best rugby on the East Coast, and both teams have long exuded an air of mystery, elitism and snobby dominance.

When I played for Boston in the mid-eighties, they fielded four sides: the eponymous first XV, the Pilgrims, the Minutemen and the Stranglers, along with an Old Boys side that was like a who's who of American rugby from the previous decade. The club was so deep, in fact, that on any given Saturday, playing for the Pilgrims, I might have two former Eagles in the second row, the white-haired

maestro Chris Vale, and Tim Moser, who'd played against the Springboks in a closed stadium during apartheid, when international test
matches with South Africa were banned. The Mosers' brother-in-
law, Boyd Morrison, a hard-charging center, played for the Eagles.
Scrumhalf Paul Male, a stocky, agile fellow, originally from Leeds,
England, was then in the U.S. Eagles pool, a strong candidate to make
the national team, along with number eight Bobby Clark, flanker
Jack Donnelly, and another scrumhalf, Rory Mather, also a British
transplant.

I got my first start for the New England Select Side that year, when
the regional all-star team scheduled a match versus the Quebec
Selects, and Boston's coach, Aiden McNally, recommended me. I drove
up to Burlington, Vermont, for the match with Mike Skiotis, one of
my Boston teammates, with Ski getting a kick out of the business card
I'd gotten from a blonde I met the night before in a bar. She worked
for a company that made graduation gowns, judges' robes and the
like, and Ski kept the card in his pocket the entire weekend, taking
it out on occasion and mentioning to our teammates that I was well
known in the world of "Fraternal Regalia."

Being on the New England team meant you were one of the fifteen or twenty best rugby players among the one hundred and fifty
senior men's and collegiate clubs that made up the regional union,
which spanned six states and was one of the strongest in the country. Those appearances with the New England team were the high-
water mark of my career, where I reached the lower aspect of the
upper gradient in U.S. rugby. That vantage point gave me enormous
respect for guys who'd made it into the pool for the U.S. and Canadian sides, or played for their respective national teams. They were
studs.

The day of the select-side match, I had a nasty cold and temperatures were in the nineties, sticky and humid, when the game com-
menced on what looked like a Vermont farmer's field. In the opening
minutes, I had so much difficulty catching my breath that I thought
I was going to pass out. Quebec nearly popped our first scrum, providing flashbacks to what had happened in Wales, and they took a
6–0 lead on penalty kicks. But we stormed back with a try, coming

on a long, three-phase possession that began with a tighthead I stole at midfield.

Nearing halftime, we were ahead 9–6. At one point, having been kicked in the thigh during a ruck, I was on the ground struggling for breath, and signaled to the referee that I needed a minute of injury time. Our scrumhalf, Bobby Poirier, a tough, freckle-faced kid who played for Providence RFC, came over and asked if I was all right. When I said that I wanted to go off for a reserve, Poirier shook his head.

"You don't want to be on the sideline when we win this game," he said.

We scored another try early in the second half, a play that started with a lineout. I threw a long ball to Ski at the back of the line; he leaped up, made a great catch and the backs took a dive pass from Poirier on the tapped ball, with Boston's star winger, Mark Cooley, dotting it down in the corner of the try zone. We missed the ensuing kick; Quebec scored a converted try; and our lead was narrowed to 13–12.

With ten minutes left in the game, the heat was so bad I could no longer run, and I made a costly mistake in a lineout when I mixed up the signals and threw the ball to the wrong spot, allowing Quebec to poach it. They were hammering us in the scrums, but on the strength of Boston fly half Nick Murphy's kicking, we chased them deep into Quebec's end of the field and were scrummaging at their five-meter line when time ran out.

Leaving the pitch, I felt nauseous, dehydrated, shaky-legged and weak, satisfied that my select side debut had been a *qualified* success. I could hardly keep my head up for the team photo, supporting myself by slinging an arm across loosehead prop Skip Barry's shoulder. I had cuts on my face and legs, a deep bruise on my thigh from getting stomped, and pulled muscles in my back that had me walking like an old man. While I sat in the shade of an oak tree drinking countless slow and steady cups of water, Bobby Poirier sauntered past with his kit bag, looking fresh enough to play another match.

"Told ya," he said.

I was nearly asleep beneath the tree when someone nudged my

foot. Gazing up through the splintered light, I saw Mike Skiotis looming over me. "Time to don your fraternal regalia," he said, handing
me a beer.

Playing for the Boston Rugby Club's firsts, seconds and thirds,
personally I was 12-1-1 that spring. In April, one of the guys from
Aberavon over in Wales sent me a picture taken on my last night on
tour: Angela Morgan looking fresh and lovely, and me with things
written all over my face that weren't even hinted at during the Centaurs' boozy flight to Toronto. Angela and I'd been writing letters
since I'd gotten home. First, there were short funny ones addressed
"Dear Chucklehead" and "To an American Poser"; but afterward,
long, detailed treatises composed in the Morgans' back garden in
Port Talbot, or out on the deck at Glenn and Jeff's beach house, where
I'd wrap myself in a blanket, looking east toward the Isle of Shoals.

Then, one Sunday morning, Angela called, her voice faint, like it
was coming down a long rubber tube. "Jay. It's me. I'd like to come
see you in America," and before I knew it, I was standing in Logan
Airport with a bunch of roses in my hand and a shit-eating grin on
my face.

I was living at my mother's house, in the corner room overlooking the garden, and it was strange to wake up in the morning beside
someone who looked like a young Elizabeth Taylor. Just before Angela came to stay, I landed a job teaching GED classes for an anti-
poverty agency in Haverhill, Massachusetts; soon after, I paired up
with the local arts foundation to organize a writers' conference. The
most famous writer in those parts was Andre Dubus II, an award-
winning master of the short story who taught at a local college. In a
telephone conversation, Dubus agreed to participate, and recommended another writer, John Smith, a young novelist who had just
started teaching at the college.

Pleased to have filled two slots with a single phone call, I acquired
Smith's number, speaking to him shortly after. To assist in promoting the conference, Smith agreed to send along an excerpt from his
forthcoming novel.

Reading it, I learned that the novel purported to be about Smith's
experiences as a combat infantryman in Vietnam. I had read exten-
sively in this subgenre, and my delight in his excerpt turned to

unease and then outright disgust when I realized that the passage Smith had sent had been lifted, pretty much word for word, from *Dispatches,* Michael Herr's harrowing chronicle of his time in Vietnam. It didn't take a linguistics scholar to figure out that Smith had stolen Michael Herr's intellectual property, and would soon publish it under his own name.

Harry Crews had given me his personal copy of *Dispatches,* and I'd read it so many times I knew many of the passages by heart, so there was little doubt. But plagiarism is a hanging offense in the literary world and as a young, unpublished writer, I wanted to be certain of the charge before talking to Smith about it. I called Dubus and made arrangements to meet him at a bar near campus called Ronnie D's.

Sitting in one of the dark wooden booths along the wall was a broad-shouldered, bandy-legged stump of a man in his late forties, with a thick salt-and-pepper beard, hobnail boots, a satin Red Sox warm-up jacket and an Aussie-style cowboy hat with one side pinned up. Dubus was about five foot six when he stood and extended his small, thick hand, callused from lifting weights.

On the surface, at least, Andre Dubus II had several things in common with my mentor, Harry Crews. Both were raised in the South (Dubus had grown up in Lake Charles, Louisiana), had served in the U.S. Marine Corps; married young, divorced, had ongoing troubles with authority and liked to fight. They were roughly the same age, and had served their literary apprenticeships with older, established writers after getting out of the service: Harry with Andrew Lytle in Florida, and Andre under Richard Yates at the University of Iowa.

In the booth at Ronnie D's, I produced my copy of *Dispatches* with the page marked and the excerpt from Smith's novel, and then sipped a beer as Dubus, working with the deliberateness of a bank examiner, read the works side by side. Each time Andre found an identical phrase or expression, he underlined it on both manuscripts with a ballpoint pen. By the time he'd reached the bottom of a single page, the text was marked up in twenty or thirty places. The conclusion was obvious.

Andre closed the book, leveling his beady-eyed gaze on me. I knew he was in a difficult spot: Dubus and Smith were colleagues, the only two professors teaching in the fiction-writing program. They'd already taken to having a few beers together on occasion, and were neighbors in campus housing. I'd also heard that Smith was a pretty big dude who went around campus in an old army jacket.

"What are you gonna do?" Dubus asked.

I told Andre that I planned to confront Smith that night when he finished teaching. Dubus offered to come along, though I knew he didn't really want to. Finishing my beer, I said it was my decision to invite Smith to the conference, and that I'd go up there by myself.

"You're certainly not a wimp," said Andre.

At quarter to nine, I left the bar and climbed the short, steep hill to the campus. Arriving at the bungalow where Smith lived, I greeted him with a firm handshake and steady eye in the front room, where he taught his classes. He was six feet tall, with a mustache and thick, dark hair, his old field jacket hung over the back of his chair. We got straight to business, and when Smith looked over the marked-up pages and knew he'd been discovered, his hand shook a little, and he groped for an explanation, though we both understood there wasn't one.

I asked him to withdraw from the writers' conference, which he did, and suggested that he contact his editor and have the passages struck from the galley. I retrieved my copy of *Dispatches* from the table and was headed for the door when I turned back for a moment, asking Smith if he was a Vietnam veteran.

"My agent thinks so, and I haven't done anything to disavow him of that notion," Smith said.

I'd taken a couple of English classes at the college while still in high school, and was familiar with the terrain, even in the dark. Andre's residence was a bright, cluttered space in a pebbledash town house near a small pond. He lived there with his third wife, the writer Peggy Rambach, a smart, lissome blonde who was twenty-three years younger than Dubus.

Dubus invited me in, asking Peggy to get us each a beer. When I'd told him what had occurred, Andre said, "I'm proud of you, son. It's a rare thing in the world to see someone pursue the truth like that."

Andre and Peggy and I became friends, though I maintained some reservations about Andre. He was a short, pugnacious man, feet splayed, canted back on his heels when he talked to you, with a braying, nasal sort of laugh. He had a gun collection, and always carried one or more of them during that period. At little blue-collar dives like Ronnie D's and McMino's, located a few miles from the college on Route 110, we'd stand at the bar and after a few drinks, Andre would start demonstrating wrestling holds on me; more than once, I'd return from a trip to the men's room and Dubus would say something like, "We're gonna go outside and fight these truck drivers." I'd have to talk him out of it, partly by saying that I wasn't going to help him fight his battles.

I began to think that Andre's greatest battle was with his inner demons, a hunch that gained some credence when he was fired from his teaching gig for discharging a gun on campus, among other transgressions. By this time, Dubus had been awarded fellowships from the Guggenheim and MacArthur foundations, and was about to publish a story collection titled *The Last Worthless Evening*, his seventh book, and third in just four years. He and Peggy were able to purchase a rustic little house, built from a kit and overlooking East Broadway in Haverhill, a half mile from McMino's bar. Then, shortly after Angela Morgan came to stay with me, Dubus phoned to invite us to dinner, saying that his grown sons, Andre III and Jeb, neither of whom I'd met, would also be in attendance, with their girlfriends.

The Dubus residence was located on a steep wooded lot divided by a gravel driveway. The house itself was arranged on two levels, with exposed beams and vast picture windows, and when Angela and I shook hands with Andre Senior and entered the kitchen, we were confronted with a dense, gamy odor that emanated from a large pot simmering on the range. Dubus asked if I wanted a drink, and when I lifted the cover off the pot, inquiring what was inside, Dubus said, "Squirrel gumbo. Shot 'em in the backyard," and I replied yes, I'd like some vodka.

A large, comfortable wooden table was set for eight people, and upon descending a couple of steps to the lower level, Angela and I were introduced to Andre Junior, a tall, angular fellow with an abundance of wavy dark hair; his girlfriend, a pretty blonde; and Jeb, a few inches shorter than his brother, a quiet guy whose look vacillated between petulant and brooding. His girlfriend was a little brunette, who said even less than he did, which wasn't very much.

Andre Senior was at the head of the table, Peggy at the other end, nearest the kitchen, and Angela and I were seated opposite Andre's sons and their girlfriends. By all accounts, Andre Senior hadn't been around very often when his sons were growing up, and was unable or unwilling to provide much in the way of financial support. That evening, there was an air about him of a man trying to accomplish three things: make up for lost time with his boys, who were now young men; impress me, his sons, their dates, and Angela; and establish himself as the indisputable alpha male in attendance. In Andre Senior's mind, I was there to see him, and only him; to curry his favor; and to jockey with Andre Junior and Jeb for the lower spots in the pecking order. You could just smell it in the room, floating along with the rancid squirrel odor.

The gumbo was served with homemade corn bread, ice-cold beer and generous amounts of vodka; the squirrel meat was scarce and bony, tasting like a bad clam. After the meal, Andre Senior held court from his end of the table, with me on his immediate right, and Andre Junior to his left. Peggy was jumping up every few minutes, bringing items to and from the kitchen, and her husband seemed to take perverse satisfaction in ordering her around, giving contradictory instructions, and so on.

Seated beside me, Angela was wearing skintight jeans, open-toed shoes, a clinging white jersey and a pair of bright red suspenders that bowed outward to accommodate her good-sized breasts. Her hair was dark and curly, flowing to the small of her back, and she laughed easily, her blue eyes flashing, as she parried Andre Senior's flirtatious comments.

Andre Senior asked if she'd fallen in love after watching me play soccer; Angela corrected him by saying I played rugby, and living near Cardiff, she could easily find more impressive and productive players of the Welsh national game. No, she said, putting her hand on me and raising her eyebrows in carnal suggestion, she'd been irresistibly attracted to my immense (here there was a comic pause) personality. Everyone laughed, and Andre Senior clapped his hands, ordering Peggy to get some more beers.

After the dishes had been cleared—Angela and I rose to help, feeling bad for Peggy—Andre Senior handed out little colored cigarettes, and he and his sons puffed away, braying to each other like long-lost chums. Cigarette in hand, Andre Senior rapped on the table, gathering everyone's attention to sing an off-key rendition of the old Guy Clark song, "Desperados Waiting for a Train." Jeb was an accomplished guitar player, showing us a few licks on an acoustic that was lying around. Prompted by table talk, he also recounted a story about sexual encounters at a tender age with distant cousins of the opposite sex.

Andre Junior, who was trying to make it as an actor then, and hadn't yet become a writer, declaimed a few lines from a play he was doing. Peggy was standing beside the table, cleaning up, when Andre Senior prevailed upon her to sing for us. It took some coaxing, but in a wonderful alto Peggy intoned the lyrics to an old English folk ballad, "John Riley":

> No kind sir,
> I cannot marry thee
> For I've a love who sails
> the deep salt sea

The applause was sustained and genuine, with the onlookers pounding the table and whistling, abetted by their cumulative vodka intake. In a way, I suppose everyone was expected to sing for his supper that night, and since Angela and I had no discernible abilities in that regard, Andre Senior decided to push us into a little improvisation: the Theater of the Absurd meets Antonin Artaud's Theatre of Cruelty.

As soon as the clamor died away, with Peggy still flushed by her performance and a tinge of embarrassment, Andre Senior leaned past me and in a calm, steady voice, said, "You're the most sensuous girl I've ever met, Angela. I'd like to fuck you. I'd like to see you in bed. But Peggy's my wife, and Jay's my friend."

Never shy, Angela replied to that brutal come-on with the Welsh equivalent of "Forget it, pal," but Dubus wasn't really talking to her. After his brief soliloquy, Andre Senior trained his small, dirty eyes on me, smirking within his beard. Nobody was *that* drunk. Beside him, Andre Junior leered as well, tilted forward, his hands and thick wrists lying on the scarred wooden table. I'd heard that he was a pretty good boxer, a light heavyweight, by the looks of him.

Wear a motorcycle jacket or a military uniform into a bar, and sooner or later, someone will challenge you to a fight. Rugby players get their fair share of that, too, especially when they're wearing a Boston Rugby Club T-shirt, as I was that night. Certainly, Andre Senior had meant to provoke me, but I remained silent, returning his stare. Who knows why he said it. Delusions of Hemingway, perhaps, though it was also clear that Andre Senior was not participating in the same reality that we'd all agreed upon.

My metric back then—and now—when faced with anything resembling that sort of boorishness, a personal insult or an imminent physical threat, is to gauge my antagonist on how he'd make out in a rugby game. It's a simple accounting, and my instant, irreducible judgment was that neither Andre would last five minutes on a rugby field, that night, in the past, or ever. So I really had nothing to say to him.

Angela and I helped Peggy with the dishes, apologizing to her by the kitchen door. We left shortly after that, understanding as we bumped down the hill that we hadn't really owed Peggy an apology: Andre Senior did.

Angela and I had plenty of good times after that, but I had to work a regular job and she got bored, sitting around the house all week. She was a spirited girl and sometimes we fought, with an intensity never felt by couples that had spent years together, with a fire kindled only by people born to be enemies.

Bedeviled by the same kind of visa problems that had affected me in Canada, Angela went home after a few months, got back together with her old rugby-playing boyfriend for a while, and then started calling me again. (She seemed to want whoever was on the other side of the Atlantic Ocean, as I'd answered late-night phone calls from the Welsh boyfriend when Angela was in Methuen.) In retrospect, there were moments of unsolicited cruelty, knock-down, drag-out fights, drunken yelling on street corners, et cetera, but I ran with it as long as I could. After all, I'd met a lovely girl from a foreign land, watched her undress by the long windows in the moonlight; the grace of a goddamn ballerina for such a big girl when she uncovered her breasts, and bent to pull off her panties, the width of a penknife. It felt like being stabbed in the heart when she left, but I came back in the spring of the following year, whistling a tune.

Chapter 26

Don't Cry for Me Argentina

I was in my office on the third floor of a repurposed mill building in a run-down section of Haverhill, Massachusetts, when the heavy, steel-reinforced door creaked open and Karen Koffler was standing there on the dingy carpet.

"Hi," she said, in that rolling, up-front way that always made me feel like we were parties to the same joke.

Though it was April in New England, with skies the color of gravy and a rustling wind, Koffler was dressed in a bathing suit, Dolfin shorts, and flip-flops, wearing a pair of aviator sunglasses with strings of beads twined in her hair.

I hadn't seen her in close to three years, although we'd maintained an intermittent correspondence, and I'd included the name of the place where I worked in a fairly recent letter I'd sent to her on the island of Majorca. She'd been kicking around Europe then, having finished a master's degree at the University of Florida, and was heading to medical school at the University of Miami.

I glanced out the window to see Koffler's BMW parked at the curb. She was driving up to Maine to visit some friends, returning that Friday to her parents' home on Long Island. She'd stopped by out of the blue to invite me down for the weekend, offering to pick me up on her way back through Massachusetts. Sure thing, I said.

"Don't talk yourself out of it," Koffler said, as she was leaving.

"Don't worry. I won't."

At ten o'clock Friday night, Koffler and I hit the interstate for the six-hour drive to West Islip. We talked nonstop, discussing her recent trip to Morocco, and how the people there wouldn't stop touching her blond hair; and the time in Spain that a guy began chasing her when she was out jogging. In the end, Koffler rocketed up eight flights of stairs to her *pensión*, leaving the guy on a landing about halfway up, where he collapsed from exhaustion.

We arrived at the Koffler residence at 4 A.M. (her parents were out of town), and while I was perusing her father's collection of Dashiell Hammett novels, she descended the stairs wearing only a starched white policeman's shirt purchased in Madrid. Her body was smooth and deeply tanned, with sensuous long legs, a swimmer's upper back and shoulders, and brilliant white teeth. And when she laughed, which was often, it came out a little husky, like Marlene Dietrich.

Koffler showed me to the guest room overlooking the swimming pool. The drive had tired me out, but I was wide awake, my system running on impulse power, eyes weary but my mind alert and relaxed. Sitting cross-legged on the end of the bed, Koffler asked if she could stay with me. Hell, yes, I said. I was afraid you were going to leave.

We wriggled beneath the comforter and fussed around, giggling like a couple of kids sleeping out in the backyard. The day had taken a toll and I went motionless there, every muscle languishing as Koffler stroked my hair and neck with her fingertips. I rolled over, and she was gazing at me with those deep brown eyes.

"Back in Gainesville, I always wanted to do this with you," I said, "and now, no matter what happens, it's done."

She kissed me. "Me, too."

I flew home on Sunday night, and the phone rang soon after I walked in. It was Koffler, saying that she was preparing to sleep in the guest room again, and that she missed me.

"I always thought there was great chemistry between us," she said. "Even when other things got between."

"I like hanging out with you," I said. "Always have."

I had a nine-to-five job in Massachusetts (a mistake I never made again), and Koffler was in the first year of a demanding program, so it wasn't easy keeping up our relationship. I flew down to Miami as frequently as possible between rugby and work commitments, and Koffler visited me during the Christmas holidays, including a drive up to Halifax, Nova Scotia, for Dag Fullerton's wedding, and a re-union of FADC charter members. The most indelible image of that trip was crossing the floodplain between Sackville, New Bruns-wick, and Amherst, Nova Scotia, most definitely border territory, the trans-Canada radio towers like something out of a science fiction movie as we zoomed past at eighty miles per hour. Reggae music was playing on the radio, and Koffler, her face serene, the beads in her hair swaying against the console, was tapping out the rhythm on my arm with her fingertips—*let's get together and feel all right*—my head bobbing to the music, and my eyes registering my old stomp-ing grounds from behind a pair of Ray-Bans.

It was a quick trip to the Fullerton nuptials, and twenty-four hours on the road out of forty-eight will tell you a lot about a travel-ing companion. What they revealed about Koffler, the tall, persis-tent character from the Florida chapters, was that she remained as genuinely charming, funny and unpredictable as she'd been five years earlier, when she spotted me hiding beneath my Astros cap at the frat party I'd crashed with Surfer.

Koffler and I would often go a month or two without seeing each other, and I missed one of our weekends together that June when I got another selection to the New England team. This time the select side was playing against Quebec up in Montreal, and once again, it was in the nineties and humid. Though I'd frequently played in that sort of heat in Gainesville, I much preferred the cool, damp weather that fueled me during the soccer practices that immediately pre-ceded wrestling workouts back at Acadia. I never seemed to get tired, if the conditions were right.

I was determined to play better than I had in my previous select side match, but against Quebec on their home ground we had our hands full with the scrummaging. Their hooker was the reigning national team representative at the position, and they crumpled our front row in the first few sets, shoving us backward so far that I was hemorrhaging my own ball even after winning the initial strike. My nose was in the dirt all afternoon, and I was reeling around in oxygen starvation after three consecutive scrums, my legs numb, pissed off at myself for not contributing very much. I hated playing rugby in June.

Finally, in the last minutes of the game, leading 10–8, we hit our scrummaging just right, a few meters into Quebec's territory beyond midfield. The referee was glancing at his watch every few seconds, and when he heeled the mark, loosehead prop Skip Barry of Providence got a tight bind on me, and for the first time we got beneath the Quebec tighthead and hooker, creating a steady platform. It was their put-in, and with my head just twelve inches off the ground, I peeked to the right, watching for their scrumhalf's feet as he approached.

Lungs burning, I swung my right leg up, outward and across the tunnel, heel first, clipping a piece of the ball immediately after the Quebec halfback flicked it in. We had enough of a surge to get over the ball, winning it cleanly—my only tighthead of the game, and at a critical moment. But we'd had two substitutions early in the match that affected our scrum, including one for our captain, Jack Donnelly. Jack was my teammate in Boston, a former football player at Colgate, and one of the best ruggers I every played with or against, anywhere. (One time we were playing a match against Portland RFC in Maine and Donnelly, a quiet, squinty-eyed fellow with a lopsided grin, was sitting in his car near the pitch listening to music. Figuring that whatever worked to psych Jack Donnelly up would do the same for me, I was surprised to hear Jack singing along to John Cafferty and the Beaver Brown Band, which you'd hear on elevators.)

The ball was hooked at an angle, passing along to my right, ending up beneath the chest of our open-side flanker—normally Jack Donnelly, a smart player who would've collected the ball with his right foot, directing it back to our number eight, Snapper, for transfer to scrumhalf Bobby Poirier, his dive pass to Nick Murphy, and a booming kick to end the match, sealing our victory.

But the substitute flanker, plucked from the sideline when Donnelly received a huge gash on his head and we'd run out of forwards, reached down and touched the ball with his right hand while still bound to the scrum—a penalty, resulting in an immediate whistle, and loss of possession. No one was expecting it and very few of our players even saw it, the infraction happened so fast.

In the moment of confusion following the penalty, their quick-thinking scrumhalf tapped the ball through the referee's mark and made a long, rapid pass to the Quebec fly half. He handled it deftly, continuing it along with just one hand, and their centers zipped the ball straight to the wing, who made it a footrace and scored with a dive into the corner of the try zone. What should've been the play that secured the win resulted in a last-minute loss, 12–10. In a weird way, it was a harbinger of things to come.

I hadn't seen Koffler in two months when I flew to Gainesville for an alumni rugby game, arriving on Friday in time for FADC; like something out of a summer night in 1981, strange but achingly pleasant to be back in that place and time. Sometime after 2 A.M., I was crashed in the spare room at Farwick's place, the old 641 Club, when there was some commotion in the living room. It was Psycho and Smitty and Surfer, just getting into town from parts unknown, and I could hear them whispering. "Jay's in there." "Jay who?" "Jay Atkinson." "No shit. No! Let's fuck with him," and they rushed through the door and leaped onto the bed, keeping me up until daybreak.

The old Gators defeated the new Gators, 14–10, the big play coming when Sergio Lopez, forty-one years old and still looking like he'd been chiseled out of stone, took one of my lineout throws and ran over their flanker and eight man for the winning try. After the game, I met Harry Crews for a beer at the Orange and Brew. I still hadn't published any fiction, though back home in Methuen I was up every morning at 5 A.M., tapping the keys of my old Olympia, working on my novel before I headed to my straight job. In his office, Harry gave me the author's copy of his latest book, *2 by Crews*, inscribing it, *"For Jay, who is my brother. Keep on fishing, fucking and fighting. Best forever, HC."*

Later that day, beneath threatening skies, the rugby boys met at the 641 Club, challenging each other to pull-up contests and drinking beer. Koffler was running late, and every few minutes I'd round the side of the house, looking for her car. I was hoping she'd arrive in time to attend a big shindig at Crescent Beach that all the boys were going to. Near dusk, I was standing out front just as Koffler pulled up to the curb, the first patter of raindrops falling from the sky. I was so excited to see her, I ran over, yanked open the passenger side door, and jumped in a half second before she sped away.

I leaned over and kissed her on the cheek, going back hard against the seat when she downshifted, turning onto West University Avenue.

"I have something to tell you," Koffler said.

"I have something to say, too. You go first."

Being in Florida with my rugby pals made me homesick for the place. Surfer, Civil, Conrad and Carlos were playing rugby for clubs on the coast, and lived close enough to see each other fairly often. Koffler was entering her residency year at Jackson Memorial Hospital in Miami, and we got along so well it seemed like the right time to make a move. All my rugby friends knew and liked her, and I was about to say that I was giving serious thought to quitting my job and returning to Florida, perhaps even moving in with her, if she'd have me.

"I'm getting married," Koffler said.

My heart jolted in my chest, like I'd been unnecessarily defibrillated with a pair of rusty jumper cables. "What?"

Koffler shifted into a higher gear, maneuvering the BMW along University like a Le Mans driver. In the white noise filling my head, I could make out something about how hard the year had been for her, lonely at times with me so far away, and how she and this guy Dane were doing the same residency . . . and then I just turned it off, like I'd flipped a switch.

"Take me back to the party."

Now it was Koffler's turn to be surprised. "Don't you want to talk about it?" she asked.

I wasn't angry, not even hurt, really. Most of all, I felt perturbed, like when your best friend announces a decision that you know is a flat-out mistake, but you also know your friend well enough to understand that discussing, analyzing and changing that decision will be exhausting, and ultimately, futile.

"Take me back to Farwick's. They're leaving soon, and I don't want to miss them."

Her lips quivering, Koffler went around the block, roared up University and turned onto Farwick's street, pulling up in front of the house. It was raining harder now.

"Jay, don't you want to talk to me? We can go to dinner or something, hang out."

"See ya," I said, as I climbed out, shutting the door behind me. After pausing for a beat at the curb, Koffler put it into gear, and drove off.

In my pique, I hadn't noticed that the 641 Club was locked up tight, the windows dark. Most of the cars that had been parked alongside the house were gone. Even the gate on the fence out back was fixed with a padlock. I jumped up, grabbed two of the pickets, and hoisted myself over. Beneath a picnic table was a cooler with a single can of Old Milwaukee in it. I popped it open and sat at the table, drinking the last beer in the rain.

A short time later, I quit my job in Massachusetts, though not for the reasons I'd originally envisioned. Since traveling to Wales with the Centaurs, I'd been on rugby tours to Edinburgh, Belfast and Dublin; Cairns, Melbourne and Sydney in Australia; and Suva on the island of Fiji; a torrid stretch of rugby barnstorming that would last for more than a decade and fill up more than forty wire-bound notebooks with my adventures. Right after Koffler dropped a bomb on me in Gainesville, I heard about a rugby trip to South America from Surfer. The Florida Select Side, coached by Bing Towne of Boca Raton RFC, was planning a three-week tour to Argentina and Chile; and Carlos, Conrad, Civil and Surfer, all of whom were playing representative rugby for Florida, the mid-South, or, in Carlos's case, the ERU select team, comprising the best players on the East Coast, had been invited to join the tour.

Carlos and Conrad were playing for Boca Raton and spoke to Towne, as well as the tour manager, "Dead-eye Dick" Elliott, a union referee, about my interest in going on tour. I'd been a candidate for the Florida Select Side before my departure from Gainesville (a situation that also occurred with the Niagara Rugby Union selects when I left Canada rather abruptly), and Bing Towne was aware that I'd been playing for the New England select team.

I had to quit my job to go on tour, since I'd used up my vacation time for a trip to Scotland and Northern Ireland a few months earlier. But I could always find something else, I figured, and rugby trips to South America didn't come along very often. Early that spring I'd begun work on a novel, *Caveman Politics,* based on events that occurred in Gainesville after a rugby teammate, a black grad student from Trinidad, was accused of raping a white girl. So it would be professionally expedient to hang around with my old pals from those days, and gather their reminiscences. (A few years later, *Caveman Politics* would become my first published book.) And after what had transpired with Koffler, I was more than ready to get on a plane headed for Buenos Aires.

On the flight, Conrad and Carlos talked to Bing Towne about selections. Two teams were making the trip: the Florida President's XV, which contained mostly select side players, and a social side, composed of old boys, friends of friends, and players from lower division clubs. After Bing finished his conversation with my old teammates, he lurched down the aisle to where I was sitting. I was fresh off scoring a try in the New England Select Side trials, a development camp held the weekend before in Providence, Rhode Island, where they invited thirty or forty players to be evaluated under game conditions. After he'd asked me a few questions, Bing said I'd be playing with my old buddies on the President's XV. The two hookers from Florida on tour, neither of whom were regulars on the select side, would each end up getting a couple of games with the social side.

Before we arrived in Buenos Aires, Towne gathered everyone in the rear of the plane for a debriefing. Argentina had been struggling with civil unrest for months, sometimes boiling over into street violence; and Chile, ruled by strongman General Augusto Pinochet ("Strong? That guy couldn't do five push-ups," Conrad said), was no bastion of human rights, either. Since the presidential election of

Carlos Menem a couple months earlier, Argentina had suffered rampant inflation, as well as a brutal devaluation of its currency, which created havoc for the poor and middle class. Reckless printing of money by the Argentine government had boosted the value of the American dollar so high that, as we prepared to leave Miami, players were advised to bring just two or three hundred dollars—in small bills hidden in a money belt worn beneath our clothes. It was like something out of a Graham Greene novel.

In the past few weeks, the value of the Argentinian currency, the austral, had plunged from approximately $1.20 U.S. to its current level of one half of a cent. People were rioting outside the supermarkets because they couldn't afford to buy food, and more than one thousand looters and rioters, most of them shanty-town dwellers from the outskirts of Buenos Aires, had been rounded up by the police and imprisoned. The situation in the capital, where we'd be staying, was tense and getting worse.

Dave Civil raised his hand. "Does this mean the women are lonely?" he asked.

At the airport, a poor-to-middle class looking family stood in a circle guarding their treasure, a half-dozen new weed whackers, still in the boxes. It appeared that nonperishable items were hard to come by in Argentina, and many more people were departing on flights than were arriving. Outside on the curb, dozens of fire-eaters were lined up, men with worn-out faces and empty stares. The fire-eaters took a swig of gasoline and then, waving what looked like a flaming cat o' nine tail, exhaled a quick, forceful breath, throwing a plume of acrid black smoke and orange flame high into the air. If you blinked your eyes, startled by this display, they'd move in fast and try to steal your wallet.

Our hotel was located on the Plaza de Mayo, the long, tree-lined avenue that contained the presidential headquarters, Casa Rosada, the Pink House, an enormous, three-and-a-half-story palace, its tall vertical windows divided by stone mullions and flanked with recessed Ionic columns. Eva Perón had addressed an adoring multitude of Argentine workers from the north balcony of the Casa Rosada, the same platform where military dictator Leopoldo Galtieri made his ill-fated declaration of war with Great Britain over the

Falkland Islands in 1982. (Conrad had never let Carlos forget about that one.)

Temporary security fences topped with razor wire encircled the building, patrolled by soldiers wearing flak vests and toting nasty-looking automatic weapons. "It's like Disney World, with attitude," Surfer said. "Don't fuck with us, Argentina."

After a meeting in the lobby of the San Francisco Hotel, where Bing informed us that rioting, looting and bloodshed in a nearby suburb had resulted in four deaths, including a nine-year-old boy accidentally shot by police, we dumped our bags and had a drink at the bar.

Emboldened by this, Surfer, Conrad, Civil, Carlos, Mark Carpenter and Chris "Stinky" Hines, a second row from Boca Raton, with a high-crowned head of swept-back hair like the actor Sterling Hayden, and I ventured out from the hotel into the plaza. Silver-helmeted police were clustered at every intersection, and squads of soldiers in riot gear were marching out from the Pink House, clearing the sidewalks as they came.

We dined at the Acapulco Room a block from the hotel, where a steak dinner of local, grass-fed beef in a gigantic bloody slab, new potatoes, grilled asparagus, and carafes of red wine cost us just four dollars apiece. Dave Civil had been handing out his business cards since the minute he'd arrived in Buenos Aires, especially to pretty girls; he must've given away dozens of them.

Dusk was falling over the spires of the city, and during a stroll north of the Pink House, we settled at an outdoor kiosk named the Bar Europa. We ordered beer in tall pilsner glasses, playing a game Stinky called "Spot the Nazi," and watching the fantastic local girls hurry home from the shops. They were dressed in well-cut European clothes, with beautiful smooth dark skin, high cheekbones, green or blue eyes and hair the color of summer wheat. Two other players joined us, Space Boy, a batty but hard-charging winger from St. Pete, and a blond-haired Miami firefighter named Sean, who was a loosehead prop and flanker.

The city had an end-of-the-world feel to it, with leggy blondes streaming past the elegant old buildings, which were topped with sandbags and loops of concertina wire. Curfew in Buenos Aires was

10 P.M., and when a squad of riot police motioned to us, pointing their machine guns down the boulevard toward our hotel, we paid for the beers and guys began walking in that direction. Soon most of them were half a block away, drifting along the plaza, their laughter echoing in the street. I was finishing my glass of beer when a half-dozen street urchins, dressed in tattered clothes, none older than eight or nine, emerged from a nearby alley. They flew up to the kiosk, chattering in Spanish, and began giving me the finger and throwing karate kicks.

One of the youngsters asked the barman for a glass of water; he was a dirty-faced kid dressed in rags, his eyes set deep in his head like an old man's, though he was probably seven years old. The barman swatted at him, but I called the guy over and asked for *"cuatro vasos de leche,"* and he delivered the four pint glasses of milk with an astonished look on his face.

I gestured to the kid that the milk was for him, but he shook his head. I told him again in pigeon Spanish, and he reached for one of the glasses and took a tiny sip, never taking his eyes off me. I told him in Spanish that the other glasses were for his friends, who were now a couple blocks away. The kid hesitated for a moment and then ran after them, waving his arms.

I waited with the barman, and when the children returned, they fell upon the milk, drinking it in quick, steady drafts, hands shaking, their upper lips whitened by the sort of milk mustache every kid should have. That end of the plaza was deserted, and when the beggars returned the glasses to the barman and ran off into the shadows, I hailed Surfer, who was waiting for me on the corner, and we followed the other rugby players back toward the hotel.

Chapter 27

In the San Francisco Hotel

The next morning, we headed to the La Plata Rugby Club for practice, and to look over the ground. La Plata is a seaport on the east coast of Argentina, located thirty-five miles south of Buenos Aires on the Rio de la Plata. Driving out of the city, we passed soldiers on street corners and behind sandbags, drinking coffee and smoking cigarettes. I was dozing in my seat when Conrad nudged me, pointing out the window.

On the outskirts of Buenos Aires our route bisected a terrible slum: ramshackle cardboard shacks arranged like a kennel on either side of a slow-moving, shit-colored stream. Mangy dogs roamed the trash-strewn ravine and people were dumping buckets of effluent upstream from where women were doing laundry and drawing water for breakfast. Even inside the bus, you could smell the stench: gasoline, shit, rotten garbage and burning tires. The U of Florida guys were seated together and we shook our heads, grimacing at the kind of poverty seen only in the Third World.

Twenty minutes later, we crossed the river into fresher circumstances: large stucco homes appearing at regular intervals, and vast green fields demarcated by rows of jacaranda trees. Down a long paved road through flat country we turned beneath a metal arch inscribed with LA PLATA RUGBY CLUB, heading toward the low-slung clubhouse and its outbuildings and playing fields. The bus sent up a funnel of road dust, the early sun illuminating the park with hazy gold shafts.

It was a posh club, with an open-air terrace dotted by fan-backed chairs, a stone-topped bar and several ornate wooden tables. Carlos had grown up here, and it was easy to imagine him and his brother Gaston and their friends dodging the tables and laughing about some prank they'd played. Bing Towne yelled to us and we trooped over the paving stones and down a long grassy path to one of a dozen rugby pitches.

Training was light: a warm-up, ball-handling drills, and a chance to go over lineout signals and get to know each other. I'd be playing with Conrad, Civil and Mark Carpenter in the forwards; the tight-head prop, always my best friend on the field, was a transplanted Chilean of Polish descent named Ivan Skulski who played for the Miami Rugby Club; a dark-haired fellow with the physique of a cir-cus strongman and a reputation as a hard player.

After practice, I ran a few laps by myself, the sun slanting across the dun-colored playing fields in long, slow, mote-filled beams; the air was cool and invigorating, and it felt good to be moving, a keen sense of South America filling me as cars passed by on the access road, and three local kids sneaked a cigarette in a corner of the field.

I caught up with the guys on the terrace, where we were treated to lunch and a couple of beers. The U of Florida boys sat with Ivan, Stinky Hines and Sean, the amiable firefighter from Miami. Playing for the social side was a muscle-bound nitwit from South Florida who wore his dyed blond hair in a Mohawk and was known as "the Boz." He styled himself after the former Oklahoma Sooner's line-backer, Brian Bosworth, which was as silly as going around dressed as Batman or Captain America. Boz thought he was a wheeler-dealer, in light of the fact that, back home, he made his living as a salesman of dubious commodities—lifestyle supplements, he called them. On tour, he planned to make a small fortune exchanging cur-rency, though he hadn't factored in a significant detail: he didn't speak a lick of Spanish. Carlos and Conrad, both of whom were flu-ent, said that Boz was the only person in Argentina flush with

American dollars who wasn't benefiting in any way. (Immediately after the tour, he told a few guys he was going back to Argentina to marry a local girl, apparently some kind of green card scheme that didn't work out for either party, as Boz ended up in prison.)

Boz's partner-in-crime on the trip was an oily, thirty-eight-year-old stock trader nicknamed Ray van Asshole. Not expecting to play, Van Asshole had purchased a seat on the plane and tagged along on behalf of American diplomacy. He was so habitually drunk, snide, condescending and boorish that he made the rest of us look like Gandhi's entourage.

On the ride home, a commotion arose on the bus when we drove back through the slums. Boz and Van Asshole had hit upon the brilliant idea of throwing money out the windows, American coins mostly, along with handfuls of australs and the occasional one-dollar bill. Children begging on the side of the road were struck by the first few coins, and began chasing after the bus, which in turn drew more ragged children and, eventually, grown men and women. They dived on the pavement and in the scrub lining the side of the road in pursuit of the money, and arguments and fistfights were breaking out in our wake. Boz and Van Asshole and a couple of other guys were laughing like idiots, keeping it up for a mile or so, until we reached the first military checkpoint. It caught us off guard at first, a real shit show, and overcoming his initial speechlessness, Civil looked over at Boz, and said, "Hey, breath of a thousand Slim Jims, don't be so fucking stupid."

That night, Carlos picked up some scuttlebutt about our match with La Plata. His old team fielded several men's sides and their first team, which we didn't expect to play, featured a handful of Junior Pumas, the under-twenty-three national select players expected to one day make the Pumas. Then, as now, Argentina was ranked in the top tier of international sides, along with the All Blacks of New Zealand, Australia's Wallabies, England, Wales, France, and South Africa's Springboks. (The U.S. national team, the Eagles, was situated near the bottom of the second tier, below Canada, Japan and Italy, among others.) Carlos heard that La Plata was putting out a strong team against us, since like most foreign sides, they loathed the idea of losing to an American team, especially at home.

In the changing room before the match, we donned the orange jerseys, white shorts and orange socks of the Florida President's XV, with the Rolling Stones blasting from a portable stereo and very little being said. By that time, Bing Towne, a curly-haired avuncular presence who resembled an aging swinger, had uttered some encouragement and departed, taking the reserve players with him. We had a decent collection of rugby players, but none, with the exception of Carlos, who regularly competed at the national select level. Nor had we ever played together as a team, while many of La Plata's fifteen had been together since they were twelve or thirteen years old.

Suddenly, Carlos began pacing up and down the room. Always laid-back and jocular, even before our championship match against FSU, Carlos surprised everyone when he stopped abruptly, banging his shod foot against a locker.

His dark eyes blazing, Carlos said, "This is a *very* good team we're playing, but they don't like to get hit. You've got to hit them like the NFL." He pounded a fist into his open palm: *Bam.* "They've never seen the NFL. They don't even have the Movie Channel."

Surfer had grown his hair out since the Marines, and when we ran onto the field, turning alongside the grandstand, kids hung over the balustrade shouting, "MacGyver! MacGyver!" thinking he was the old TV star who made grenade launchers from tennis ball cans, et cetera. It was an immense park: thick, well-trimmed grass rising in a cambor in the middle, perfectly lined and flagged—at the corners, the try line, twenty-two meters and midfield. Two professional-looking touch judges were standing out there, flags in hand, talking to the referee: a trim, long-legged fellow with an Argentina refereeing society crest on his gray jersey.

If the officiating crew looked like a glossy magazine advertisement, the La Plata side resembled something out of a movie: they cantered across the field in their bright yellow jerseys, young, fast and loose-limbed, each segment of the team reflecting the standards of central casting. The backs, with their longish hair and dashing good looks, were all six feet tall and 185 pounds; the scrum-half, an extraordinarily nimble fellow, threw incredible spinning passes to them as they moved around the pitch; and the back row, made up of the two flankers and their number eight had sunburned faces and thick legs. La Plata's second-row forwards looked like the Übermensch twins: six foot six or seven, wide shoulders, freakishly long arms, their ears pinned to their heads by a halo of black electric tape.

But the front row intrigued me the most. Not a day over twenty years of age, yet with the hardened faces and cauliflower ears of forwards a decade or more older, La Plata's front row averaged 210 pounds straight across, with shoulders an ax handle wide, tapered waists and bulging legs. Yet they ran around the field with incredible pace, handling the ball with the dexterity of our halfbacks—a discouraging sign.

All six U of Florida guys were on the pitch: Dave Civil, Conrad, Mark Carpenter, Carlos, Surfer and me. We were in the try zone, waiting in the hot sun for the ref to blow the whistle; it had been nearly eight years since we'd played in a meaningful game together. Bing and Dick Elliott and a couple of reserves were the only people on our side of the pitch, looking tense and somewhat resigned. Having met with the captains, the referee signaled that La Plata would be kicking off.

In Gainesville, we were never a rah-rah bunch. I kneeled quickly, ripped a few blades of grass from the try zone and made the sign of the cross, kissing my fingers and discarding the grass ends. One of the UF boys spit over the touchline and said, "Let's go," and we trotted out to our positions.

La Plata's kicker put the ball in the air, and the instant Stinky Hines touched it, six of their forwards engulfed him in the tackle. The ball was lost in the pileup, and the referee awarded the first scrum to our side. By this time, lifting in the front row was discouraged, if not banned outright, and when we formed up, bound ourselves together, and were about to engage, I discovered that the opposing forwards were tight and low, at the level of our knees if we'd been standing up. I'm fairly long legged for a hooker, and this posed a new difficulty: getting low enough to engage the rush when we packed down, while having enough leeway to swing out from my right hip to strike at the ball.

I needn't have worried. As soon as the referee gave the command,

La Plata took us so low that my nose was ten inches off the ground; even if I could've lifted my foot, probably resulting in a serious injury if the scrum collapsed, I was certain that even Gumby couldn't get his leg around at the necessary angle.

It was uncomfortable enough before the ball came in, but as soon as it did, La Plata seemed to focus all the pressure directly on me: a reasonable strategy considering how important the hooker is to offensive continuity. I couldn't move, or breathe; it felt as if all the air had been sucked out of the park, and that temperatures had risen somehow. It was like being expected to conduct an athletic movement in a blast furnace.

Working as eight, they moved us backward over the ball, consuming it with a foot rush when they got close. It was only the second occasion in my long career that I *wanted* our second row to give way, choking up the ball as we retired, if it came to that, so great was the discomfort—and so disconcerting.

The ball was spoiled at the back somehow, and the referee blew his whistle for another scrum. This one was even worse because we knew what to expect, and though resisting with every bit of strength we had, they pushed us off the ball again, leaving us in a heap on the turf. La Plata ran a play off the back with their loose forwards, employed a skip pass in the centers, and put the ball through the hands of six or seven players before scoring a try beneath our goalposts. Forty or fifty seconds had elapsed, just two scrums, and we were losing, 6–0 after the conversion, without ever touching the ball.

I knew it was going to be a long afternoon when, right after the second scrum, our loosehead prop fell to the ground, signaling to the referee that he'd injured his left knee. Precisely at that moment, one of their flankers was sprinting past with the ball and our loosehead, a sturdy tackler, jumped up from his supposed injury, leveled the flanker just as he off-loaded the ball to a teammate and then collapsed again, rubbing his knee—the right one this time. After the try was scored, our prop took himself out of the game, limping off the field with his arms slung over the shoulders of two reserve players.

It wasn't the first time a player faked an injury to avoid what was shaping up to be a physical and psychological beat-down, but I'd never seen a front-row player do it before. In the front row, you're at the point of attack on every scrum. There's a level of pride in that, and a palpable sense of camaraderie that makes those three players inseparable on the field and off. Biting down on my mouthpiece, I looked over at Ivan, our tighthead prop, and he spat in the direction of the sideline and looked away. It just wasn't done: in the front row especially, you'd risk everything before you'd quit like that, leaving your teammates to fend for themselves.

There's no other way to win in rugby than through the forwards—through battering the other team in the rucks, mauls and scrums—and no more demoralizing way to lose. My strategy of hanging on until the other forwards began to tire out didn't work, either; they never seemed to slow down. La Plata was a premier division club, with several young, elite players on the field that day, operating at a superior level of skill and fitness. No matter how I approached the lineouts: go short, long, alley-oop-style balls, or attempts to thread the needle with quick high spirals, they took down our possession like I'd intended to throw it to them. And their scrummaging got tougher, lower and better as the game wore on; or it stayed exactly the same, as ours wore down.

They were piling up the points, and in my fatigue only bits and pieces of the match were clear to me, like the park had been overrun by a thick, encompassing fog, though the sky was clear and bright. About twenty minutes in, they were advancing downfield with a rolling maul that had the precision of a close-order drill, sealing off each player that took the ball so tightly that if you had your hand in the seam, it felt like an iron gate was closing when they switched up, left-right, right-left, driving it down our throats.

I was peeling off the maul on the defensive rotation, and stepped out to the right for a peek into the gap; I advanced into that narrow space just as their flanker took the ball from the back of the maul, and was going to break it open. I had a bead on him, and he was surprised to see me there. Quick over short distances, I scuttled forward, lowering my shoulder, and just as I was about to make contact, the La Plata player floated sideways, eluding my tackle, and shifted into a higher gear. It was a remarkable move: He appeared to hover above the ground and shimmy to my right, like the disk in an air hockey game.

He was a tall, dark-haired youth of nineteen or twenty, thick in the shoulders and narrow in the waist, with a hurdler's striated legs; it was like being humiliated by a Calvin Klein model. The flanker linked up with their center and fullback and they scored again on the break. I was getting tired just running back to stand on the try line for their conversion kicks, they were scoring so frequently.

With minutes left in the half, something finally went our way. La Plata was counterattacking from deep in their end, after Carlos put a towering up-and-under kick into the corner. Their backs were capable of long, precise passes, and they'd already cut through our defense when their fullback made a lazy pass to the wing. The ball hung in the air just a millisecond too long and when the wing gathered it, Conrad angled over and just flattened the guy, causing him to spill the ball. Dave Civil was there, scooping up the loose ball on the run, flying along the touchline in front of the grandstand.

From playing together for so long, the U of Florida guys had a kind of sonar, like dolphins, all streaming toward the ball before it even became available. Surfer, Carlos and I were in a loose triangle behind Civil, offering him a few options in support, and there were thirty yards of empty grass between the ball and the try zone.

Civil had decent speed, and a long, loping stride. As he closed in, twenty, fifteen meters from the line, I sensed movement over my right shoulder, and La Plata's number eight came flying by like he was wearing a jet-pack and drove Civil off his feet, over the touchline and out of bounds. He hit him so hard he knocked Dave right out of his boots; they were left there, in bounds, exactly where they'd been when Dave got hit, like something on a Saturday morning cartoon.

The ball bounced crazily away, remaining in bounds. Their fullback swung around, picked it up as coolly as you please, and they began to counterattack again; a more conservative reaction would've been to kick it away, into touch, but our opposites played with an enviable flair—and a thirty-point lead.

While Civil sat in the grass putting his boots on, dozens of people in the grandstand waved his business card, shouting, "J. David Civil, Realtor!"

At halftime, Bing came out with the water and we stood beneath the goalposts in silence. It was the middle of the worst loss most of us would ever play in—there wasn't much to say. When the referee blew his whistle to start the second half, Bing gathered up the plastic jugs and said, "Go get 'em, boys," and trotted away.

What little consolation the game would provide occurred in the last minutes. The Miami firefighter, Sean, had entered the game as a replacement at loosehead prop, and though he only weighed 190 pounds, light for the position, he was strong and willing and handled pressure well. Near the end of the game, La Plata, ahead by fifty points, was awarded a scrum five meters from our try zone. Ivan and I glanced at each other, and I nudged Sean: they aimed to push us over for one last, late try: the ultimate sporting insult.

The sun blazed overhead, and we were exhausted from getting pushed backward all afternoon. At the first engagement, we retreated a yard, but then held fast, the scrum collapsing to the ground. La Plata got the ball on the reset, and again we were pushed back, nearly to the try line this time, and the front rows went down hard, the scrum was so low. Setting the mark back at the five meter line, the referee motioned to the La Plata scrumhalf to put the ball in for a third time. Upon contact, we anticipated the shove, and for the first time in the match, we didn't budge; the ball hovered in the tunnel for an instant, and just as I began to strike at it, La Plata collapsed the front row intentionally, which was a penalty.

The ref blew his whistle. But instead of awarding us a free kick, he induced a near mutiny by requiring another five-meter scrum and awarding the put-in to our opponents. "That's bullshit," said Carlos, who was the captain.

Some of our forwards were still on the ground, completely spent. Crouched on one knee, I eyed the ref, shook my head, and spit into the grass. They were beating us by fifty points, for crissakes, and the right call was the penalty. But the referee heeled the mark, and blew his whistle: if we didn't scrummage again, he could award La Plata a penalty try, a final indignity.

Ivan was already on his feet; Sean reached over and hauled me upright, we took our binds, and Ivan looked back at our second row, and said, "C'mon. We love this shit!" It was a moment that made me proud to be a rugby player.

The ball came in, and we held our ground. Their number eight tried to pick it up at the back of the scrum and make a dash for the line, but Civil and Stinky tackled him. The game ended a short time later.

We shook hands with La Plata, and then filed through the gate and across the terrace toward the changing rooms. Kids asked us to sign their programs, and though it seemed a farcical exercise, we obliged them. In the room, we slumped on the benches in disappointment, every speck of energy used up. No one said a word.

Finally, Stinky said, "I'm goin' out on a limb here, but I feel a lot of love in this room," and everyone laughed.

After we showered and dressed, an incredible display of rugby hospitality awaited us in the clubhouse. Inside, we were directed to the players-only bar; behind a velvet rope meant to separate us from other visitors was a large, stainless steel barrel filled with gin and tonic. Halved limes bobbed on the surface, and we were each handed a plastic cup and invited to fill it as often as we liked. One wall was open to the air, and beneath a bower of grapevines, white-jacketed cooks were attending a brazier that must've been thirty feet long.

There, above a red-coaled fire, well over two hundred pounds of the famous Argentine beef sputtered and sizzled: flank steaks, rib eyes, T-bones, fillets and chops, some of it marinated in a rich wine sauce and the rest sprinkled with salt and pepper, the aroma heavy in the air. Nearby were a dozen wooden tables, scattered over with mounds of empanadas, baskets of green salad, and carafes of the local wine.

I'd come onto the terrace with my drink, gravitating toward the perimeter fence, where I rested my foot on a wooden rung and surveyed the acres of playing fields, stretching west to a border of trees. I was gazing at the sun dropping into the forest, the gin cold and bitter and medicinal, when I noticed Dave Civil, also wearing a jacket and tie, had wandered out of the bar. We didn't get to see each other very much anymore, and certainly we'd come a long way since Big Daddy's and the Sin Sity Saloon. Civil was standing in the far corner of the patio, watching the sunset, and when I caught his eye, he raised his glass and we smiled at each other, shaking our heads.

The team stayed in Buenos Aires for several nights, and on the way back that evening, the bus stalled against hundreds of people milling about in the street. Entering the Plaza de Mayo, we watched soldiers erecting barricades, stringing razor wire and pulling their armored vehicles right up to the Casa Rosada. Someone said a bomb had gone off a few blocks from our hotel, killing at least one person, and that a state of civil emergency had been declared. The San Francisco Hotel was a narrow, yellow brick building that looked onto the plaza, and until Bing got word on the curfew, we were told to stay inside, either at the bar or in our rooms.

On the street somewhere, Boz had met a guy, a local fixer, who provided two ladies of the evening for five dollars apiece. Word spread through the bar that the girls were putting on some kind of show up in Space Boy's room. Outside the hotel there was pandemonium—sirens, people yelling and the rotten smell of collapse: a whiff of tear gas and cordite and heaps of garbage. There was the feeling that anything could happen, and when I got to the room, traveling up in the rickety cage of the elevator with Surfer and Civil, half the guys on the team were crammed in there. The bathtub was filled with ice and bottles of Quilmes beer. A soccer game was being played on the little black-and-white television, and one of our guys was sitting in a chair by the door collecting bets. He had a huge fistful of dollar bills.

Tending to cheerful anarchy to begin with, rugby players, faced with a possible South American revolution, had reacted in the typical way, by drinking and gambling. With so many guys crowded in there, it was difficult to see what was going on until I got closer to the action. But what I encountered on the fifth floor of the San Francisco Hotel was like something out of Jean-Paul Sartre, by way of Henry Miller.

Space Boy was sprawled out on the bed closest to the windows, a little straw hat covering his face while one of the whores performed a salacious act on him. Another player, with a baseball cap hiding his face, was in the adjacent bed with the other sex worker, doing the same thing. The gambling was on who'd finish first.

With such a large audience, stage fright set in, and the sprint had turned into a marathon. Guys were drinking beers, making new bets as the fortunes of the participants rose and fell. There was a ten-dollar bonus for the winning whore, so the contestants were using every trick and technique in their professional repertoire to earn the extra money, glancing over at each other like a pair of rival jockeys.

"I hope Space Boy tackles this better than he did that fuckin' winger," said Surfer, putting a couple of bucks on him.

Someone remarked that it was like Vegas, only under martial law. "Debauchery along the lines of Byron and Shelley," I said, going him one better. "Only without the tedium of writing all those poems."

It went on so long it was like an army training film, and I took a chair from against the wall and sat with my feet on the dresser, watching the soccer game on TV with Ivan and Stinky. At some length, Bing stuck his head in, telling us the curfew was nine o'clock, and to be careful if we went out. Glancing around, he was taken aback by the ongoing sideshow, then achieved a see-no-evil look, and withdrew.

Never a gambler or interested in prostitutes, I quit these shenanigans just before 7 P.M., shaking hands on the way out. I had a date with a girl named Tatiana, a beautiful young Bolivian travel agent I'd met on the first night. We were supposed to rendezvous at the Acapulco Room for dinner and dancing, so long as the police let us through. (I found out later that Space Boy won the contest, and gave both girls an extra ten bucks beyond the winner's share. Hand-tooled leather jackets were selling for fifty bucks in the marketplace, and the girls were happy about the American money.)

The streets near the hotel were empty and quiet, eerily so. Even the slick young hombres who loitered on every Latin American street corner were absent, their spots occupied by stone-faced policemen in silver helmets, draped with bandoliers and carrying automatic rifles. It wasn't yet dark. Tatiana and I had a drink at the bar, and were seated at a table across the dining room; I took the gunfighter's seat, with my back against the wall.

Although Tatiana didn't speak any English, and all I could muster was some pigeon Spanish I'd learned at Acadia, we had a pleasant dinner of Cornish hen and fresh local vegetables while listening to the orchestra. She wore a clinging black dress, a lively, narrow-hipped girl with exquisite cheekbones; touring around on a junket with other travel agents, Tatiana was staying at a hotel on the far side of the plaza. After we danced to marimba and had a couple of drinks, it was nearing curfew and we said good night beneath the marquee, making plans to rendezvous in Mendoza, the next stop on both our tours.

It was quarter to nine, the rumbling sound of an army truck carrying over the houses from the next block. Quickening my pace, I took a shortcut through a seedy neighborhood just beyond our hotel. Beneath an old crown-and-bulb streetlight was a small café, lit up and doing business. I stopped to look in through the window, then glanced up and down the empty street, and ducked inside for a quick one.

It was a long narrow bar shaped like a hallway with a dozen patrons clustered at the far end, watching a soccer game on television and drinking beer. I stood at the rail about halfway down and gestured to the bartender. He hauled up a bottle of Quilmes from the cooler and then a bowl of peanuts; shells were scattered all over the floor. Just then the home team scored a late goal, and the man nearest me, a round-shouldered, middle-aged gent with a few dark hairs stretched across his pate, grinned and touched his bottle to mine.

It occurred to me that it was no different than watching the Celtics at Sully's Tap, a dark alley of a bar near the old Boston Garden; or the Methuen crowd, groaning over the Red Sox at Norm's White Horse on a pleasant fall evening. It didn't seem to matter that Argentina was coming apart at the seams. Men and their ball games: same the world over.

On the bus to practice the next day, Carlos read aloud from the newspaper account of our game versus La Plata: "The only thing colorful about the Florida side's play was their socks." In our next match, a day later, we played the Bel Grano Athletic Club's under-twenty-three side at their ground, located on the piedmont over-looking the city. The match was tight at halftime, with Bel Grano leading 10–9.

With about ten minutes left, we were rucking near midfield when our scrumhalf, Scotty McLaughlin, who grew up in North Andover, Massachusetts, picked up the ball and ran to the weak side, break-ing into the clear. Anticipating Scotty's move, I sprinted into the gap beside him, with Space Boy coming up hard in support to my left.

Scotty had just the fullback to beat for the go-ahead try. He ran straight at him; I was four or five meters to Scotty's left, and two meters back, in the right place to receive his pass. The best play here was to get right up on the fullback, commit him to the tackle, and then lay it off to me. A good pass would leave the defender flat-footed, and I'd clear him, and then give it back to Scotty, who was much faster than me. Or, if the fullback tackled Scotty right after his pass, I could run a short distance with it and then off-load to Space Boy, and he'd race in for the try.

A second before the breakdown occurred, Scotty glanced over at me—I looked him right in the eye—and when the fullback stepped up, Scotty threw a dummy—a fake pass—in my direction, retaining the ball in his hands. The fullback didn't bite on the dummy, lung-ing forward to take Scotty off his feet, spoiling a good ball. It died in the ensuing pileup, and we wound up losing, 18–9. Twenty years later, I mention those four or five seconds every time I run into Scotty McLaughlin.

Next, we traveled to Mendoza, a medium-sized city in west central Argentina. We left Buenos Aires at 5 A.M., with the Rolling Stones' "Sympathy for the Devil" playing from the stereo. A block from the Pink House, the bus rattled over the cobblestones, past groups of soldiers behind the barbed wire and sandbags, Mick Jagger's shrieks rolling out behind us.

The political and social conditions in Mendoza were even worse than we saw in Buenos Aires. The local citizenry, upset with the skyrocketing inflation, were looting the supermarkets—men and women using their children as human shields, if you could believe the newspapers. Right away, we heard that police had killed some of the rioters, and hundreds were arrested, many of them without any sort of due process. The streets were a mess, but at the Plaza Hotel, where we were staying, things were incongruously serene. The polished mahogany bar was long and elegant, watched over by tuxedoed barmen, and the casino was doing a booming business at blackjack and roulette.

Despite being told to stay close to the hotel, several of us became restless and decided to venture out, with Carlos as guide and interpreter. Near downtown was an open-air market, teeming with hawkers and their pushcarts. Somewhere in the marketplace, Carlos purchased a live chicken, secreting it beneath his jacket when we brushed past the concierge at the hotel. That night, after we'd lost our match against the local club, and were partying in the bar and on the veranda, Carlos sneaked up to Bing's room with an extra key he'd acquired at the front desk. He unlocked the door, threw the chicken inside, and locked it up again.

Late that night, busted flat at the casino and sweating vodka, Bing fumbled with his key, swaying against the doorjamb and humming show tunes. Switching on the light, he was dumbstruck when he found the room in total disarray, chicken shit everywhere.

In the morning, no one spoke about it when we boarded the bus, and Bing certainly wasn't going to volunteer any information. The brain trust had decided to head for Chile a day early, and as soon as Bing stood up to make a few announcements, Carlos began a chant: "Bing fucked a chicken! Bing fucked a chicken!"

Soon everyone had picked it up, shaking the windows of the bus and startling passersby on their way to riot at the supermarket. It continued for some time, Bing's ears turning red, until he sat back down and stared out the windshield with his arms folded. Finally he got to his feet, turned toward the back of the bus and executed a deep formal bow, and we all cheered.

We were headed for Santiago, Chile, an eight-hour ride over the pass through the Andes mountains. Bing's travel agent, a paunchy, slick-haired fellow who was acting as our guide for the border crossing, announced that anything illegal in our possession had to be discarded before we reached the first customs stop. Soon after, a great cloud of pot smoke rolled out from the back of the bus; and when a sign marked the Argentine customs station as three kilometers distant, Boz and Ray van Asshole could be seen stuffing things out the window.

Looking on, Conrad said, "A pair of idiots on the midnight express."

The Andes were tall, jagged outcroppings of red rock dusted with snow. We made two stops, at the Argentine and then the Chilean side, where an implacable border guard carrying an AK-47 lurched up the aisle of the bus and went sifting through our passports. Then we watched through the windows as a trio of young men in a superannuated VW were rousted out and searched by the side of the road. Cut right into the mountain was some kind of man-made cave with a huge steel door like a bank vault, and we shuddered when a Chilean Army sergeant formed the three youths into a line and marched them through the door. To say that the Chilean president, General Pinochet, was not widely recognized for his support of human rights is a gross understatement, and you had to wonder what was going to become of those three guys.

Somewhere above eight thousand feet we stopped at Portillo, a world-class ski resort located astride the mountain road. It was off season, not enough snow yet for skiing, but they had an enormous rustic dining room that was open for business, with latticed bay windows overlooking the upper slopes, deep forested ravines, and a glacial lake at the foot of the mountain. Local red wine was incredibly cheap, and Surfer, Carlos, Stinky and I sat at a table fashioned out of an old cartwheel, having lunch and watching Conrad, Civil and some guy from West Palm Beach descend the slope toward the icy-looking lake.

Over by the fireplace, Ray van Asshole sat at a table with the only other Americans we'd encountered in South America: two men in their early thirties, dressed in sport shirts and pressed khakis. Whereas Boz annoyed us with his ill-advised currency exchange and Latin American marriage bureau, he was essentially good-natured; and though clueless on the rugby field, at least he tried hard and wasn't afraid to run into people. On the other hand, Van Asshole was loud and abrasive, the quintessential American jackass who made you cringe every time he opened his mouth.

If he cornered you in a bar, Van Asshole liked to brag about what a football player he'd been, two decades earlier at some junior college. In La Plata, when we had a rash of injuries, both real and imagined, he was pressed into service at second row in the social-side match. Half drunk on the sidelines, he stumbled into a motley-looking kit of basketball shorts, borrowed rugby boots, and a team jersey, running onto the field to join a scrum. He grabbed on to the other second row, a podiatrist and UF alum, Dennis Frisch, and bellowed like a constipated hippopotamus.

Unaware that he was supposed to wedge in between the prop and the hooker, Ray stuck his head between our prop's legs, appearing in the middle of the tunnel like a perverted ventriloquist's dummy. Watching from the sidelines, a bunch of us fell down laughing when Van Asshole's face protruded from the loosehead's crotch. The social side lost the game, 70–3, their only points coming on a penalty kick from a La Plata reserve they'd picked up from the sideline.

Now, at the resort, after learning that the two Americans hailed from Chicago, Van Asshole delivered an obscene monologue about his experiences there, selling vacuum cleaners door to door: "Man, I got more great pussy on Lake Shore Drive than Raquel Welch's bicycle seat. This one time, three of my units were going in the kitchen, all roaring at once, bumping against the furniture, and I had this broad bent over the sink and was giving it to her in the ass. She was yelling something, but I couldn't hear what she was saying over the racket, and finally, without stopping, real loud she said, 'MY HUSBAND JUST PULLED IN THE DRIVEWAY, SO HURRY UP!' Isn't that the funniest thing you ever heard? What do you guys do for work?"

Arms crossed, the strangers eyed Van Asshole, and one of them said, "We're Baptist missionaries."

Mortified, Van Asshole slid out of his chair, rolling beneath the table where he hugged himself, babbling incoherently. Just then, Conrad and Civil returned from their swim, dripping water on the dining room floor. Having heard the tail end of the exchange, Civil glanced over at us and pointed at the door, where we could see the other guys climbing onto the bus, many of them lugging cases of wine.

We hustled out, leaving Van Asshole under the table. When we mounted the stairs of the bus, Dick Elliott and Bing each tried to do a head count, but guys were shifting around.

"Is everybody here?" asked Bing.

Conrad was looking out the window and saw Van Asshole staggering from the resort. "Yeah, we're all here," he said. "Hurry up. Let's go."

Ray fell to his knees as the bus began to pull out, and Civil had a weak moment. "Bing, you forgot the asshole," he said.

At the resort, Dennis Frisch had negotiated a deal for thirty cases of wine and a corkscrew: $100 U.S. We started guzzling the wine, and by the time everyone was pretty lit, Space Boy came up with something called "riding the rails." Space Boy was a select side wing from St. Pete, a short, muscular fellow, not nearly as fast as Psycho Taylor, but darting and quick; a fast thinker, clever in his boots and out of them, a great deal of his success built upon the fact that he didn't really give a shit about anything.

The bus was a luxury coach with faux-leather seats and a luggage rack running along both sides of the aisle. Riding the rails, as Space Boy soon demonstrated, meant stripping naked, downing half a bottle of red wine, then grabbing the luggage rack with a hand on either side, kicking one's feet up to catch the railings with your heels. Swinging to the bumpy rhythm of the coach, Space Boy yodeled along with the Stones' tape, making lewd thrusts at the ceiling. Soon Conrad had joined in, and Civil, and Surfer, and then Carlos, hanging from the luggage rack like demented monkeys, while the tour guide, suffering paroxysms of existential dread, twisted this way and that, looking around for Pinochet's secret police.

Arriving in downtown Santiago, our driver eased up in front of a posh-looking hotel. Space Boy was first off the bus, and when the doorman extended his hand, our enterprising winger puked on the sidewalk in front of him.

The final match of the tour was against Catolica RFC, in the mountains outside Santiago. Their field and clubhouse were located on the high sierra overlooking the city, and I couldn't even get warmed up properly because of the smog and elevation. Catolica was a bunch of fleet young schoolboys who played dirty, punching and kicking in the rucks and mauls. It didn't make any difference to me, since I was huffing and puffing right from the kickoff, my lungs burning like the gaseous elements in a lantern. After nearly three weeks of touring, I didn't have enough aggression left to get pissed off.

Catolica ran us silly in the loose play. But there was one funny moment that led to our first score. About twenty meters from Catolica's try line, the referee called for a lineout. As I prepared to throw the ball in, signaling that I was going to Stinky, Dave Civil, at the very end of the lineout, waved his arm. I noticed there was separation between him and his opposite number and heaved a long spiral over the back, twenty yards on the fly. Our six man leaped up to tap it; Civil swerved over, caught it on the bounce, and dashed in for the try. When I jogged over to congratulate him, Civil swore at me; apparently, he was so hungover he'd been waving to the coach that he wanted out of the game. No way Bing was going to take him out now.

Catolica won the match, 37–14, and I couldn't help think that we'd have beaten them easily if we'd played them in the first match on tour, instead of La Plata. Afterward, we were treated to yet another steak barbecue and lots of beer, and I left mine and wandered off to stare at the hazy mountains and ponder my future in the sport. I had a fine panoramic view of the city; the gleaming skyscrapers, crowded train yards, with industrial stacks belching smoke to the north and west. The air was rarefied and dirty, permeated with the exhaust from a million cars, scurrying everywhere at once.

In Argentina, I'd felt like a millionaire for about a week: the best booze, the best-looking women, and the choicest tables at the fanciest restaurants. Here in Chile, the last few days had been spent in near exhaustion, too little sleep and too much rich food, wandering around the trash-filled streets like some hapless out-of-towner. I was nearly broke, had no job or girlfriend to return to, and no idea what I was going to do next; a penniless rugby adventurer reduced to living by his wits.

That night, the team dinner was held in a crowded nightclub in Santiago. The entertainment consisted of a musical review, and when the entire troupe of six-foot babes got up for the final number, Dave

Civil rushed up to dance a can-can with them, kicking so high he danced himself right off the edge of the stage, landing in the orchestra pit. I was at the bar, having a laugh with Stinky, Conrad and Surfer, autographing tour programs for a few of the guys, when Bing Towne came over. Shouting in my ear because of the din, he thanked me for my efforts and asked if I'd be interested in another tour he was planning. He and Dick Elliott wanted to take the Florida President's XV to Mexico City for a game against the national club champions. Sure thing, I said.

None of the locals spoke any English, and though the nightclub was teeming with beautiful girls, we were reduced to pantomime, trying to charm them with charades. When the floor show ended, one of the guys found a jukebox against the wall, pumped in a few coins, and selected a familiar song. A minute or two later, the entire crowd, numbering close to three hundred souls, was unified in song, raising their voices in a phonetic rendering of Don McLean's "American Pie," which could've been our theme song.

> Them good old boys were drinkin' whiskey and rye
> And singin', "This'll be the day that I die"

The thing that most people wouldn't understand is, after a hard day of rugby, win or lose, nothing bothers you, and you're not afraid of anything, neither Argentina's social volatility or Pinochet's secret police. In the midst of singing, I glanced down at my tour program, lying open on the bar. Beneath my photograph, one of the guys had scrawled his name, writing that I was a *"un buen jugador que le gusta jugar"*—a good player who loves to play—the highest sort of praise you could get from another rugby player.

Epilogue

Are You a Vandal?

Last summer, we arrived at Nagog Park in Acton, Massachusetts, at 8 A.M., lugging our kits, coolers, chairs and a large yellow sun tarp, the temperature near eighty degrees and rising. After a long, often brutal rehab, I was about to play in the annual New England X's Rugby Tournament, my first game action since the Fort Lauderdale Ruggerfest, two and half years earlier. A grassy ridge divided four rugby pitches on one side of the park from the natural amphitheater on the other side, with a small iridescent lake and the public beach located just beyond.

I'd come a long way from my first baby steps in Chris Pierce's clinic to the grassy confines of Nagog Park. It had taken a major act of will to push through the early setbacks, including a second eye operation and a badly sprained right ankle suffered in a hockey game. A million toe raises later, I'd pared away all the inessential aspects of my life, focusing almost exclusively on getting back onto the rugby field. A strict vegan diet; intense workouts six days a week; attending Mass, and praying every morning and night; the avoidance of alcohol; and an early bedtime—everything aimed at proving I could still do my job out there, even at the age of fifty-three, a year older than my father was when he died.

With Piercey's help, I'd put an invitational side together for the New England X's (calling ourselves Vandals North, and drawing on other Vandals who live in New England, as well as several first-side players from Amoskeag), in order to prepare for the venerable Can-Am Rugby Tournament at Saranac Lake, New York, three weeks hence. One of the premier tournaments in the country, the Can-Am was the Vandals choice for a summer trip, and I needed to get some rugby under my belt if I was going to play at that standard after such a long layoff.

The format at the New England X's is ten men per side, for ten-minute halves. Pool play meant games against the Seacoast Alumni and Mystics I (there were eight pools of three teams apiece), after which the teams would be reseeded and put into single-elimination brackets for the Bowl, Plate and Cup divisions. In our first match, against Seacoast Alumni, I ended up with the ball in my hands on the opening kickoff, mauling upfield with three other Vandals until transferring the ball to Bubba MacIntosh, a hard-charging fireplug, who crashed through the first tackle and spun the ball outside. I joined a ruck at the opposition's twenty-two-meter line, then cleaned a fringing player off the next ruck a few yards deeper and half the width of the field away. Digging at the pileup, Todd Hathaway, a stylish halfback who plays for Amoskeag's first XV, brought the ball back to the near side and we scored a quick try.

Hands on hips, gasping for breath, I asked the referee how much time was left in the half. "We've only played three minutes," he said, with an amused look.

We defeated Seacoast Alumni 19–12, in a match that wasn't really that close, as they got two late, runaway tries from dropped or messy ball. We threatened their line throughout, and should've won the game by twenty points or more. In our second game, we lost to Mystics I from Boston, a first division powerhouse and the pretournament favorites, by a score of 12–7. It would be their closest match of the day. Both Mystic tries were similar: weak-side, end-to-end breakaways from a misplayed ball right near their own goal line, lucky in defense. The Mystics had a U.S. Eagle 7's winger and he scored the first try, and set up the second. We were right on their goal line, hunting for the tying score, when time ran out. I knew we were going to make a run at a trophy, and with the sun blazing overhead, retreated into the shade right after the match.

In the seeding round, Vandals North came out 1–1 and went to the Plate division. In our first match in the bracket, we defeated Springfield I, 60–0. Tries upon tries, especially by Sam Rabb, our fleet-footed winger from Brown University. I had the ball three or four times in the first half, including a quick lineout from far behind the play that Billy Bishop threw to me. I was in the backline and daisy-chained the ball to Bubba and Piercey on the relay, who ran it wide, touching down a try in the corner. That sure felt good. My lineouts were uneven, but the set scrums were low and solid; we won our own ball, and went forward consistently. Because we ruled play in the Springfield game, I began to get my legs under me. It was hot, though, and the temperature rose toward ninety after lunch.

Against Central Maine, we went up by two tries early, led 12–0 at the half, and continued to follow the disturbing pattern of giving up long tries off a dropped or poorly presented ball right near the opponent's goal line, which led to breakaways. They converted one of the tries, and missed the other, as we had missed ours, and it was tied 12–12 at halftime.

We scored an unconverted try near the six-minute mark of the second half, and things looked promising. With barely any time left, a Central Maine player ran onto a loose ball near his own twenty-two meters and hacked it forward thirty or forty yards by kicking it on the fly. He was long-legged and fast. Piercey gave chase, and about forty yards from our try line the guy hacked it again as the ball grubbed along, running onto it in our try zone with Piercey right on top of him. They both lunged, fully extended, as the ball tumbled in the end goal. From thirty yards away, the referee indicated their player had touched the ball first, and awarded Central Maine a try as the clock ran out.

Ballsy call. Lucky for us, they missed the conversion. Now we were tied, 17–17.

The tiebreaker for the tournament, other than in the finals, was kicks at goal. Piercey, a former soccer player at Ithaca College, handled our dead ball kicking; with increasing tension, both kickers made it through the uprights from twenty-two, twenty-seven and thirty-two meters. Piercey was locked in, and his fourth kick, from nearly forty meters, was straight down the middle with room to spare.

I leaned over to Bubba and Paul Godbout, our try-scoring second row, and said, "Better to go first, as Piercey did. You miss it, the other guy still has to make his to win. You make it, the pressure is square on the other guy."

Central Maine's fly half, a stocky, blond-haired guy, lined up his kick. "He's been shorter on his kicks than Piercey," said Bill Bishop. "He's going to be short here."

He was way short, and wide left, and we were through to the Plate final.

By then it was late afternoon, and ungodly hot. Muscles get stiff between matches, and it's a psychological challenge to gear up for a new opponent every hour or so. Just after 6 P.M., we trudged down the hill for our fifth game of the day. We stretched a little and rubbed our chins, squinting up at the sun. We were playing Springfield II, which meant they'd also "won through" in their bracket. They were bigger, more grizzled, and faster than Springfield I. We could see them across the dusty reaches of the park, looking over at us.

"This is the existential moment," I said to Piercey. "When dread intersects with the potential for reward. When fear crosses the line into desire."

"The existential moment," said Piercey, stretching his hamstrings. "I can dig it."

He walked away, said something to our longtime teammates, Todd Hathaway and Billy Bishop, and came back. "Okay," he said, drawing up. We'd spent over a hundred hours together in his clinic, getting my foot and ankle in shape for this very thing. "You're talking to me. You're saying this and that. Now talk to me with your eyes," Piercey said.

Our faces were inches apart; we looked at each other without blinking. "You're ready," Piercey said. "Let's DO IT!"

I played my little heart out, and though tired, contributed my most spirited rugby of the day. Their front row was short, squat, strong and quick; the scrum hits were teeth chattering. But Matt Medina, a rugged kid from Providence, Rhode Island, was very solid at prop for us, as I knew he would be. Their hooker was low to the ground, a good striker, and against the toughest competition of the day, I had my best game. Off the kickoff, which they booted into touch, we were awarded a put-in at midfield and I won it, but saw that my opposite number had a quick foot. In a format mostly devoid of scrums and even lineouts, with lots of rucking and mauling, we had three scrummages in the space of a couple minutes. Twice I disrupted their ball, one heading straight out the tunnel, and the next shooting out the back of their abbreviated, five-man scrum. From the backline, I could hear our guys saying, "Get one, Jay. Steal it."

I never did, and one of our hooked balls was kicked back through Springfield's half of the scrum by the second row (aggravating most hookers, no end), giving them a cheap tighthead. One time, the opposing hooker thought he had the starboard side of his foot on my ball and I stayed calm, using my leverage to force his leg out of the way, and push the ball into channel three, the best place to attack from. We went up by three tries late in the match, winning 26–12. I shook hands with Piercey and Bubba, and had a good laugh when Paul Godbout said, "I'll have one of those vegan sandwiches now."

After all three championship matches had been played, there was a brief ceremony at the referee's table on the edge of the park. When they announced that Vandals North had won the plate, I went up to accept it, still dressed in my grubby kit. Shaking hands with several teammates as I passed through the crowd, I noticed two or three guys I'd played with years before in Boston: now they were coaching, refereeing, or merely spectating. One of them smacked me on the back, and said, "Still playing in the Tens. Fucking A."

The referee handed me the trophy, and I held it over my head for a moment, and said, "Thanks very much to our opponents, and to the referees. It was hard rugby." When I came back over to the guys, Piercey handed me a beer. "The existential moment," he said. "Well done."

Three weeks later, Piercey and I drove up Route 89 through the steep, forested valleys of the Green Mountain State, listening to the Grateful Dead on the stereo and shooting the breeze. Our destination was the Thirty-seventh Annual Can-Am Rugby Tournament in Saranac Lake, New York, which attracts dozens of premier teams to the Adirondacks every summer, and where I'd been competing for decades. After playing in Fort Lauderdale a couple years earlier, I'd missed the Vandals trips to the Montreal Irish Rugby Tournament, which garnered the club a first-place trophy; the Wild West Rugby Festival in Scottsdale, Arizona, resulting in a second-place finish; Fort Lauderdale again, second place in the division; and last year's Can-Am, consolation finalist. Increasingly, guys from various clubs were fishing for invitations to play for the Vandals, as the standard of rugby and the quality of the socializing continued to improve.

Reaching the ferry at Grand Isle, Vermont, over to New York State, Piercey leaned out of the driver's side window. Ensconced in a glass booth was an obese woman with stringy hair and old-fashioned tattoos dotting her arms, neck and upper back.

"How much does it cost to cross this river?" asked Piercey.

"It's not a river. It's Lake Champlain," said the woman, like she was talking to an idiot. "There's no river that wide."

"There's the Mississippi," Piercey said. "It's wider than that. Have you ever seen the Mississippi?"

"I have. It's not that wide."

Piercey handed over twenty-four dollars for a round-trip ticket. "Oh yes, it is," he said. "You must've seen one of the skinny parts."

After we'd driven down to the queue, I said, "What are you talking about, Piercey? Why are you arguing with her?"

Piercey was laughing. "BECAUSE I LOVE IT, BROTHER. I LOVE IT," he yelled over the strains of Bob Dylan's "Visions of Johanna."

We arrived in Saranac close to midnight, and met up with Spencer Cackett, our Aussie flanker, who was rooming with us. Joining the rest of the guys, we had a few beers beneath a gazebo alongside the hotel. The captain of the Vandals, Frank Baker, and I've been playing rugby together for two decades, and went through an elaborate series of bows and nods and hand gestures, as we always do upon seeing each other. There were the obligatory vegan jokes, as Solly from the Washington Irish and Mike Zizza from the Boston Irish Wolfhounds asked if I was eating grass and dirt as part of my new regimen, et cetera.

Spencer thought this was hilarious. I first met Spencer Cackett seven or eight years ago, when we both played for the Vandals at the Washington Irish Rugby Tournament. A burly, sunburned, ruddy-faced loose forward from Perth, Australia, Spencer makes his living on oil rigs as a deep-sea diver. His father and grandfather were divers, and he thinks nothing of descending to one thousand feet during his twenty-eight-day "shifts" at sea.

While we were standing there, Spencer handed me a business card from the West Australian Marauders Rugby Union Club, a very keen side he plays for when he's back home. Among the rules of the club are *"Thou Shalt Not Question the fact that Rugby Union is the game they play in Heaven, or that, come the Second Coming, His Son, Jesus Christ, may be considered for a game at inside centre for the Marauders."* This was the same sort of rubric that applied to the Vandals; there were certain rules and rituals when you traveled with the club, such as left-handed drinking only; no "dangerous" beers (those left closer than two inches from the edge of the bar or table); and no stacking, or accumulation of new, full bottles or cans of beer. Violators were penalized during the kangaroo court sessions following the end of play on Sunday.

Furthermore, when approached by a fellow Vandal, in any setting, and asked the question, "Are you a Vandal?", the one and only appropriate response is, "You bet your sweet ass I am!"

The next day we convened at the local high school, one of several venues where the more than eighty teams in attendance would be playing all weekend, to square off against Blackthorn of Pennsylvania. My old buddy, Super Dave Laflamme of Providence, Rhode Island, was supposed to play the first half and I the second, at hooker, but he was injured in the opening minutes and Baker called me into the match. After the restart, our opponent made a break down the right sideline, ending up inside our twenty-two meters, rucking the ball forward in little three- and four-man pods. By the time we organized our defense, they were a meter from our try line, and as several big bodies crashed in the tackle, I thought I saw the white of the ball showing for an instant amid the grinding progression of a maul that had formed.

I stepped over the try line, my hips low, auguring into the maul. Just as Blackthorn's sandy-haired flanker picked the ball out of the massing bodies to channel it back to their scrumhalf, I reached in, sinking my arm to the point of the shoulder against his chest, and tightened up on the ball. I ripped it back and downward, toward our try line, and quickly bent over, serving the ball between my legs while maintaining a solid grip with both hands, like a center snap in football.

I shouted, "Todd! Todd!" but Hathaway was already there, taking the stolen ball from my hands and kicking it beyond our twenty-two-meter-line and out of bounds. The half ended shortly thereafter.

These are just tiny moments in a rugby game, individual links in the chain of possession, unnoticed by anyone but a connoisseur. In that particular sequence, Blackthorn was very close to scoring a try between our posts, which would've been the first points of the match. But working with our big guys and Todd, and using a bit of savvy, I'd helped turn five and perhaps seven points for Blackthorn into a clearing kick. When the ball sailed into touch, Todd looked over and grinned at me.

In the second half, I lost one of my own scrums, won a tighthead on the next set piece and cleaned up a few loose balls, including one I came up with in heavy traffic, developing it into a ruck by falling on my right shoulder and hip and thrusting the ball straight out from my chest as soon as I gathered it in. An opposing player was caught offside, and the whistle blew. On the ensuing penalty, Spencer took a quick tap fifteen or twenty meters for a try, carrying their eight man over the line, which put the Vandals up by four points.

My rugby fitness was pretty marginal, and after playing seventeen or eighteen minutes, I was substituted for. We beat Blackthorn 17–5, so the spoiled maul counted for something; then we lost a close game to White Plains, 15–8, though I didn't appear in that match.

The next morning at 8 A.M. we drew a match with Cortland, New York, and I played in the second half. Our Kiwi prop, a dark-featured behemoth named Royal Orbell, was having trouble engaging with Cortland's tighthead (the referee said later that the Cortland prop was very inexperienced), and there was a dangerous moment at the first set piece when the scrum collapsed. I was half up and half down with the weight of their pack surging forward, and I felt my left leg bow outward for a second—I thought my tibia and fibula might snap, or my knee give way.

Instinctively, I felt a little space to my right and fell in that direction onto the turf, avoiding serious injury. I yelled "Fuck!" when I rolled on the ground, more relieved than anything else.

Two more scrums collapsed, but none as dangerously as the first one. I won a very sloppy hook with two strikes at the ball, the second one with my left foot, and we gained possession and cleared the back of the scrum. I had begun the match by going forward in the tight-loose, but the three bad scrums had "ruined my mojo," as Piercey put it.

I won a clean, fast strike about twenty minutes into the half, made a tackle, and was substituted for a short while later. We tied the match on a late try, and won it 22–17 on Piercey's beautiful crashing run for a try in sudden death overtime. We played the Ottawa Indians right after that, the eventual champs in our bracket, and got skunked 38–0. Thus, our tournament was over by midafternoon, as we finished 2–2.

Kangaroo court, always a highlight of a Vandals trip, was convened in a stuffy function room at the hotel. Thirty-four players occupied two banks of chairs arranged auditorium-style, facing a wooden table acting as the judge's bench with a podium off to one side. Among the gallery several players were nursing injuries; a few chewed tobacco, spitting into plastic cups; everyone was drinking beer. The Vandals are equal opportunity ballbusters, ignoring race, color and creed during their harangues; and the proceedings took a raucous turn when I was called up before Judge Baker on charges of providing "untested food products" to the team—the implication being that the vegan energy bars, drink powders, and protein shakes that I'd supplied (I'd arranged for a sports nutrition company to sponsor the team at the Can-Am) had affected players' performances in a negative way.

Though I was congratulated for landing the Vandals their first corporate sponsor, Judge Baker also pointed out it wasn't a beer company, sports apparel manufacturer or porn site, drawing a chorus of boos. Before I could begin lecturing on the benefits of these products, several members of the gallery began making outrageous claims related to their consumption of the supplements over the weekend.

My old Amoskeag teammate, tighthead prop Butch McCarthy, once a rotund 335 pounds, insisted that his current, anemic-looking physique, weighing in somewhere around 210, was the result of drinking a single packet of the sports energy drink. Daniel Carter of Tennessee and Walt Davis of Alabama, whose pates were as smooth and shiny as billiard balls, each claimed to have had a full head of hair prior to eating an energy bar. Someone asserted that Frank Kelley, a hard-hitting, but excitable and marble-mouthed center, also from Amoskeag, had been "articulate" and "intelligent" before drinking a protein shake that morning.

Someone yelled out, "that stuff made Frank retarded," while Kelley grinned like a madman.

In a particularly tumultuous interlude, Steve "Duma" Johnson, a wide-bodied, African-American center/prop from the Washington Irish RFC, announced that he "used to be white" before trying several of the products. (Johnson's nickname, bestowed on him by his Irish teammates, was actually one of the all-time great rugby acronyms: DUMA, or Don't Underestimate My Ass.)

This created an uproar when Tom "Reggae" Rege, and Lyle "the Vulture" Jones, both black, said they'd experienced the same transmogrification. They looked at each other from their respective locations in the room, marveling at their new selves. Baker called out that Scooter Lefkowitz and Jeff Levinson had "been God-fearin' Christians" before sampling the recovery drink. Bedlam ensued, and I was in fear of a "public canning"—being pelted with dozens of empty and half-empty beer cans—as well as a forced shot or two of Maker's Mark, which would certainly put a damper on my plans to drive back to Massachusetts after court adjourned.

I glanced over at Baker, who was wearing his long fluffy white judge's wig, and we both laughed, bowing to one another in comic deference. Rugby socializing doesn't get much better than that, and I signaled to Baker that I had a few tricks up my sleeve that hadn't yet been revealed. Baker used his gavel to restore order, noting that the "sixty-five year old plaintiff" had a statement to enter into the record.

A day earlier, prior to our match with Ottawa, I was standing beside the pitch with Crab (the wild-hearted flanker, Jim Chrabolowski, a longtime teammate at Amoskeag) and Tom Rege, when Reggae noted that one of the Vandals rookies, a guy from California who he didn't know very well, had pointed to Duma the first night under the gazebo and said something like, "We've got our quota of black guys."

Leaning against the fence, Reggae said, "What the fuck is that? I don't know the guy well enough for him to be telling 'black jokes.'"

As if on cue, the guy trotted over and handed Reggae the baseball hat he'd been wearing. "Here," he said. "Hold this for me." Then he jogged away, to warm up for the game.

Reggae tossed the hat on the ground, and Crab and I laughed. "That's the second time he's done that," said Reggae. "What am I, his fuckin' hat rack?"

In court, as I stood to mount my defense, I said, "Before I deliver my opening statement, Tom, here, hold my hat for me." I walked across the front of the room and handed Reggae my visor. Bill Bishop, Piercey, Todd and about half the room—the guys who'd heard the story—began laughing. Other guys were saying, "Why did you give Reggae your hat?"

Lyle Jones stood up. "Your Honor, why didn't I get the hat? I'm just as black as he is."

I took off one of my shoes and gave it to Lyle, and then ran down the center aisle and handed my other shoe to Duma, who was stumped. He threw the shoe into the aisle, as guys began to roar.

"As to the notion that I have been distributing 'untested food products,'" I said, quieting the assembly. "Why, earlier this morning, while touring a local winery with Bubba and Lyle and Piercey"—more hoots, laughter—"I gave Bubba one of the energy bars, which he'd expressed interest in sampling. He put it in his mouth and began to chew it, right as we drove out of the parking lot. We hadn't traveled very far, Your Honor, when Bubba stopped the car, opened his door and puked. So it's not true that the products are untested. And, let it please the court, Bubba is still very much alive, and very short in stature. He hasn't changed one iota."

More laughter. Bubba grinned. At that moment, I walked down the aisle and said to Bill Bishop, "Give me the bag," referring to a large plastic bag I'd stowed beneath my chair before court started. I returned to the prisoner's dock and said, "Now, some of you may not have experienced much success in rugby"—more hoots, catcalls— "but I want to point out that just a few weeks ago, several Vandals, powered by these same products, took part in the New England Ten's tournament in Acton, Mass, playing as Vandals North."

I reached into the bag and removed the silver plate we'd won at the tournament. I stepped dramatically into the center aisle, mentioning that several Vandals—Bill Bishop, Todd Hathaway, Bubba MacIntosh, Piercey and Matt Medina—had all played in Acton.

"And we won it, baby! HAHAHA. WE WON THE PLATE, YOU ASSHOLES."

Much laugher and shouting ensued. Frank Baker, and his sergeant-at-arms, tighthead prop, John "Solly" Solomon, from the Washington Irish, bit the edge of the silver plate, testing its authenticity. They seemed impressed. Then Judge Baker levied a rather mild penalty: I'd be required to drink an entire beer from the plate, without spilling any of it. (At my last Vandals appearance, I'd been required to sing with our Kiwi center, Julian Bristow, a natural ham who'd charmed his way into being named the "rugby consultant" on Clint Eastwood's movie, *Invictus*. For our duet, Julian chose the theme song from *Annie*, and though he sang reasonably well, I did not, and our run ended after a single performance.)

Solly carefully poured a can of beer onto the shallow plate, then handed it to me. "Monkey butt," shouted Piercey, suggesting that I bend my knees, sticking out my posterior while keeping my back straight and shoulders square in the basic athletic position.

I steadied the plate, the golden puddle of beer shimmering under the lights. In my twilight years, I've become a rugby-playing Prufrock, measuring out my beer with coffee spoons. Slowly I began to tip up the plate, drinking the beer almost without incident until remarks from the peanut gallery caused me to snort some of it back out. But I finished without spilling any, and thrust the plate over my head while the Vandals chanted, "Angry Vegan! Angry Vegan! Angry Vegan!"

"Take that, you assholes!" I said, as a chorus of laughter startled people outside the window. It was the best beer I'd had in a long, long time.

Acknowledgments

In the course of human events, it seems rather a small matter to write and publish a rugby memoir. Although this was something I've long been interested in doing, until my agent, Jake Elwell, of Harold Ober Associates came along, with the rock solid conviction that he could help me shape a proposal and then sell that proposal to a major New York publisher, I had begun despairing of ever completing such a book. So, to Jake, a scrappy, hockey-playing guy from Portsmouth, New Hampshire: here's the book, and my sincere thanks for your faith and all your hard work. (I trust you will soon be occupied with selling the second volume.)

Equal to Jake Elwell in this endeavor is Pete Wolverton, editorial director of Thomas Dunne books and a longtime supporter and reader of my writing. I met Pete several years ago when I was shopping a proposal for a book called *Ice Time,* and since then we've stayed in touch and occasionally kicked a few ideas around. By editing and publishing this book, Pete is either the most prescient and talented literary man in New York, or the most sentimental; either way, I am grateful for his stewardship and his suggestions. Pete's colleagues, Anne Bensson and Joe Rinaldi, are talented, skillful, sympathetic pros who contributed mightily to this project. As a writer, you could do a lot worse than having them in your corner.

This project also benefited a great deal from the support of my many friends in rugby. Surfer John Hearin, Noel Carpenter, Stormin' Norman Litwack, Martin England, Kenny "Wee Wee" Alabiso, Dave Civil, Dr. Dennis Frisch, Matt Allen, Greg "Psycho" Taylor, Carlos Ballbe, Brian Friedman, Jon van Blokland, Chris "Veggie" Roehm, Rob "the Groper" Spadafora, Dave Farwick and several other teammates from the University of Florida RFC came through with funny stories, photographs and poignant reminiscences, as well as the dates, details and final scores of matches played long ago. (Conrad Merry even returned my phone calls, a small miracle in and of itself.)

My teammate and personal body guard, former U.S. Eagle pool scrumhalf, Paul Male, of the Boston Rugby Football Club, has an amazing memory despite being kicked in the head innumerable times, and answered a slew of questions in his usual patient, wry fashion.

Amoskeag RFC pals Fred Roedel, Butch McCarthy, Glenn Gallant, Troy "Chi Chi" Nickerson, Chris Pierce, Randy Reis Esq., Joe Raczek, Duke Cronin, Dan "Original Sully" Sullivan, Sean Markey, Dick Grise, Tim "Big Sully" Sullivan, Greg Cihlar, John Belviso, Paul Godbout, Todd Hathaway, Marc Murray, Ken "Bubba" MacIntosh, Jim Chrabolowski, Mark Maloney, Freshy, Matt "X-man" Kaminsky, Bobby Greenwood, Chase Martel, Tim Moser, Kevin Moore, Jim, Tom, Sean and Patrick Connolly, Dave Rolla, Jason Massa, Mark Broth Esq., Scott "The Body" Souza and Chris Scuyler all chipped in, on the book, and whenever I couldn't afford to buy myself a beer, which was fairly often. I have been particularly touched by how well they have treated my son, Liam, over the years, the greatest bunch of Dutch uncles in the world.

It's also been my great privilege to play rugby with the Vandals, who gather from the four corners of the rugby universe like a bunch of nitwitted superheroes to enter—and often win—competitive tournaments in Florida, Quebec, Arizona, Nevada, New York and other exciting locales. I have enjoyed quite a few memorable evenings over the course of my rugby career, but never have I laughed so hard as when I'm having a few drinks with Frank Baker, Drew Cooper, Mike Zizza, Julian Bristow, Spencer Cackett, Jim Merklinger, Steve "Duma" Johnson, Super Dave Laflamme, Alex Mandel, Jerry "Lumpy" Loeffler, Tom "Reggae" Rege, Walt Davis, John Solomon, Daniel Carter, Geoff Ormsby, John Jablonski, Nate Heiselt, Jake Fraser, Walker Larson, Lyle "the Vulture" Jones, Matt Medina, Lee "Burgers" Bartlett, Royal Orbell, Andrew Fowler and the rest of the Vandals. You guys truly make life worth living.

I am also indebted to my old sporting chums from Acadia: remnants of the Coolen's Gang hockey team, the varsity wrestling team, varsity soccer, the European handball squad and the rugby club, including Dag Fullerton, Ron Martin, Scooter Riddell, Pinky Stevens, Terry Tapak, Dave Barnes, Jay Buckler, Joe Fleming, the late Marty DeMarzo, Ralph Stea, Bill Barlett, Rob Murray and George Lefort.

A good reference librarian is like found money to a writer, and I feel like a millionaire every time I walk into the Nevins Memorial Library in my hometown of Methuen, Massachusetts. For their assistance on this project (and many others), special thanks to Krista McLeod, Kirsten Underwood, Tatjana Saccio, Sue Jefferson, Maureen Tulley, Beth Safford and Sharon Morley. Also, librarians Frances Magro, Tracy Pekarski, Ellen Paine, Cynthia Christie and Patricia Graham were always eager to answer questions and help with elusive facts. If you have this book in your hands, please thank a librarian today.

Special thanks to honorary rugby player Harry Crews, who taught me everything I know as a writer. And to my family: Liam, Jodie, Jill, Jamie and Patrick; Matt, Katie, John and Gramps; Nick, Michaela and Sparky; Owen, Reese, Shane and Deanna; Uncle Johnny and Jackie; Scott and Mary; Auntie Barb; Auntie Shirley, Uncle Paul, Steve, Larry, David and Lisa; Karen Koffler and family; Auntie Nat and the late, great Uncle Arthur; Candy and her family; Cheryl and Kerry and Tasha; as well as my late parents, Lois and Jim; so, you guys, I love you all.